Migration Studies
and Colonialism

SOAS Library

A 275/

D1434877

:9

SOAS LIBRARY
WITHDRAWN

SOAS, University of London

18 0869772 7

Migration Studies and Colonialism

Lucy Mayblin and Joe Turner

polity

Copyright © Lucy Mayblin and Joe Turner 2021

The right of Lucy Mayblin and Joe Turner to be identified as Author of this Work has been asserted in accordance with the UK Copyright, Designs and Patents Act 1988.

First published in 2021 by Polity Press

Reprinted 2021

Polity Press
65 Bridge Street
Cambridge CB2 1UR, UK

Polity Press
101 Station Landing
Suite 300
Medford, MA 02155, USA

All rights reserved. Except for the quotation of short passages for the purpose of criticism and review, no part of this publication may be reproduced, stored in a retrieval system or transmitted, in any form or by any means, electronic, mechanical, photocopying, recording or otherwise, without the prior permission of the publisher.

ISBN-13: 978-1-5095-4293-2
ISBN-13: 978-1-5095-4294-9(pb)

A catalogue record for this book is available from the British Library.

Library of Congress Cataloging-in-Publication Data
Names: Mayblin, Lucy, author. | Turner, Joe B., author.
Title: Migration studies and colonialism / Lucy Mayblin & Joe Turner.
Description: Cambridge, UK ; Medford, MA : Polity Press, [2021] | Includes
   bibliographical references and index. | Summary: "Why colonial histories
   are crucial to understanding migration today"-- Provided by publisher.
Identifiers: LCCN 2020022233 (print) | LCCN 2020022234 (ebook) | ISBN
   9781509542932 (hardback) | ISBN 9781509542949 (paperback) | ISBN
   9781509542956 (epub)
Subjects: LCSH: Emigration and immigration--Social aspects. |
   Postcolonialism--Social aspects. | Imperialism--History.
Classification: LCC JV6033 .M39 2021 (print) | LCC JV6033 (ebook) | DDC
   304.8--dc23
LC record available at https://lccn.loc.gov/2020022233
LC ebook record available at https://lccn.loc.gov/2020022234

Typeset in 10.5 on 12pt Sabon
by Fakenham Prepress Solutions, Fakenham, Norfolk NR21 8NL
Printed and bound in Great Britian by TJ Books Limited

The publisher has used its best endeavours to ensure that the URLs for external websites referred to in this book are correct and active at the time of going to press. However, the publisher has no responsibility for the websites and can make no guarantee that a site will remain live or that the content is or will remain appropriate.

Every effort has been made to trace all copyright holders, but if any have been overlooked the publisher will be pleased to include any necessary credits in any subsequent reprint or edition.

For further information on Polity, visit our website:
politybooks.com

Contents

Acknowledgements   vi
Foreword *Gurminder K. Bhambra*   vii

1 Introduction   1
2 Time and Space: Migration and Modernity   26
3 'Race' and Racism in International Migration   49
4 Putting Sovereignty, Citizenship and Migration in
   Dialogue with Past and Present Colonialisms   78
5 Deconstructing Forced Migration, Rethinking Asylum   110
6 Towards a Colonial Account of Security and Borders   136
7 Gender, Sexuality, Colonialism ... and Migration   166
8 Conclusion   195

References   204
Index   243

Acknowledgements

We would like to thank Gurminder K. Bhambra, Thom Davies, Katie Bales, Arshad Isakjee, Sara de Jong and Marcia Vera Espinoza for their helpful and constructive feedback and for generously reading parts of/the whole manuscript. Thanks also to the organizers and participants of the 'Colonial Mobilities' workshop at Linneaus University Sweden in summer 2019 for their inspiration, especially Aurora Vergara Figueroa, E. Tendayi Achiume, Peo Hansen , Debbie Samaniego and Gunlog Fur. Thank you to our friends, families and partners for their patience and support whilst we completed the book. Lastly, we remain indebted to the scholarship, social movements and ongoing struggles that shape this book and that we hope we have done justice to.

Foreword: On the Beginnings of Migration: Europe and Colonialism

Recent years have seen much attention, media and political, given to the movement of people. This is especially the case in terms of the extraordinary movements precipitated by war, famine and the ravages of global warming that have produced refugees in seemingly greater numbers. They have also produced hostile responses with the building of walls and fences, the denial of aid and solidarity and changes to citizenship laws which have often turned citizens into migrants to be policed even more harshly. Global crises related to the movement of populations recur with relative regularity, and yet each is presented as unprecedented, reproducing the idea of crisis in the process. This occurs not just in media representations and political debate but also in academic accounts of migration, which often use similar framings in their analyses. In this superb new book, *Migration Studies and Colonialism*, Lucy Mayblin and Joe Turner contest the idea of the unprecedentedness of the movement of peoples and seek to locate both contemporary migrations and our understandings of migration in the historical contexts that produce them.

Our modern world has been significantly shaped by historical processes and structures that have been in place from the late fifteenth century onwards. These have shaped our institutions and our understandings. We can use the figure of Columbus and his voyages to stand for the beginning of these processes and structures and how they have been understood within Europe. As Locke wrote in the late seventeenth century, 'in the beginning all the World was America'. That is, in their discovery of the Americas, Europeans believed that they were encountering earlier versions of themselves.

This laid the groundwork for particular understandings of hierarchies among and between populations across the world. If those peoples encountered by early European travellers were effectively understood as being their ancestors, then Europeans could both show them the (predetermined) future and be unconcerned about their elimination. The first justifies the belief in 'development'; the second suggests that the disappearance of other cultures, peoples, is not a consequence of European actions but a quasi-natural phenomenon.

Columbus, and the Europeans who followed him across the subsequent centuries, are often presented as heroic figures – as travellers and pioneers. They are seen to move in what has been called the age of free migration when, apparently, there were no obstacles to movement. Traders, merchants, travellers, mendicants and explorers had long criss-crossed the globe, encountering new cultures, trading with them and learning the ways of others. The population movements from Europe to the New World and beyond coalesced, over four centuries, into a phenomenon that was markedly different from these other quotidian movements and encounters. This is because European movement was linked to colonial settlement which was central to the displacement, dispossession and elimination of populations across the globe. It was also central to the creation of the global inequalities and injustices that mark the worlds we share in common and that are the basis of contemporary movements of peoples. Without understanding the histories that produced these inequalities, we are unlikely to understand contemporary movements.

Taking Columbus, and the Americas, as the beginning is not the same as taking him, or them, as the origin. As Said (1995 [1978]) argues, whereas the idea of 'origin' presupposes that which develops from it, that of a 'beginning' is developed as a complex of connections which allows for construction and reconstruction. Columbus is not the origin of what followed but can be seen as one of the beginnings of the processes and structures that have shaped the modern world. Acknowledging beginnings permits shifts in perspective and understandings of knowledge by taking different points of departure. Events, in this view, are best understood as located in, and constitutive of, particular historical interconnections. Columbus, then, is *an* event in a world of events which together brought into being our modern world.

Christopher Columbus, born in the Italian city-state of Genoa, patronized by the Spanish Crown of Castile, landed in the islands of what we now know as the Caribbean, searching for a direct route to the treasures of the Indies. His exploratory voyages in the late fifteenth century opened up an entire continent to European populations who travelled in increasing numbers to the New World. Some were in search of adventure, others fleeing poverty, famine, religious persecution and economic disadvantage. Whatever their motives, the decades and centuries subsequent to Columbus's 'discovery' were marked by the subjugation and elimination of indigenous populations and the extraction and appropriation of their resources and land (Dunbar-Ortiz 2014).

In the journal *Nature*, Simon Lewis and Mark Maslin note that the arrival of Europeans in the lands that would come to be known as the Americas – lands which had been known by their pre-existing (and continuing) inhabitants as Turtle Island and Abya Yala – 'led to the largest human population replacement in the past 13,000 years' (2015: 174). They suggest that the continent had had a population of around 61 million prior to European contact and that this 'rapidly declined to a minimum of about 6 million people by 1650 via exposure to diseases carried by Europeans, plus war, enslavement and famine' (Lewis and Maslin 2015: 175). In this way, Abya Yala was gradually, although not without resistance, transformed into the Americas.

If subsequent waves of Europeans – and across the nineteenth century this involved around sixty million Europeans (Miege 1993) – found these lands to be available to them, then this ought not to be regarded as a natural fact but a social and political fact that requires further analysis. It is a fact that should be central to all subsequent discussion of the movement of peoples, to all discussions constituting migration studies. As I have argued elsewhere, migration is a movement of people across political boundaries, and migrants are people who live in societies other than their own, but according to the rules and norms of the societies of which they come to be a part (Bhambra 2019). Within this understanding of migration, those who do not, en masse, live according to the rules and norms of the societies of the lands they come to are not migrants. They are better understood as colonial settlers and colonial settlers are not migrants, even if much of the scholarship on migration describes them as such. Failing to acknowledge the ways in which colonial histories are the context for the consolidation of particular patterns of European

movement and the ways in which these come to be the reasons for
subsequent movements is problematic to the extent that we are interested in effective solutions to the problems of global inequality.

Where we start from, and which histories and epistemologies we
acknowledge, will profoundly shape our understandings. This is the
central premise of this vitally important book. Mayblin and Turner
start from an understanding that the field of migration studies is
poorer – in terms of both intellectual coherence and policy applications – if it does not take colonial histories seriously. While they do
not suggest that colonialism explains everything about migration,
they do argue that migration can rarely be adequately understood
without taking it into account. While there is plenty of literature at
this nexus, in a global context, it does not often form the basis of
migration studies as it is generally conceived in Europe or the United
States. Mayblin and Turner ask those of us located in migration
studies who have not addressed the histories of colonialism to
consider what difference would be made to our understandings if we
were to do so. It is urgent that this call be answered.

Gurminder K. Bhambra, University of Sussex

1
Introduction

Migration studies and colonialism

Between 1600 and 1950, the vast majority of mobile subjects (what some might now call 'economic migrants') originated in Europe and sought their fortunes on other continents. An estimated 62 million people – settlers, labourers, colonials, imperialists, invaders – moved around European empires in the period 1800–1950 (Miège 1993). Indeed, colonialism was characterized by conquest, exploitation and domination through migration. From the massive forced migrations of the triangular slave trade and circuits of indenture to the almost unfettered mobility of many (but not all) white Europeans within their various empires, from the large-scale population displacements which the turbulence of decolonization gave rise to to the migration of people from the former colonies to the former metropoles in the mid- to late twentieth century, the history of migration globally is very much entangled with colonialism. It should be unsurprising to us, then, that patterns of mobility and immobility today follow these colonial-era logics in what Steffen Mau and colleagues call 'the global mobility divide' (Mau et al 2015). Or that border regimes effectively amount to 'multilateral projects for the regional containment of Third World persons beyond the First World' (Achiume 2019: 1515). And yet, when consulting the indexes of a selection of key texts of migration studies today, it is very rare to find any mention of colonialism, postcolonialism or decolonization. If the absence of empire as a relevant context to migration studies is a surprise, so too is the general lack of interest in the legacies and continuities of colonialism for contemporary migration governance and the experiences of 'migrants' and 'hosts' today.

This book starts from the premise that colonial histories should be central to migration studies. We argue that colonialism is so fundamental to contemporary migrations, mobilities, immobilities, receptions and social dynamics that it is certainly not something that should only be of concern to scholars of colour, indigenous scholars and/or those working in formerly colonized countries. Our overarching aim is to explore what it would mean (acknowledging that it will not in fact mean one thing but many) to take seriously the centring of colonialism in researching migration, not through forging new theories but through learning from, and being inspired by, the wealth of literature that *already exists* in the world to engage with this task.

Migration studies is of course a diverse multidisciplinary field. Yet even critical migration studies has tended, according to Tudor (2018: 1065), 'to forget about postcolonial racism and racialization and instead promoted an understanding of migration that is disconnected from postcolonial analysis'. Gayatri Spivak (1999) calls this type of silencing 'sanctioned ignorance'. Sanctioned ignorance is not necessarily an issue of individual malice but is an institutionalized way of thinking about the world which operates to foreclose particular types of analysis or considerations from entering into the debate. One of the enabling factors of this type of silencing is the real urgency of contemporary issues and 'crises' relating to migration. Certainly, presentism is engendered within the field as every year brings new crises, displacements and patterns of migration and new politicians and laws seeking to control it. The present is, it seems, always new.

This underlying framework of 'the unprecedented present' within migration studies and migration policy making does not lend itself to a deep engagement with history. Nevertheless, a sense of history does quietly frame most analyses of the present. We see this in claims to 'unprecedentedness' itself – the common assumption that because a phenomenon is highly visible, contested and difficult to administratively manage, nothing like this has happened before. Because the world's population is growing all the time, even if the percentage of people that migrate always stays the same, each year will see unprecedented numbers of migrants crossing borders. But that isn't quite the same as 'nothing like this has ever happened before'. More explicit nods to history appear in the context sections of books or articles which briefly explain how rights emerged, or how things have changed since previous periods, before moving on to the topic at hand. Sometimes these contexts mention colonialism but most often not.

We think that sanctioned ignorance of histories of colonialism, and of the wide-ranging debates around the legacies of colonialism in the present, within migration studies is a problem. First, because ignoring vast swathes of human history leaves us with theories which are inadequate to the task of making sense of the present. Second, because without acknowledging these histories, the common usage of dehumanizing phrases associated with racial science such as the animalistic 'migrant stocks' and the disaster-like migrant 'flows', 'mass influxes' and 'waves' can appear objective rather than historically and culturally emergent. Third, it facilitates the denial of ongoing colonialisms in the present, and in doing so silences struggles for justice.

While, at the time of writing this book, it is common to attend a migration studies conference and fail to find a single paper that mentions colonialism (or indeed 'race'), questions of mobility and 'migration' have been taken up by those working beyond the field of migration studies, in postcolonial, decolonial and related intellectual projects. From the start, postcolonialism, decoloniality, indigenous studies, Third World Approaches to International Law (TWAIL) and many other projects have been interested in migrations, diasporas, conquests and hybrid transnational identities, and the power relations that they gave rise to on multiple spatial scales. This means that there already exists a substantial body of work which presents concepts and frameworks for analysing migration in the (post/neo-)colonial present. Much of this work in postcolonial studies has been in the arts and humanities but it is ripe for application to social scientific phenomena. Other areas of scholarship such as decoloniality and TWAIL have more directly engaged with social scientific questions. Indeed, there are numerous bodies of work across the social sciences internationally which both address migration *and* place colonialism at the centre of their analyses. Yet the core of migration studies, which is highly influential in international policy-making circles, appears to remain largely unaffected by this work.

This book responds to this disconnect. Its purpose is not to spend endless pages critiquing migration studies as it is articulated in hegemonic journals, conferences, policy fora and textbooks in the

Global North. Rather, our aim is to demonstrate what paying attention to colonialism through using the tools offered by postcolonial, decolonial and related scholarship can offer those studying international migration today. We do not present a new grand theory or claim that every single thing that people want to research can be explained with reference to colonialism. What we do offer is a range of inspiring and challenging perspectives on migration that are less often seen in influential migration studies research centres in Europe and North America, not least because students are so often asking us for reading lists along these lines. We also, by extension, suggest that in raising the colonial question, those engaging in research on migration may then need to consider the politics of knowledge production – the underlying assumptions, categories and concepts – which they rely on within this academic field.

While literatures already exist which should make ignoring colonialism seem like a bizarre and naive omission, these literatures seem still to be inaccessible, or unimportant, to many. This book seeks to showcase some of this work for people who research migration and yet never encounter such perspectives. If you are well versed in these debates, the issues that we discuss will doubtless seem obvious. Indeed, we are 'white' academics working in British higher education institutions and for this reason our perspectives are of course particular and limited, and undoubtedly readers will spot omissions and parochialisms throughout the book. Whilst we have sought to frame our discussion of the literature and examples in a global manner, we still broadly rely upon the legacy of intellectual projects from the Americas (North and South), with engagements from scholars from Asian and African traditions. For those not familiar with these literatures, we hope that this book will raise questions such as how broadly postcolonial and decolonial perspectives might change the kinds of research questions that we ask in migration studies, as well as the ways in which we analyse our data. Do such perspectives allow us to frame our research in terms that accord with the interests of policy makers? No. Are such perspectives policy friendly in the current terms of debate on migration? Rarely. If, and how, these perspectives can therefore be used in challenging migration policy, as most critical work hopes to do, is a topic for contemplation in the coming years. This volume, we hope, will spark discussion as part of what some have termed the 'postcolonial turn' in migration studies (Koh 2015; Tudor 2018). Our aim is *not* that you cite this book, but that in the future you cite some of the scholars discussed within it.

The growing call to 'decolonize' the social sciences

Recent years have seen the intensification and spread of calls to 'decolonize the university' and it would not be appropriate to write a book on the theme of migration studies and colonialism without discussing this agenda. While 'decolonizing' is a highly contested issue, the content and praxis of which is unresolved, at its heart is an agreement that we put colonialism and its legacies and continuities at the heart of our understanding of the contemporary world (Bhambra, Gebrial and Nişancıoğlu 2018; Ndlovu-Gatsheni and Zondi 2016). Academia is an important site of knowledge production and, as Dalia Gebrial argues, 'consecration'. She goes on:

> It has the power to decide which histories, knowledges and intellectual contributions are considered valuable and worthy of further critical attention and dissemination. This has knock-on effects: public discourse might seem far from the academy's sphere of influence, but 'common sense' ideas worthy of knowledge do not come out of the blue, or removed from the context of power – and the university is a key shaping force in the discursive flux. (Gebrial 2018: 22)

Decolonization in this context includes, but is not limited to, renewed questioning, or uncovering, of the colonial origins of some of the core concepts of the social sciences (e.g. 'modernity', 'development', 'capitalism', 'human rights', 'demography'); a focus on the Eurocentrism inherent to much social science research; and a critique of the ways in which contemporary research (and teaching) practices sometimes/often (depending on the field) reproduce colonial power relations.

There are disparate political and intellectual projects that all coalesce around these themes. The political projects have largely been student led and have particularly centred on 'addressing issues of racial exclusion and racialized hierarchy within the university, including its teaching and research practices' (Bhambra 2019: 1). 'Rhodes Must Fall' is widely seen as triggering a wider global movement. This campaign, based at the University of Cape Town in South Africa, centred in part around a campaign in 2015 to have a bronze statue of Cecil Rhodes removed from a prominent location on campus (Gebrial 2018; Nyamnjoh 2016). Cecil Rhodes was a wealthy British businessman and politician, who was prime minister of the Cape Colony in the late 1800s, founded the colony of Rhodesia (now Zimbabwe and parts of Zambia) and was an ardent white supremacist who laid the legal groundwork for apartheid. Challenging his reification on campus was, for the students studying there, urgent and necessary in the post-apartheid context. 'Rhodes Must Fall' Cape Town drew the attention of students at the University of Oxford in the United Kingdom. They too had a statue of Rhodes on campus and, as part of a much broader agenda of drawing attention to the colonial entanglements of the university, they campaigned for its removal (Gebrial 2018; Rhodes Must Fall Movement 2018). Of course, this is set within the context of a long history of anti-colonial movements in South Africa but also globally.

These explicitly de- and anti-colonial protest movements have been linked to other campus-based protests such as those against caste privilege at Hyderabad and Jawaharlal Nehru Universities in India, and Black Lives Matter on campuses in the United States, United Kingdom and elsewhere (Bhambra, Gebrial and Nişancıoğlu 2018). Related to these disparate events is the broad-based campaign 'Why Is My Curriculum White?'. This student-led movement, often headed by students of colour, asks that teachers in higher education take a look at their reading lists and consider whether there are any scholars of colour on them at all. Where there are scholars of colour on reading lists, how many of them are present to offer core theory, as opposed to place-specific case studies? How many courses address questions of race, racism, colonialism or its ongoing legacies? These questions are most poignant when the courses under consideration cover topics such as international development or international migration. 'Why Is My Curriculum White?' is a challenge: it should not be possible to teach a course on international development without putting colonialism and neo-colonialism centre stage, and the First World should not be the source of every theoretical perspective relating to the topic of poverty in the Third World. For us, the same is true for migration studies: it should not be possible to teach a course on migration without mentioning colonialism or having any discussion of 'race' and racism, and the First World should not be the source of every theoretical perspective relating to the topic of migration globally. The point is not necessarily to stop teaching Marx, Foucault, Agamben or

Carens, it is to also make sure that you are teaching Fanon, Quijano, Wynter and Spivak alongside them, while also asking how colonialism frames the work of all of these scholars.

In light of the debates sketched out above, what does it mean to 'decolonize' a field of scholarship? Is such a task even meaningful or is it just paying lip service to a live political issue which is having a fashionable moment and tokenistically mentioning it while carrying on as normal? For Gurminder K. Bhambra, Dalia Gebrial and Kerem Nişancıoğlu, decolonizing in the university context involves the following activities:

> it is a way of thinking about the world which takes colonialism, empire and racism as its empirical and discursive objects of study; it resituates these phenomena as key shaping forces of the contemporary world, in a context where their role has been systematically effaced from view … [then] it purports to offer alternative ways of thinking about the world and alternative forms of political praxis. (Bhambra, Gebrial and Nişancıoğlu 2018: 3)

This definition places emphasis on epistemology and on the underlying Eurocentric frameworks which cut across a lot of research that is undertaken in universities around the world (see also Alatas 2006; Amin 1988; Mignolo 2011a). It focuses on academic knowledge production and particularly on the sanctioned erasure of histories of colonialism and ongoing anti-colonial struggles from many (most) fields of study. It furthermore argues that the ways that we think about the world can lead to political praxis which seeks to change it.

There have been challenges to this perspective in recent years which must be acknowledged here. The most well-known intervention has been from Eve Tuck and K. Wayne Yang (2012), who are interested in decolonization in the field of education studies within the context of settler colonialism. Their point is that in settler-colonial states such as Canada, decolonization should always refer to the relinquishing of stolen land to indigenous peoples, and that 'until stolen land is relinquished, critical consciousness does not translate into action that disrupts settler colonialism'. They argue that:

> curricula, literature, and pedagogy can be crafted to aid people in learning to see settler colonialism, to articulate critiques of settler epistemology, and set aside settler histories and values in search of ethics that reject domination and exploitation; this is not unimportant

work. However, the front-loading of critical consciousness building can waylay decolonization, even though the experience of teaching and learning to be critical of settler colonialism can be so powerful it can feel like it is indeed making change. (Tuck and Yang 2012: 19)

When they write about decolonization, then, they 'are not offering it as a metaphor' or 'an approximation of other experiences of oppression'. Decolonization, for Tuck and Yang, 'is not a swappable term for other things we want to do to improve our societies and schools. Decolonization doesn't have a synonym' (2012: 3). University-based intellectual and pedagogic activities are, for Tuck and Yang, 'white moves to innocence', which allow settlers to feel better about the horrors of settler colonialism without actually doing anything practical to change it since to do so would involve (at a minimum) a loss of privilege.

This is an important intervention and decolonization of intellectual thought should not be simply another 'move to innocence' which assuages 'white guilt'. We need to sit with the discomforts which their intervention may give rise to and take them seriously in approaching our own work. Building critical consciousness should always, necessarily, lead to action in the contexts and varying positions of power that we occupy. Nevertheless, we concur with Bhambra, Gebrial and Nişancıoğlu (2018) in that we do not take the position that struggles against colonialism are *only* about settler-colonial dispossessions of land. Colonialism was/is not only a series of settler projects, it also entailed slavery and slave trading, commercial imperialism and direct rule (to name but three examples). It was furthermore accompanied by a whole host of legitimating intellectual projects, in which many universities in former metropoles played a central role, as 'Rhodes Must Fall' so aptly demonstrates. With Bhambra and colleagues, we take colonialism as a global project and acknowledge the role of universities, academic knowledge and disciplines as key sites through which colonialism – its moral justifications, racial theories and Orientalist imaginaries – was produced. These different projects require different, but related, responses in different contexts. We take this position, undoubtedly, as a consequence of our location in the British context and acknowledge that any blind spots on the specificity and structures of settler colonialism may be a consequence of this position.

But we also do not subscribe to the idea that all intellectual work to reveal systems of colonial knowledge should be viewed as moves towards (white) innocence (although this remains an active risk that we should be reflexive about). This is in part because intellectual work should never be the only work that we do, but also because knowledge production has long been an important part of colonizing and decolonizing work; thinking and acting are interconnected. What is of particular concern to us as scholars interested in migration is the extent to which colonial perspectives in many ways continue to dominate scholarly output and teaching in the contemporary period, as the 'Why Is My Curriculum White' and other projects of 'decolonizing the university' have so clearly shown. While this book engages with some theoretical work which challenges migration studies as it is currently articulated in the Global North, then, the perspectives discussed are not simply 'add-ons' to be included while the core stays the same. Instead, taking such interventions seriously upends much of what we think we know about migration.

But bearing in mind Tuck and Yang's (2012) intervention, it is important also to state again that the intellectual sphere cannot and should not be the only sphere in which we seek to enact change. We may observe, therefore, that migration studies has tended as it has emerged to be a predominantly 'white' field and this may not be unrelated to the fact that the colonial past and its legacies and continuities, including a focus on race, have not been central to migration studies projects, textbooks or the agendas of research centres. Those who have provided answers to the question what would it mean to make colonialism central to how we understand migration are rarely self-declared 'migration scholars'. We need, then, to reflect on (and act to change) structural hierarchies in higher education which are themselves connected to the legacies of colonialism, as other critics of the project have argued, at the same time as thinking about our intellectual commitments. This will include recognizing structural racisms – racial and ethnic inequalities (and silences and absences) in terms of student attainment and staff appointments and promotions. It is also to recognize that as migration studies has a historical relationship to policy making, the type of knowledge produced by scholars and taught to students does shape (if not often in a direct way) material conditions and policies. Challenging the intellectual foundations of the field is always part of broader struggles which are not always, or only, 'academic'.

Sitting with the unease and tension around calls to decolonize which Tuck and Yang articulate, we have decided to not call this book 'decolonizing migration studies'. However, we see this work as connecting with activities encapsulated in decolonizing agendas within 'the university' as an institution, a site of power relations and a place for the validation of knowledge claims. We also need to recognize our privilege within the existing systems of power and political economy which made the writing of this book possible. We are both white 'cis'-gender scholars, with relatively secure positions in elite institutions, and this has shaped our ability to write this book, perhaps over other people systematically marginalized within, or excluded from, the academy. This is important to acknowledge. But challenging the colonial and racialized systems of academic knowledge (in this case on migration) is not simply a job for people of colour. Nor should centring colonialism be a niche research interest; it is a fundamental reorientation which is often/ always contested, incomplete and imperfect, a work in progress and *everyone's* responsibility. With this in mind, we hope this book will form part of broader conversations, challenges and critiques which we openly welcome and encourage.

Does migration studies need to think about colonialism?

As the discussion above indicated, 'decolonizing' is a highly contested agenda. But the idea that colonialism should be an important part of how we make sense of the present is, surely, less contentious, particularly in contexts where it has been elided. Recent years have seen a growing number of scholars arguing for greater acknowledgement of colonial histories and their legacies for contemporary migration issues. For example, Mains et al. (2013: 132) observe that 'despite the material links between colonialism, postcolonialism and migration, social scientists in general have been slow to address this intersection' (see also McIlwaine 2008, cited in Mains et al. 2013). Tudor (2018) and De Genova (2018) specifically articulate this lack of attention in terms of a neglect of postcolonial racism and racialization, and observe that there is a strong sense in the field that to speak of racism is either to be racist, or (relatedly) that such observations are (or should be) the exclusive interest of scholars of colour (see also El-Tayeb 2011; Boulila 2019; Grosfoguel, Oso and Christou 2015; Michel 2015; Walia 2014). Rivera-Salgado (1999) noted twenty years ago that race and ethnicity are 'frequently either ignored or treated as a consequence of migration flows and considered to be a problem "here" not "there"', but this pattern has not significantly shifted. Certainly any increased recognition of ethnicity rarely also then understands ideas of racial or ethnic difference to be rooted in long-standing practices and processes of colonialism (see Hall 1978 for more on this).

The interconnectedness of migration *studies* as a project of university institutions, with migration *management* as a project of national and international policy-making institutions, is relevant here. Because migration scholars do not only speak to each other and have esoteric intellectual discussions about the dynamics of migration, they are also invited into these national and international policy-making fora. The language of migration scholarship and that of migration governance are therefore deeply entangled and interdependent. Institutions such as the United Nations High Commissioner for Refugees (UNHCR) and its non-refugee, migration-focused sister organization, the IOM (International Organization for Migration), are key players in this relationship and themselves emerged from colonialism. The UNHCR was founded to support European refugees exclusively following the Second World War because the colonial and settler-colonial powers did not want people of colour to have full access to human rights (Mayblin 2017). Its remit expanded as a consequence of the demands and activities of movements for decolonization. The IOM, meanwhile, was founded to settle Europeans (at a time when Europe was thought to be overpopulated) in Africa (at a time when African countries were not thought of as sovereign nations) (Hansen and Jonsson 2014).

Bridget Anderson (2019: 2) has suggested that 'perhaps we are experiencing not an "age of migration" but an age of migration *research*' (emphasis in original). Studies of migration first emerged at the end of the nineteenth century. Gabaccia (2014) argues that in the United States studies of migration were primarily based in social anthropology and revolved around the application of 'assimiliationist theory' to different social groups who were deemed 'immigrants' (see Fitzgerald 2014). When we tend to speak of the institutionalization of migration studies as a 'field', we are referring to the period after the Second World War when states and international organizations began funding research on migration and refugees. The development of migration studies thus presents an interesting example of a 'state science' (Gabaccia 2014). Whilst interdisciplinary, the field grew around the demands of states and the international community to track and account for the movement of people 'globally' (Donato and Gabaccia 2015). But, more specifically, this was concerned with the mobility of people from the Global South to the Global North in periods of decolonization and under what would later be called 'globalization' and the further entrenchment and expansion of neo-liberal capitalism. The provision for this type of research grew in the United States and in Europe, in the latter under the emergent funding landscape of the European Union (EU) and within a broader biopolitical interest in the cost and benefits of migration, demographics and population management (for example, see the establishment of Osnabrück's Institute for Migration Research and Intercultural Studies (IMIS) in 1991).

This history of course shapes the field today. Whilst it would be a mistake to see all migration studies as overdetermined by the need to create policy-relevant research and to produce research that maps onto the interests of states and international organizations for the capture of funds, these factors strongly shape what constitutes appropriate knowledge and determines research agendas across migration studies (see Hatton 2018 on the United Kingdom and German context). To Scholten (2018), the dangers of this 'co-production' of knowledge have led to migration scholars reproducing forms of methodological nationalism and reifying state concepts such as 'integration', 'sovereignty' and the 'migrant versus citizen' divide (also see de Genova 2013). Whilst more 'critical' intellectual projects have shaped the field in terms of engagement with theories of 'transnationalism' throughout the 1990s (see Blanc-Szanton, Glick Schiller and Basch 1992), and more post-structuralist-influenced approaches to mobility and spatiality (Urry 2007), this environment has not been conducive to a sustained engagement with postcolonial and decolonial theory or even a broader engagement with historiography (Gabaccia 2014). The often superficial engagement with history is evidenced by the long-held view in key migration study textbooks that continue to periodize 'contemporary migration' (i.e. after the Second World War) as 'new', 'unprecedented' and 'unique' (see, for example, Castles, de Haas and Miller 2014).

In spite of the colonial blind spots within migration studies, it would be disingenuous to suggest that the field has completely ignored colonialism. Migration theories which draw on world systems theory (which is also an intellectual point of departure for decoloniality) are notable in taking account of colonial histories in their analyses (Richmond 1994; Satzewich 1991), and textbooks on migration studies almost always cover this theoretical field (see Brettell and Hollifeld 2008; Castles, de Haas and Miller 2014; Martiniello and Rath 2012). World systems theory (see Wallerstein 2004) makes sense of the world in terms of the incorporation of increasing numbers of states into the global capitalist economy and the consequent emergence of a worldwide division of labour which has uneven impacts on different societies. It divides the world into core, semi-periphery and periphery and argues that the core and periphery are locked into a relationship of exploitation and dependency which structurally prevents peripheral countries from developing. There are clear implications for migration studies here in that migration would then be understood as part of much broader relationships between states and societies. As wealthy 'core' economies became increasingly dependent upon low-paid migrant labour from the peripheries from the 1970s, international labour migration came to be seen as an important element in relations of domination between core and periphery. What is now called South–North migration therefore, from this perspective, reinforces relations of dependency.

There are criticisms to be made of the extent to which world systems theory adequately accounted for, or then instrumentalized, race and gender in the world system (Grosfoguel 2011). Nevertheless, this is undeniably a corner of migration studies which has sought to incorporate an account of historical colonial power relations in seeking to make sense of the present. Equally, Latin American decolonial work on the 'coloniality of power' is indebted to world systems theory even as it departs from its primarily economic focus (Quijano 2000). It is here that we see emerging some decolonial analyses of migration which are alive to the importance of colonial histories, and indeed presents (Grosfoguel, Oso and Christou 2015).

A postcolonial awareness is also visible in, if not central to, other areas of migration studies. Scholars who research the European context often, for example, note the movement of migrants from former colonies to former metropoles in the second half of the twentieth century (Geddes and Scholten 2016). These 'postcolonial' migrations have given rise to many studies which, though more often cited in sociologies of race and ethnicity or cultural studies (for example, Cohen and Jonsson 2011; Gilroy 2002b, 2004; Hall 1996c;

Wemyss 2009), nevertheless overlap with the concerns of migration researchers (for example, race and racism as legacies of empire are strong themes in Joppke 1999). Those who research the settler colonies as 'countries of immigration' also often note the colonial history of those countries, albeit often too briefly and rarely with an engagement with settler colonialism as an ongoing phenomenon. Those who work on what is increasingly dubbed 'South–South' migration are, furthermore, offering a wellspring of non-Eurocentric analytical frameworks which, if not necessarily centring colonial histories, are certainly working against Eurocentrism and are very much alive to the connected colonial histories that link different parts of the world (Fiddian-Qasmiyeh 2015; Fiddian-Qasmiyeh and Daley 2019).

There are, nevertheless, prominent volumes in the field which barely mention colonialism, postcolonialism or decolonization (e.g. Brettell and Hollifield 2008; Carens 2015; Faist 2000; Kivisto and Faist 2010; Sassen 1999; Soysal 1994). Likewise, postcolonial and decolonial scholarship is frequently ignored as a way of theorizing migration in key textbooks (even those professing to 'diversify', for example Castles, de Haas and Miller 2020). There are also many postgraduate 'Refugee and Forced Migration' programmes at 'world-leading' universities which cover neither these themes and theories nor issues of race and racism. As historical-structural approaches, such as those deriving from world systems theory, have been dismissed as overly structurally deterministic and have fallen out of favour, with them we have lost a focus on global racism and the legacies of colonialism as structuring axes of inequality and im-mobility. The focus has moved towards the more agential meso- and micro-level theories of 'communities', 'networks', 'circulations' and individual migrants within the context of globalization. But at the same time as acknowledging people's power to act upon their own lives, these approaches pay too little attention, as previously noted, to structures of race and racism.

Refocusing on race and racism necessitates a renewed focus on the legacies of colonialism in contemporary power relations and particularly on the continued relevance of racial hierarchy for contemporary social, political, legal and economic life. Migration scholars tend to shy away from 'race' as a concept, as noted above, since it is associated with histories of racial science which we do not wish to lend legitimacy to. When studies do at least show an awareness of colonial histories, it is too often the case that colonial knowledge, racism and power are treated as something 'in the past' (see, for example, Castles, de Haas and Miller 2020: 312–16). Nevertheless, 'race' continues to hold meaning in the social world and racial ideas continue to significantly impact upon people's lives (Bonilla-Silva 2003; Lentin 2020; Yancy 2016), as the recent renewed focus on racial capitalism has shown (Bhattacharyya 2018). In order to develop more adequate analyses of migration in the contemporary world, we need to acknowledge this and incorporate such analyses into migration studies.

A further issue is the extent to which migration studies continues to be quietly invested in 'modernization theory' (see Bhambra 2014). This is the idea that Europe and the white settler colonies at some point became 'modern' (wealthy, democratic, rational, secular, rights-based, egalitarian, capitalist, etc.), and that this process (the 'European miracle') was endogenous. In order for other parts of the world to become like Europe and its settler colonies (an aim assumed to be desirable), and particularly for them to eradicate poverty, modernization theory advocates that they can and should follow the path laid out by Europe and the wider Global North. This idea of modernization underpins the idea of 'development' (Escobar 1995). It centres Europe and European history as the reference point from which a road map into the future is imagined for countries deemed 'underdeveloped'. The concept of 'development' is important in migration studies and is rarely paid critical attention. There is an assumption that development is the same as poverty reduction and that migration may facilitate or hinder this desirable process, or that from the opposite perspective development can facilitate or curtail migrations. That is not to suggest that poverty reduction is a problematic aim, but that we do need to acknowledge: (a) the colonial history which facilitated wealth accumulation in 'the West' – development in this part of the world was not endogenous and unrelated to impoverishment and exploitation in other parts of the world (Rodney 2018 [1972]) and cannot therefore be simply mimicked elsewhere; and (b) the ongoing power relations which facilitate inequality in both mobilities and immobilities but also in concentrations of wealth and poverty globally. An interrogation of the colonial origins of the idea of development facilitates an alternative framing of the issues at stake.

A growing number of scholars argue that our analyses of

migration-related phenomena are enriched by an analysis which acknowledges histories of colonialism, and related racisms. On this theme, Adeyanju and Oriola (2011: 952) observe that 'there is no notable scholarship in the existing body of literature on African migration that deals with the influence of the colonial discourse and ideology on Africans' desire to immigrate to the West'. This is despite the fact that these discourses, which have endured the end of formal colonialism, are for them central to understanding the motivations behind African migration to the West, and despite the fact that African migration to 'the West' has received a significant amount of scholarly attention. Mains et al. (2013: 131) suggest that the critical interweaving of postcolonial theory and migration studies offers 'a unique opportunity to reflect and ground our understandings of mobility in more complicated and (hopefully) sensitive ways'. A call to complication and complexity, then, goes to the heart of the potential of the bodies of literature discussed here.

But there have also been recent suggestions that a post- or decolonial frame risks reconfirming the national territory as a site of analysis (Anderson 2019; Sharma 2020). A central danger, some argue, is that migration researchers might be cementing or confirming the migrant/native distinction by working from such perspectives when what we should be doing is denaturalizing such binaries through de-nationalizing and de-territorializing our work (see also Davies and Boehmer 2019). We contest this reading of post- and decolonial perspectives though concede that too often binaries are reinforced rather than complexities embraced. Undeniably, anti-colonial movements have historically drawn on nationalist discourses as a move to resist colonial definitions of belonging, but this has not been without significant intellectual critique (for example, see Fanon 2008 [1952]). Equally, indigenous studies have been criticized for promoting an exclusionary 'nationalist' agenda and the debate rages about how solidarities can be built across colonial/modern lines of racialized distinction which were the very basis of the formation of settler-colonial states (Lawrence and Dua 2005; Sharma and Wright 2008–9; Tuck, Guess and Sultan 2014). While we would distinguish between projects of self-determination under conditions of colonial occupation on the one hand and anti-migrant nationalism on the other, the point here is that such struggles are certainly not the totality of intellectual discussion within decolonial or related fields.

The project of questioning colonial frameworks of hierarchical distinction (Mayblin 2017; Mignolo 2011a; Ndlovu-Gatsheni 2018a; Wynter 2003), of understanding histories as made up of movements and interconnections between societies and peoples rather than separateness (Bhambra 2014; Krivonos 2019; Nisancioglu 2019), of challenging Eurocentrism (Alatas 2006; Amin 1988; Bhabha 2005 [1994]) and critiquing the ways in which legal, social and economic definitions and functions of border regimes produce certain migrants as a problem (Achiume 2019; Anghie 2008; Pahuja 2011) is the very antithesis of parochialism, nationalism and 'us and them' politics. We hope to show this at length through the course of this book but also acknowledge that all fields and perspectives have their own blind spots, contradictions and unrealized aspirations – we are certainly not arguing that there is not a lot of work to do in this area. In the next section, we sketch out some of the key foci of three fields of work that have offered significant inspiration to us in our own work and in exploring in this book what a migration studies that centres colonialism might look like.

Postcolonialism, decoloniality and Third World approaches to international law

In relation to the intellectual projects which are associated with the agenda of 'decolonizing the university', postcolonialism, decoloniality, TWAIL, indigenous studies, global histories, South–South relations, black studies and subaltern studies, amongst other projects, are all seen in a variety of different disciplines and geographical locations to have contributed to this agenda. Three of particular relevance to the perspectives presented in this volume are postcolonialism, decoloniality and TWAIL. Here we briefly sketch out the main foci of these intellectual fields, but for an extended discussion of some of the broader theoretical issues at stake refer to chapter 2.

Leela Gandhi (1998: 4) describes postcolonialism as 'a theoretical resistance to the mystifying amnesia of the colonial aftermath'. In other words, postcolonialism is a critical theoretical perspective which engages with and contests the enduring uneven relations between formerly colonized societies and former colonizing societies. Postcolonialism is rooted for many scholars in 'Third World' struggles for decolonization, both in a practical political sense and in terms of ongoing decolonizations of thought, knowledge, economic power and cultural practices (Young 2001). Academic postcolonialism, as a general orientation, originated in the humanities and is better established in English literature, history and cultural studies (which offers a key bridge into sociology, anthropology and human geography) than in the social sciences (Bhambra 2007, 2011; Go 2013). In theoretical terms, postcolonialism has sought to contest dominant western ways of viewing the world and to challenge the assumed universalism of ideas which emerged in Europe from the eighteenth century to the present day. In this sense (and rather confusingly), it is very much not about seeing colonialism as something which has finished and is now in the past, despite its name.

Three authors are often cited as being the founding theorists of postcolonialism within the humanities and social sciences. They are: Edward Said (1995 [1978]), Gayatri Chakravorty Spivak (1988, 1999), and Homi K. Bhabha (2005 [1994]). Said's 'Orientalism' takes a Foucauldian perspective in uncovering the discursive production of colonial meanings beyond the end of formal colonialism. Said is primarily concerned with the way in which the western academy reproduces the colonial difference, the inherent 'otherness' of non-European societies, through textual and non-textual (e.g. art) media. Colonial power, Said urges, is not separable from colonial knowledge since the Orient, and the Occident, are the products of systems of representation. He reminds us that 'human history is made by human beings' and that 'since the struggle for control over territory is part of that history, so too is the struggle for control over historical and social meaning' (Said 1995 [1978]: 331). The Orient, then, is an invention of intellectuals, commentators, artists, politicians, writers and others, but it does not exist as a cohesive entity outside of that representation or outside of its relation to the Occidental self-understanding. What is at stake is not 'that there is a real or true Orient that could have been known, but rather [Said] is provoking us to consider how what we know is itself framed as knowledge through particular systems of representation and the practices of colonial governance based upon them' (Bhambra 2014: 212). There is a broader challenge here. For migration researchers, that is about questioning whether the subjects of academic research exist as 'migrants' outside of our definitions of them as such, and how those definitions connect to colonial modes of defining the world and the various people within it.

Spivak extends this. Her key contribution is to problematize and question how the Third World subject is represented in western discourse, taking up some of the themes addressed by the Subaltern Studies Collective in the early 1980s. In 'Can the Subaltern Speak?' (Spivak 1988), Spivak seeks to complicate the concept of representation, borrowing the *vertreten/darstellen* distinction from Marx. While *vertreten* means to represent in the form of a substitute or proxy, *darstellen* is to represent in the form of a depiction or portrait. Spivak is here interested less in the subjective experience of oppression and more in the mechanisms and structures of domination. She argues that the subaltern, by virtue of being the subaltern, cannot speak in the ways we demand of her, yet too often European academics present themselves either as objective observers of others or as allowing the oppressed to speak for themselves. What this hides, Spivak argues, are the power relations at stake, as well as the historically rooted worldviews of academic 'observers' who interpret as they translate.

Finally, Homi K. Bhabha contributed the next keystone publication in what have now, retrospectively, become the key pillars of postcolonialism. In *The Location of Culture*, Bhabha (2005 [1994]) investigates identity through the lens of representation within the context of colonialism. He suggests that the value differential between the original and the copy, with western culture always representing the former, consistently places the mimicking colonized subject in a position of 'otherness'. Identity here is therefore either 'presence' (the real thing) or 'semblance' (similar to but not the real thing). Thus the point that to be anglicized is 'emphatically not to be English' demonstrates the place of knowledge as a form of social control: whether such knowledge is implicit or not, it cannot be learned (2005 [1994]: 125). The copy can thus always be identified and therefore controlled. For Bhabha, the writing out of colonial spaces from the narrative of modernity, the spatializing of time, instituted a particular theory of cultural difference which installed 'cultural homogeneity into the sign of modernity' (2005 [1994]: 349). The crux of the critique therefore becomes apparent: modernity is fundamentally limited by its built-in ethnocentrism.

While postcolonial studies is often associated with South Asian scholars working from post-structural perspectives in the humanities, decoloniality is associated with Latin American scholars working from world-systems perspectives in the social sciences. In a key founding article of the field, Anibal Quijano articulated a theory of the coloniality of power. Quijano argues that the 'modernity' of

Europe has become the context for its own being, but that this is in fact 'so deeply imbricated in the structures of European colonial domination over the rest of the world that it is impossible to separate the two' (Bhambra 2014: 130). Coloniality and modernity are therefore 'two sides of the same coin' (Mignolo 2007: 464). Many other scholars, particularly those from, or working in, Latin America, have explored this co-constitutive relationship between coloniality and modernity (Maldonado-Torres 2007; Mignolo 2000, 2011a; Vázquez 2011; Wynter 2003).

In the same vein as the postcolonialists discussed above, decolonial scholars are interested in the ways in which colonial power has not only been used to physically and materially dominate groups or societies identified as racially inferior, it has also entailed the subjugation, dismissal and erasure of whole systems of knowledge identified as *intellectually* inferior. Thus Maldonado-Torres has identified three key realms of coloniality which are of interest to their project: coloniality of power, coloniality of knowledge and coloniality of being: 'while the coloniality of power referred to the interrelation among modern forms of exploitation and domination (power), and the coloniality of knowledge had to do with the impact of colonization on the different areas of knowledge production, [meanwhile] coloniality of being would make primary reference to the lived experience of colonization and its impact on language' (Maldonado-Torres 2007: 242)

In dialogue with Levinas, Maldonado-Torres explains that 'coloniality survives colonialism' and this has implications for political and economic power and for knowledge production, but it also affects our ways of being in the world: 'It is maintained alive in books, in the criteria for academic performance, in cultural patterns, in common sense, in the self-image of peoples, in aspirations of self, and so many other aspects of our modern experience. In a way, as modern subjects we breath[e] coloniality all the time and everyday' (Maldonado-Torres 2007: 243).

Decolonial scholars are, then, in part, interested in exploring the means by which we can 'delink' from coloniality/modernity and in doing so recover alternative knowledge systems (Mignolo 2007). Decoloniality is, therefore, a diverse project which has developed through an intellectual tradition distinct from postcolonialism, but which shares many of the core concerns (see Bhambra 2014).

TWAIL is centred on principally legal concerns from a broadly

'Third World' perspective. TWAIL begins from the position that international law is a 'predatory system that legitimizes, reproduces and sustains the plunder and subordination of the Third World by the West' (Mutua 1994: 31). Despite the fact that international law is meant to be universally applicable and purportedly delivers global stability, TWAIL scholars argue that the development of international law was 'essential to the imperial expansion that subordinated non-European peoples and societies to European conquest and domination' (Mutua 1994: 31). In other words, the very establishment of international law as an international legal framework went hand-in-hand with colonial enterprise (Anghie 2008). TWAIL is deeply connected to movements for decolonization and is seen by many as being inaugurated at the 1955 Asian–African Conference in Bandung, Indonesia (Kanwar 2015). Though it is a wide-ranging intellectual and political project, the TWAIL agenda, according to Mutua (1994: 31), has three foci:

1 'to understand, deconstruct, and unpack the uses of international law as a medium for the creation and perpetuation of a racialized hierarchy of international norms and institutions that subordinate non-Europeans to Europeans';
2 'to construct and present an alternative normative legal edifice for international governance';
3 'through scholarship, policy and politics to eradicate the conditions of underdevelopment in the Third World'.

Chimni (2006: 3) argues that 'international law is the principal language in which domination is coming to be expressed in the era of globalization' and suggests that part of the (as yet unfulfilled) potential of TWAIL is the promotion of the equal mobility of human beings. A TWAIL perspective, then, draws attention to the ways in which international law does not necessarily offer universal justice precisely because unequal power relations following the patterns of the colonial era are maintained through international law today.

This brief overview gives a flavour of the large bodies of work in postcolonialism, decoloniality and TWAIL which can be drawn on in migration studies in order to think through the legacies of colonialism for migration governance and migrant experiences today.

There are also many other bodies of relevant work which will be drawn upon through the course of the book, including the work of black studies scholars, indigenous scholars, critical race theorists, and decolonial, postcolonial and black feminist and queer scholarship. These bodies of work offer theoretical tools for researchers interested in centring colonialism in migration studies, though it should be noted that they are not always in agreement, or compatible, with each other. We do not seek to smooth the edges of these disjuncts. In this book we nevertheless aim to further explore how such scholarship might contribute to understanding migration-related phenomena, and to showcase the work of scholars who have already taken up this agenda.

Structure of the book

The book is structured as follows. Chapter 2 discusses a central concern for scholars working with postcolonial and decolonial theory: modernity. We discuss two key aspects of the conceptual framework of modernity: the temporal and the spatial, and how these aspects are deeply connected to colonial histories. These debates are vital for centring colonialism in migration studies and have significant implications for how migration is researched and understood in, and between, different parts of the world. The chapter also discusses the concept of 'Eurocentrism', and how Eurocentric perspectives emerge from, and are fed by, the uneven global politics of knowledge production. The penultimate section discusses a specific idea, that of 'development', and how ideas of development follow colonial ways of understanding the world. The final section asks whether Eurocentrism can be overcome since, as Walter Mignolo argues, we are all trapped in the 'colonial matrix of power'. As a whole, these discussions lay the groundwork for much of what follows in the book and as such the discussions follow through and are elaborated through the subsequent chapters.

Chapter 3 demonstrates the relevance of interdisciplinary work on race to the central questions of contemporary migration studies. We thus explore the connections between colonial racism and mobility and explain how an analysis of race can help us understand contemporary migration and mobility. The chapter focuses on the centrality of race to the shaping of the modern world through European colonialism. Here we demonstrate how race was bound to colonial rule and imperial capitalism and, as importantly, how systems of domination relied on the management of mobility globally. We tie the more 'historical' way that race related to the control of movement to the modern push towards state immigration regimes and explore what this means for studies of migration. We also examine how different bodies of scholarship have theorized race. Race is foregrounded here as a 'sociopolitical fact of domination' (De Genova 2018: 1770). Throughout the chapter, we demonstrate in more detail how race informs the politics of mobility, but also how an analytics of race helps us understand migration in a more rigorous and historically accurate manner. In short, we are better able to understand what underpins mobility, what structures responses to certain people moving and how people experience migration if we centre race and racialization in our analysis.

Chapter 4 focuses on questions of sovereignty and citizenship. While sovereignty is typically defined as 'authority over a territory occupied by a relatively fixed population, supposedly necessary to protect that territory and its citizens from external [and internal] threats' (Leigh and Weber 2018, cited in Nisancioglu 2019: 2), an engagement with colonial histories, and the colonial present, significantly complicates this definition. This is in part because the myth of equality between sovereign states is brought into question, and in part because the sovereignty of settler-colonial states especially is directly challenged (Mathieu 2018; Moreton-Robinson 2007, 2015). This chapter therefore explores the relationship between ideas of migration, sovereignty and citizenship when set within the context of colonial histories and presents. It does this through an engagement with three very different areas of scholarship which have centred colonialism in relation to such issues: connected sociologies (postcolonial), migration as decolonization (TWAIL), and indigenous studies. Together, these interventions present modes of thinking about migration in the context of citizenship and sovereignty regimes which denaturalize their formation today.

All of the perspectives discussed in chapter 4 take seriously the importance of colonialisms of various kinds in shaping the present, and they concur that what results are racially grounded global inequalities and injustices. But between them there are contradictions and disconnections. This in part arises from the different modes of colonial relations that are foregrounded in the work of scholars. These different emphases do not necessarily sit easily together, as the discussion on 'no borders' at the end of the chapter makes clear. It is not our intention to smooth over these differences but to draw attention to the multiple possibilities raised by a commitment to centring colonialism and then the subsequent importance of local contexts in making sense of them in place.

Chapter 5 focuses upon forced migration and looks at three key interventions on this theme which have sought to rethink forced migration and asylum from a postcolonial, decolonial and TWAIL standpoint. The first section addresses colonial histories in relation to asylum as a human right in order to draw out some important reflections on the exclusivity and Eurocentrism of the category of 'man' and 'human'. The next section focuses on the work of Aurora Vergara-Figueroa, whose writing on deracination in Colombia offers an important new perspective on forced migration. The next section discusses the concept of 'necropolitics', first proposed by Achille Mbembe but recently taken up by numerous scholars seeking to understand the role of violence, suffering and (especially) death, particularly 'letting die', in migration governance. Collectively, these perspectives disrupt many of the dominant ideas about displacement and forced migration within the field and ask us to rethink both how we understand refugee histories and what that then means for how we understand the present.

Chapter 6 examines the relationship between security and borders as part of the colonial present. The chapter responds to work on border security and the 'securitization of migration' which has become an expanding area of scholarship in the context of the global 'war on terror' since 2001. In order to challenge some of the assumptions of this research agenda, the chapter maps out how engagement with postcolonial, decolonial and non-Eurocentric scholarship can change how we analyse the seemingly rapid expansion of border security. It does so by demonstrating how border security should be considered part of the reformulation of colonial rule, grounded in an analysis of colonial racism and what this means for studies of border security in both the Global North and South. Through engaging explicitly with Islamic and decolonial African scholarship, the chapter also seeks to challenge how we understand borders, security and political violence labelled 'terrorism'.

In the final substantive chapter, we aim to take up and expand the burgeoning scholarship in migration studies on the theme of gender and sexuality by arguing that scholars interested in gender and sexuality need to engage more seriously with the role of colonial modernity and racism in contemporary systems of oppression. This is particularly important with scholarship in migration studies because of the field's historical amnesia over questions of colonialism and race. After outlining the benefits and limitations of feminist approaches to gender and intersectionality as a theory and methodology, we suggest that we are better able to comprehend how gender and sexuality work within coloniality by engaging with three authors' work and three key concepts: Maria Lugones and the concept of the 'coloniality of gender'; Hortense Spillers and the concept of 'ungendering'; and Roderick Ferguson and the concept of 'taxonomies of perversion'. Each of these scholars speaks to different but interrelated traditions within postcolonial and decolonial feminism, black feminism and queer-of-colour critiques. In doing so, they represent radical departures for how we think about interconnected questions of gender, family, intimacy, sexuality and, importantly, their deep connection to racialized violence and the imposition of colonial and imperial rule. What is so instructive about these authors' work is that it challenges us to start by understanding that the struggle against patriarchal society (and more specifically heteropatriarchal society – the dominance and 'superiority' of both men and heterosexual gender and sexual relations) is at once a struggle against imperial racialized capitalism and colonial dispossession. This is increasingly important in a world where claims to protect 'women's' and 'LGBTQ+' rights are being used by states to justify racist and imperial policies (see Farris 2017; Luibhéid 2018; Puar 2007).

Finally, the conclusion brings the key themes and threads together and calls again for readers to appreciate the urgency with which migration studies scholars need to engage with the history and ongoing structures of colonialism.

2
Time and Space: Migration and Modernity

Introduction

This chapter discusses a central concern for scholars working with postcolonial and decolonial theory: modernity. These debates are vital for centring colonialism in migration studies. The idea that some parts of the world became modern through, inter alia, the Renaissance, the French Revolution, the Industrial Revolution, and beyond, and that others did not, is fundamental to much social scientific enquiry (Bhambra 2007). Some of the key features of modernity are scientific progress, democracy, human rights and capitalism. Where these features are absent, it is often suggested that they must be promoted in order that societies who are 'behind' might 'catch up'. This distinction between the 'modern' world and the 'traditional' world endures today in distinctions between developed and developing countries. It has also structured the academic division of labour in terms of the legitimate objects of study, and particularly the legitimate societies for different types of enquiry. Sociology, for example, tends to focus on 'modern' societies such as France or Australia, countries which are not within the purview of development studies. In turn, this framing then has significant implications for how migration is researched and understood in, and between, different parts of the world.

This chapter thus explores the concept of modernity within the social sciences and explicates the ways in which modernity has been denaturalized and parochialized by postcolonial and decolonial studies. We discuss two key aspects of the conceptual framework of modernity, the temporal and the spatial, and how these aspects are deeply connected to colonial histories. We then discuss the under-recognized darker side of modernity. This darker side draws attention to historical omissions, erasures and silences, which complicate our understanding of the emergence of modernity. The next section focuses on the issue of Eurocentrism, and how Eurocentric perspectives emerge from, and are fed by, the uneven global politics of knowledge production. This discussion is very important for rethinking contemporary migrations because it unsettles the underlying framework from which much research into international migration begins. Following this, we explore how ideas of Eurocentrism link to dichotomies around West and East, North and South, and how these types of distinction emerge from histories of colonialism. At the same time, imaginaries such as 'the West' and 'the Global South' are shifting symbolic geographies of territory, race and culture whose content changes over time.

The penultimate section discusses a specific idea, that of 'development', and how ideas of development follow colonial ways of understanding the world. The final section asks whether Eurocentrism can be overcome since, as Walter Mignolo argues, we are all trapped in the colonial matrix of power. We present some perspectives that have sought to overcome or think from the borders of modern/colonial thinking as indications that this work is indeed being done already. As a whole, these discussions lay the groundwork for much of what follows in the book and as such the discussions follow through and are elaborated through the subsequent chapters.

Problematizing the concept of modernity in the social sciences

'Modernity' is a key orienting concept within the social sciences within many universities globally (Bhambra 2007). Indeed, for most scholars, modernity is a relatively uncontroversial and useful shorthand for a series of events which occurred in Europe between the seventeenth and nineteenth centuries, and which fundamentally changed European societies for ever. Anthony Giddens, for example, explains that modernity refers to 'modes of social life or organization which emerged in Europe from about the seventeenth century onwards and which subsequently became more or less worldwide in their influence' (Giddens 1990: 1). This generality, he notes, leaves the exact content of 'modernity' (and its effects) open for discussion; but two things, when and where it emerged, are undisputed.

Colonial expansion led to the proliferation of forms of knowledge for making sense of the world, as well as ways of organizing this knowledge (Mignolo 2005). As the social sciences developed through the nineteenth and twentieth centuries, the divisions between the disciplines often followed colonial modes of thinking about the world in relation to 'modern' societies and, conversely, 'traditional' societies. For example, sociology historically (and to a large extent contemporaneously) dealt with 'modern' societies and the conditions of living in modernity (Bhambra 2007), while anthropology and human geography dealt with 'traditional' societies and 'primitive' peoples (Asad 1979; Deloria 1988). Disciplines such as political science and economics started from the position of understanding politics as a western phenomenon (usually originating in ancient Greece), or the capitalist economy as a product of modernity, and later expanded out from this geographical starting point (Hay 2002; Marx 1990 [1887]; Skinner 1979; Waltz 1959; for debates on this in international politics, see Anievas and Nişancioğlu 2015; Hobson 2004). Modernity, then, has both *explicitly* preoccupied many social scientists and *implicitly* provided the underlying framework from which the world today is understood. That is, as comprised of, for example modern and traditional, developed and developing, societies. For migration studies, this dichotomous way of construing the world, distinguishing between developed and developing countries, or more recently the 'Global North' and the 'Global South', has been the central assumption upon which all else rests.

Postcolonial and decolonial scholars agree that modernity is centrally a concept rooted in the project of European (and later western) self-understanding which went hand-in-hand with colonial expansion. It is about understanding how some societies came to be 'modern' (and superior), in relation to 'others' who are 'traditional' (and inferior). The whole idea of modernity is therefore dependent on the story of the 'European miracle'. As Gurminder K. Bhambra has argued (2007), this story rests on two fundamental assumptions: rupture and difference. She writes of this in terms of 'a temporal *rupture* that distinguishes a traditional, agrarian past from the modern, industrial present; and a fundamental *difference* that distinguishes Europe from the rest of the world' (2007: 1, emphasis added). The Renaissance, the French Revolution and the Industrial Revolution are central to this narrative as they demonstrate how modern societies endogenously produced the unique features that distinguished them from elsewhere: rationality and science, art and literature, human rights and democracy, and technological advancement. From Europe, this was first exported to the white settler colonies but has long been seen to have much broader relevance. As Bhambra (2007: 4) points out, 'the Western Experience has been taken both as the basis for the construction of the concept of modernity and, at the same time, that concept is argued to have a validity that transcends the Western experiences'. But the world was very much globally interconnected through this period, and none of these developments or struggles happened in isolation. Indeed, the story of the 'European miracle' itself is selective in that it more often than not ignores colonialism and enslavement and is therefore incomplete.

Central to understanding modernity are the vectors of time and space. Temporally, modernity happened, or happens, at particular times in particular places. The temporal aspect of modernity (its arrival) is usually thought of as occurring within the context of a linear conception of time and progress which originated with the Enlightenment. Thus 'the present was described as modern and civilized, the past as traditional and barbarian. The more you go towards the past, the closer you get to nature' (Mignolo 2011a: 152). Europe, therefore, progressed from nature, through tradition, to enlightenment, others did not. But because progress towards modernity occurs within a linear conception of time, Europe (or 'the West' as a symbolic geography) will always be 'ahead'. If others accelerate, they may 'catch up'. The achievement of modernity is thus a kind of long-drawn-out race. But the rules are not always clear. For example, if a country is seen to have caught up economically, because it has become wealthy, it is likely that other aspects, such as the religiosity of the population, or dominant cultural practices, will be viewed as 'backward', indicating that the country (and its nationals) is indeed still 'behind' in time (Shimazu 1998).

A linear conception of time allows for the periodization of events and for the tracking of progress from a state of nature to that of civilization. A linear conception of time is therefore a precondition for the western understanding of history. As Zygmunt Bauman explains, 'the history of time began with modernity. Indeed, modernity is, apart from anything else, perhaps even more than anything else, *the history of time*: modernity is the time when time has a history' (Bauman

2000: 110). Europe transcended its past through developing a historical consciousness articulated through the practices of academic history, archaeology, archiving, periodizing and cataloguing. As these conventions were thought to be absent elsewhere, other places were thought to lack a historical consciousness. Other forms of knowledge were therefore inferior, and non-western cultures either lacked history or needed Europeans to properly record their history and recount it to them (Bhambra 2007; Cohn 1996, cited in Bhambra 2007: 22).

Societies outside of Europe did have alternative conceptions of time in general, for example approaching time as cyclical, and alternative ways of making sense of the relationship between past and present events. But this fact did not diminish the assessment by colonizers that these places were *without history*. This was the case in India. British colonials did not find evidence of the recording of history which correlated with their understanding of what history should look like, and they determined that because Indians had a cyclical conception of time they were incapable of knowing their own history or of deciphering between myth and fact (Thapar 2002). Thapar (2002) argues that in fact early Indian texts indicate both cyclical and linear conceptions of time in operation, but this was not apparent to British colonials during the colonial period, in part because they were making sense of India within the context of colonial worldviews which rendered the inferiority of Indian society an existential necessity.

Mignolo (2011a) draws our attention to the fact that in the first centuries of colonialism the difference between colonial conqueror and the objects of conquest was articulated in terms of barbarism: 'others' were barbarians. With the development through the Enlightenment, following Hegel, of ideas of linear time, and thus progress from barbarism, 'barbarians' became 'primitives'. Primitives are still barbarians, but they are very specifically defined in temporal terms: as being of the past and capable of change (enlightenment, civilization) into the future. Over time, and into the present, the concept of linear time has thus facilitated the classification of cultural differences according to their proximity to either modernity (the present and future) or tradition (the past). But as we know from Said (1995 [1978]), places elsewhere to the western academy only exist in these ways to the extent that Occidentals understand them as such. The Orient exists only in the minds (and works) of Occidentals.

Of course, this view of time as linear is only one way in which human beings have theorized the temporal, as noted above. The contemporary western and now globalized understanding of time as linear is relatively recent and is not the approach to time that dominates everywhere. Equally, the emphasis on progress, and particularly on western history as a story of progression towards civilization, necessitates the telling of history in a particular, incomplete way. Spatially, modernity first emerged in Europe as a way of making sense of perceived changes that were happening *there* in relation to *elsewhere*. In other words, the European miracle is a place-specific, or parochial, way of understanding world history. This is significant because, as Bhambra (2007: 11) points out, 'the way in which we understand the past has implications for the social theories we develop to deal with the situations we live in today'. The self-conception of Europeans as modern therefore depends upon the conceptualization of other places as not modern: 'the translation of geography into chronology was the work of colonization, of the coloniality of knowledge and power' (Mignolo 2011a: 152).

While migration studies has tended to be dominated by well-funded research undertaken in the 'developed' or 'First World' of the 'Global North' or 'the West', it has then disproportionately focused on migration from the 'developing' or 'Third' World to the 'First World'. That research institutions in the 'Global North' are better funded than those in the 'Global South' is (generally speaking) a consequence of long histories of colonial-era plunder, appropriation, exploitation, and wealth accumulation (Collyer et al. 2019; Keim et al. 2014). But the fact that this is not generally understood and reflected upon in the North then has implications for the social theories we develop to deal with international migration today (to paraphrase Bhambra). Because without acknowledging colonial history, South–North migrations become the primary migrations of interest in the world, become potentially illegitimate, become something detached from sedimented and unequal global racial and economic power relations. They become about individualized aspirations and motivations for a 'better life' set apart from the broader global historical contexts in which they might be understood.

How can we start to think against this current? Decoloniality offers us some of the theoretical tools to start to unthink what we have learnt about modernity. From decolonial scholars we gain the concept of coloniality/modernity, which articulates the intertwining of colonialism and colonial ways of viewing the world in hierarchical and civilizational terms (coloniality) with the rise of 'modernity' as a structuring frame through which the specialiness of Europe can be conceptualized (Escobar 2007; Mignolo 2000; Quijano 2000). Coloniality and modernity, then, are two sides of the same coin. Or, in other words, modernity was 'colonial from its point of departure' (Quijano 2000: 548). Capitalism, for example, did not endogenously emerge in Europe as a consequence of enlightenment, rationalism and industrial development. Rather, slavery and colonialism produced a concentration of wealth in European societies which funded the Industrial Revolution, allowed for global trading dominance and also offered technological inspiration for the emerging industries. For example, the cotton mills of Northern England used technologies taken from India (Bhambra 2007). Thus the emergence of capitalism is first and foremost a global colonial story, a story of racism and differentiation, despite the seductive power (for some) of the story of inherent European brilliance (Anievas and Nişancioğlu 2013; Banaji 2007; Bhattacharyya 2018; Hobson 2004). The point, really, is that modernity has its darker sides (Mignolo 2011a). It is not all wealth, democracy, freedom of speech and expression, employment, consumerism, and clean drinking water. It is also exploitation, appropriation, racism and subjugation.

No longer exclusively an affair of Europe or 'the West', modernity appears now to be everywhere: 'the triumph of the modern lies precisely in its having become universal. From now on, it's modernity all the way down, everywhere, until the end of times', as Escobar (2007) has pointed out. In this context, 'not only is radical alterity expelled forever from the realm of possibilities, all world cultures and societies are reduced to being a manifestation of European history and culture' (Escobar 2007). By 'radical alterity', Escobar refers here to different ways of living; different sets of ambitions for the political, economic and social organization of societies; different ways of understanding and being and acting in the world beyond the hegemonic ideology of modernity spreading globally from an imagined western epicentre. The 'coloniality' concept in coloniality/modernity does not, therefore, simply refer to colonialism. Instead, it is about a colonially inspired Orientalism in Said's (1995 [1978]) terms, a worldview.

This 'coloniality' has been analytically disaggregated into a range of spheres, notably power, knowledge and being, as discussed in the Introduction. The coloniality of power refers to 'the inter-relation among modern forms of exploitation and domination', or how western global domination is dependent on exploitation (Maldonado-Torres 2007: 242). Coloniality of knowledge relates to the 'impact of colonization on the different areas of knowledge production' (Maldonado-Torres 2007: 242). That is, where authoritative and influential knowledge is produced and proliferated, which knowledges are produced by which people, and which languages and media hold legitimacy and have greater global reach. This concept has clear relevance for migration studies and should give us pause to consider who produces 'global' knowledge, in which languages is it disseminated, where are they located and who is excluded from this conversation? Paul Gilroy (1993: 6) has articulated this from a different perspective (that of cultural studies) as 'the struggle to have blacks conceived as agents, as people with cognitive capacities, and even with an intellectual history'. The coloniality of knowledge either denies this to be the case or admits it to be plausible but scratches its head in terms of where to find such an intellectual history. For the western academy, and indeed beyond, intellectual history is white.

'Coloniality of being' refers 'to the lived experience of colonization and its impact on language', or the way in which one speaks and thinks of one's place in the world through the filter of coloniality (Maldonado-Torres 2007: 242). We might think of this in relation to W. E. B. Du Bois's work on double consciousness. To be African American was, for Du Bois, to live with a double consciousness, simultaneously black and American, always living with this 'two-ness' and always seeing oneself through the eyes of white America. This concept of double consciousness has been elaborated and applied beyond the nineteenth-century US context (see Gilroy 1993) and its overlap with Maldonado-Torres's (2007) concept of the 'coloniality of being' (in the Latin American context) might help to elaborate our understanding of both concepts. How we think about our place in the world is therefore related to how we imagine our geographical and temporal location in relation to modernity.

These insights into the spatial and temporal dimensions of modernity, which problematize the idea of traditional developing societies who are behind in time and need to catch up through modernizing, unravel many of the dominant understandings of contemporary international migration. They raise a set of questions which, if taken seriously, would alter the basis upon which much funded research on migration is undertaken. For example, whose mobility is, in this context, problematized and whose is not? When we look at this problematization in the context of colonial histories, what sorts of explanation for it appear plausible and which do not? What kinds of historical and contemporary interconnections have given rise to particular migration patterns and responses to them? Why would migration from a generalized 'Global South' be construed as threatening in the North? How do migrants understand the relations and differences between the places they have come from, and are going to, and how is their migration understood against the backdrop of histories of colonialism and ideas of modernity and unmodernity? In short, through thinking of modernity as a culturally produced time/space construct, we must then start to think through the lens of historical, as well as contemporary, interconnections. This is a theme we return to below.

Eurocentrism

The concept of Eurocentrism is closely aligned with these discussions around contesting the dominant conception of modernity. Knowledge production – the questions that we ask, the hypotheses that we come up with, the research methods that we employ, the frameworks through which we interpret our findings, the places we publish and the audiences that will consume our ideas – emerges from historically contingent social conditions and contexts. Alatas (2006) argues that because some countries (for him, the United Kingdom, France and the United States) are 'world social science powers', scholars in Asia must engage with their frameworks and scholarship, even as scholars in the world social science powers can completely ignore scholarly debates happening within Asia (or indeed elsewhere) (see also Gamage 2016). This is because these powers generate large volumes of published social science output, are well funded to undertake research internationally, have global reach and hold a global prestige that makes them impossible to ignore. They have both the resources, and access to visas, to conduct international research projects and the social position to make their findings about a variety of contexts plausible. Indeed, even within the fields of postcolonial and decolonial scholarship, the most famous scholars internationally are more often than not based in Global North institutions (Cusicanqui 2012). We have, then, according to Alatas (2006), dominant producers of global knowledge, who can write with authority about anywhere, and peripheral consumers of global knowledge, who can only write with authority about particular places and when doing so must use the frameworks of the global knowledge producers. Even when research focuses on the Global South (or racialized, migrant communities in the Global North), this is all too often an extractive research process (see Tilley 2017). When scholars in the Global South are engaged with the power structures of global knowledge production, this often means that they are treated as empiricists or area specialists rather than producers of 'theory' (often still seen as universal and generalizable). Keguro Macharia (2016a) calls this 'being area-studied'. This, briefly put, is what Eurocentrism amounts to in the global academy.

Intellectually, Eurocentrism is an orientation which puts some places (Europe and 'the West' more broadly) at the centre of world history as well as of contemporary knowledge production. Only upon entry into modernity do other places enter that world history (Dussel 1995). Eurocentrism therefore requires us to ignore connected histories, colonial interconnections and the actual role of the non-West in world history. But it also requires us to ignore non-European philosophical traditions and intellectual projects oriented to making sense of the world in which they found themselves – just as Europe's philosophers were doing. Eurocentrism is about an orientation to a 'normal' political, philosophical, economic and historical reference point. That reference point may not be explicit; it may be implicit. But it would suggest, for example, that in thinking through moral arguments for immigrant inclusion or exclusion globally we look only at European-origin philosophers.

Eurocentrism is not therefore simply about a disproportionate focus on geographically European societies. Amin (1988: 185) charges that Eurocentrism incorporates 'an inability to see anything other than the lives of those who are comfortably installed in the modern world'. Not seeing here is not the same as ignoring. Rather, it is not seeing people as themselves but instead seeing against the measuring-stick of the West. Gayatri Chakravorty Spivak (1988) has made an important contribution to this discussion in elaborating beyond the inability to 'see' to an inability to represent more broadly. In her seminal article 'Can the Subaltern Speak?' (also discussed in the Introduction), Spivak problematized the way in which the Third World subject is

represented in western discourse. She argues that while western intellectuals often express a belief that subaltern groups understand their
oppression and can speak for themselves, such an argument ignores
the inaccessibility of the subaltern as a 'subject'. For her, the subaltern
is destined to remain mute as a result of mistranslations emergent
from the relations of power involved in the colonial encounter.
The 'true' self-conscious voice of the subaltern is therefore inaccessible because the subaltern, by virtue of being the subaltern, cannot
speak in the ways demanded of her by western academics. Spivak
therefore argues that academics too often present themselves either
as objective observers of others or as allowing the oppressed to speak
for themselves, rendering scholarly representations as unproblematic.
What this hides, Spivak observes, is the economic, cultural and intellectual power relations that are at play in such representations, as
well as the historically rooted institutional contexts, categories and
worldviews in which academic observers are situated.

Singaporean scholar Sin Yee Koh (2015) argues that Eurocentrism
in migration studies manifests itself in, amongst other things, a
disproportionate focus on immigrant-receiving states in western
countries and a dearth of studies which focus on the perspectives of
sending contexts, except as a developmental concern. The *continuity*
(as opposed to contemporary novelty) of migration patterns from
former colonies in Asia to former metropoles in Europe, as well as
between former colonies within Asia, is a particular area of scholarly
silence, according to Koh. But, at the same time, concepts which
are derived from 'the Anglo-western experience', such as typologies
of different types of migrant, ideas of liberal citizenship or ideas of
'development' (discussed further below), are applied unthinkingly in
other places as though they are universal and not context specific.

North, South, East and West in colonial modernity

One of the challenges of discussing Eurocentrism is the tendency to
see it as having a bounded geographical content, in other words,
as referring to Europe and things from the geographical space of
Europe exclusively. This is true even of more fuzzy binary categories
such as the 'Global North' and the 'Global South', 'developed'
and 'developing', or the slightly more disaggregated 'First World'
(wealthy capitalist countries), 'Second World' (post-socialist) and

'Third World' (postcolonial). The latter rubric mimics the East/West dichotomy in that the Second and Third World only make sense in their relation to the First World, as post-socialist or postcolonial. The Cold War has ended and yet the 'three worlds' thesis continues to resonate. Indeed, while 'the East' is less often used, 'the West' is in common parlance. Some people, following Bangladeshi photographer and activist Shahidul Alam, use the distinction 'majority world' (less affluent) and 'minority world' (more affluent) in order to draw attention to the fact that those who hold most of the wealth are in fact the minority of the world's population. Rather than arguing that one of these typologies is better, or more geographically accurate, and should therefore be viewed as superior to others, we understand all of these labels as shifting symbolic geographies which, like 'the Orient', rarely map onto actual places. They are deployed by different actors as necessary conceptual generalizations to help them (and us) to articulate particular ideas about the world and the various people and places in it. They hold social and political meaning, but they should not be mistaken for 'real' places. Indeed, this conceptual fuzziness can open up fertile terrain for contemplation over the 'common-sense' content of these ways of articulating the world.

As noted in the introductory chapter, the separation of the world into either three groups in the 'three worlds' thesis, or two in the West/East, North/South, developed/developing, minority/majority dichotomies, is central to the academic division of labour in the social sciences (Bhambra 2007; Chari and Verdery 2009). While disciplines such as sociology focus on First World, western, developed, minority-world, Global North societies, disciplines such as development studies and anthropology focus on its antithesis. The Second World is then left to area studies that are conceptualized as in 'transition' (Baker 2018; Kangas and Salmenniemi 2016). Pletsch (1981) suggests that this division of intellectual labour emerged in the 1950s and is indebted to the dominance and mainstreaming of modernization theory in, particularly, US research institutions. For him, the two key axes emerging from this period, communist/free and traditional/modern, can *both* be understood as relations of modernity. They locate modernity (science, rationality, freedom) in the First World, with the Second World and Third World both ruled by different forms of irrationality: ideology and propaganda in the former; and traditionalism, economic backwardness and religiosity in the latter. The Second World can thus 'transition' into modernity by abandoning communist ideology, while the Third World can modernize through civilization; both can 'progress' through capitalism.

Migration studies has the *potential* to disrupt such categorizations through its knowledge of interconnection, transnationalism, complexity and hybridity. More often, however, the 'three worlds' lens is applied, with scholars offering expertise in one of the worlds, and disciplinary affiliations accordingly fitting into one of the 'modern/developed' disciplines, those concerned with developing countries and those exploring post-socialist contexts from the perspective of post-socialist area studies. But what if we ruminate on the nature of colonial modernity and what it might mean for how we carve up our analysis of the world? For example, Chari and Verdery (2009) have argued, in light of the insights of Pletsch (1981) noted above, that in the post-Cold War period we need to look between and beyond the 'posts' of post-socialism and postcolonialism. They write: 'an integrated analytical field ought to explore intertwined histories of capital and empire' and in doing so interrogate 'the ongoing effects of the Cold War's Three-Worlds ideology' (2009: 19). The Cold War, they point out, was not just about analytically organizing the world but also about representing it.

A dialogue across 'posts' may therefore be helpful in order to explore the messy reality of the world beyond the neat categories that we have created to aid our understanding of it (Kangas and Salmenniemi 2016; Krivonos 2019; Krivonos and Näre 2019). When we look at the histories of colonialism, socialism and capitalism, what we in fact find are connected histories (Bhambra 2014). Chari and Verdery (2009) think 'between the posts' because post-socialism and postcolonialism are not just about particular geographical spaces, they are about historical representations of space and time which have implications for knowledge and practice everywhere, not just in locations which were colonized. Thus what they draw attention to is that in order to comprehend the world, we need to explore the consequences of colonialism and decolonization, and Soviet socialism and its end, for spaces beyond those directly involved. The concept of coloniality allows us to do this; the coloniality of power, knowledge and being are not geographically limited in their reach, and the colonial articulation of modernity is pervasive but differentially experienced around the world.

Important in this discussion is the symbolic power of 'the West' as a container of modernity, where the West is differentially conceived, depending on where one is positioned. For example, Krivonos (2019) has found that for young Russian migrants in Helsinki (Finland), the city represents western modernity, and indeed whiteness, even while the location of Finland as European, western or ethnically 'white' has historically been contested (see also Krivonos and Näre 2019). The West, then, is a *symbolic geography*, as are all of the other taxonomies of civilization. They are bound up with how we imagine other peoples and places and how we imagine and represent ourselves (Bhabha 2005 [1994]). Postcolonial scholars have argued that each makes sense only in terms of its opposite(s) (Said 1995 [1978]). The Orient, for Said, was a fiction invented by Occidentals and only contained meaning as a site of tradition, exoticism, chaos and magic in its relation to the modernity, normality, order and reason of the Occident. In this context, where modernity is located in the symbolic geography of the 'West', the uncivilized can only mimic the civilized – the copy is not the same as the original (Bhabha 2005 [1994]).

Where and who is and can be modern changes over time. This is also intermeshed with ideas of racial inclusion and differentiation. Because modernity has a racial (biological but also cultural) content rooted in colonialism, coloniality is at all times imbued with a racial sorting logic. That is not to suggest that racial categories are static or always about phenotype. For example, the Irish are now generally considered to be modern and white, and Finns are more modern and whiter than Russians through joining the European Union (Ignatiev 1995; Krivonos and Näre 2019). These common-sense logics of inclusion and differentiation are not rational, but they do appear rational to many people, including academic researchers. Thinking with modernity therefore draws our attention to the ways in which whiteness, Europeanness, Christianity and 'the West' occupy a semantic field with shifting emphases (Hall 1996a; Hesse 2007). To reduce this field to economics (GDP, income per capita) is to miss many layers of understanding.

Modernity, migration and development

Where these discussions of modernity and Eurocentrism find their most immediate and obvious application in migration studies is in the field of migration and development. There are two main perspectives on this: the developmental perspective, which is interested mainly in the effect of migration on development; and the migration perspective, which is mainly interested in the effect of development on migration. In relation to the former, for a long time, a key question within migration studies has been 'whether migration encourages development of the countries of origin or, conversely, hinders such development' (Castles, de Haas and Miller 2014: 69). On the one hand, migration is thought to aid development in sending countries through 'brain gains' and remittances, and on the other hand migration is thought to lead to 'brain drains' and to therefore hinder development. The general consensus appears to swing, pendulum-like, between these two perspectives (de Haas 2010, 2012). From the migration-focused perspective, which is of great interest to (perhaps even led by) governments and policy actors in the Global North, the argument has been about whether development increases rates of migration through providing people with the financial means to migrate, or whether it allows them to stay in their countries of origin as a wider range of jobs and opportunities open up (see Clemens 2014). As Raghuram (2009: 104) has pointed out, 'almost all theorisations of this link assume migration to be something that can be contained, regulated or influenced, [and] development as normatively good'. Few of these perspectives challenge the idea of 'development' itself as a problematic colonial framework.

De Haas (2012) dates the migration and development debate back to the post-Second World War period. Indeed, this is the period in which decolonization began apace and in which 'development' replaced civilization as the primary language of progress through which the modernization project was articulated because 'development' as a project, we must recognize, is a project of modernization in which 'developing' countries are engaged in an externally facilitated effort to catch up with the West (Escobar 1995). Development, as a discourse, aspiration, project, practice and set of social relations, then, cannot be understood without recognizing the colonial context from whence it emerged. The idea of development has of course come under significant critical scrutiny for its damaging Eurocentric assumptions (Ake 2000 [1979]; Escobar 1995; Esteva and Babones 2013; Sardar 1999). Nyamnjoh, writing on the expansive topic of development discourses in Africa, explains:

> Development for Africa is a theme fraught with a multiplicity of
> western-generated ideas, models and research paradigms, all with the

purported goal of alleviating poverty. This discourse is carried on mainly by economists and other social scientists who limit the question of development to the problematic of achieving economic growth within the context of neo-liberal economic principles. Notwithstanding the fact that there are now novel paradigms of development that search for solutions under the theoretical rubric of alternative development, the problem is rarely studied in a holistic manner. (Nyamnjoh 2004: 162; see also Ake 2000 [1979] for an earlier intervention in this vein)

In 1992, Sachs described development as 'like a ruin in the intellectual landscape', obsolete owing to its clear failure to achieve what it had set out to do (Sachs 1992: 6; see also Rutazibwa 2018). Yet the post-Cold War period has not seen development become obsolete as a discourse or project; it seems to receive as much attention, funding, focus and effort as ever before. In this vein, Sardar (1999: 49) succinctly explains that 'development continues to mean what it has always meant: a standard by which the West measures the non-West', though we must of course acknowledge that it is not only western governments and NGOs that buy into the development discourse.

Nevertheless, the development discourse, according to its critics, does centre western knowledge about how to develop, and it decentres non-western knowledge systems which might offer an alternative to development (Escobar 1995). In more extreme critiques development has become something to be feared in many places, as it brings pollution, consumerism, the destruction of communities and cultures, and all of the individual and collective harms of global market capitalism – though such perspectives have not gone uncontested (Cooper and Packard 1997; Esteva and Babones 2013; Nilsen 2016). Nevertheless, these critiques, most vocally under the 'post-development' agenda (see Rahnema and Bawtree 1997), have, as noted above, not decreased the dominance of 'development' as a discourse within or outside of the academy.

In a widely cited article tackling the migration and development agenda, Raghuram (2009: 104) argues that the development industry has achieved very little, even as development has morphed from a concept of economic growth 'to basic needs ... [to] poverty reduction and sustainable livelihoods', and yet it continues to look for new solutions. Migration has recently received renewed focus as a possible solution since migrants undertake activities which could be construed as international wealth redistribution through remittances. Northern governments are also concerned about whether migration is a desirable mechanism for development since it moves people out of place and leads to concern over terrorism, integration and cohesion. For Raghuram, the growing interest amongst policy makers in the dynamics of migration and development has led to a concomitant increase in academic research on these dynamics. Particular 'forms of migration and certain kinds of development come to be visible in this debate', she argues, 'occluding other imaginaries of the relationships between migration and development' (Raghuram 2009: 104; see also Bettini and Gioli 2016; Sinatti and Horst 2015).

The harms of the discourse of development have, of course, been challenged by social movements around the world who have both fought for the rejection of development as an ideology and also sought to manipulate or alter the meaning and understanding of development in particular contexts for the benefit of the people who live there (see, for example, Moore 1998; Rangan 2000; Vergara-Camus 2014). Equally, as Elena Fiddian-Qasmiyeh (2015) has pointed out in her work, there is a risk of maintaining and reinforcing North–South dichotomies in critiques of development, rather than challenging them. Acknowledging South–South responses to development would enable us, she argues, to include rather than erase Global South actors within the history of development.

The challenge for migration studies, then, is how to listen to critiques of development and seriously engage with them without continuously erasing the agency and endeavours of 'southern' actors from the picture (see Rutazibwa and Ndushabandi 2019). How might we research and write about the relationships between international migration and, for example, poverty as a phenomenon and at the same time root our understanding of poverty in colonial histories and neo-colonial relations, and as connected to global processes of accumulation, dispossession and liberal capitalist ideology? Escobar (1995: 215) argues that better futures will not be found in 'development alternatives, but in alternatives to development, that is, the rejection of the entire paradigm altogether'. By thinking with alternative discourses, might we imagine the search for equality, dignity, 'a better life', beyond the confines of the 'development' discourse? Might we also follow Fiddian-Qasmiyeh's (2015) lead in decentring the Global North in our understanding of such phenomena? Perhaps by being more specific about the actual processes that we seek to understand, that are being wrapped up in the idiom of 'development', and exploring how migration is related to those factors, migration researchers need not fall prey to the pitfalls of Eurocentric modernization orthodoxy.

Can Eurocentrism be overcome?

As Aníbal Quijano (2007) has argued, we are all stuck in colonial modernity, which suggests that finding a path out is challenging. Structural barriers are important here. As noted earlier, particular languages, most notably English, are privileged in the world of academic publishing, and people such as ourselves, who are located in wealthy European and white-settler states, are more likely to have the support and resources to then successfully publish in influential journals and with well-resourced publishing houses (Cabral, Njinya-Mujinya and Habomugisha 1998). Those ideas which conform to established norms of 'good' theory or scholarship from recognized figures of the 'canon', which is usually itself made up of European and US-origin scholars, are then also more likely to be accepted for publication. Global South scholarship is more likely to be seen as particular to the context in which it is produced or to similar 'developing' contexts. Philosophical or policy ideas produced in the Global North are thus readily applied globally or to a wide range of international contexts, but ideas produced in the Global South are more likely to be seen as context specific (Alatas 2006). These are barriers to scholars in Global South countries publishing and influencing debates in international journals, but they are also barriers to the publishing of any work from any location which challenges dominant modes of thinking. Nevertheless, there are several schools of thought that have sought to imagine, or move, beyond Eurocentrism or colonial/modernity, depending on their perspective. We will briefly describe four of them here: delinking; border thinking; the pluriverse; and connected histories/sociologies.

Amin (1988) proposed 'delinking' in the late 1980s as a response to the problematic entanglement of 'development' in Third World countries and international political and economic power relations which sought to both control development and ultimately stymie it. Amin argued that Third World countries could not improve the living standards of their populations by engaging with targets set within the highly unequal global capitalist system. Instead, he argued, they should 'delink' from the global system and pursue domestic development priorities. This idea, as a practical economic policy proscription, was highly contested (see, for example, Smith and Sender 1983) but the concept of epistemic 'delinking' was taken up in the discourse of decolonizing knowledge articulated by Latin American decolonial scholars. Scholars such as Walter Mignolo and Aníbal Quijano started to argue in the 2000s that what was needed was to 'change the terms of the conversation' in order to challenge 'hegemonic ideas of what knowledge and understanding are' (Mignolo 2007: 459). Delinking here is about denaturalizing concepts and conceptual fields that are considered to be universal and yet are approached from particular perspectives. For example, what does religion, democracy, culture, society, art or family look like, and how do we know them when we see them? Denaturalizing accepted ways of knowing the world is fundamental to decolonizing knowledge from this perspective. Approaching international migration as something which is embedded in multi-generational patterns of bordering, mobility, immobility, uprooting, colonialism and imperialism would, then, constitute delinking from the accepted ways of knowing which focus on the present as unprecedented and separate from (particularly global) phenomena in the past (Vergara-Figueroa 2018).

One approach to delinking is 'border thinking' (Anzaldúa 1987; Mignolo 2007). Border thinking does not need to be newly invented; it is theory which already exists (but is rarely acknowledged away from the spaces in which it is practised) that sits at the borders of the colonial matrix of power. It comes from the lived experiences of people familiar with the darker side of modernity. Border thinking does not happen separately to modernity but in response to it, as part of live struggles against oppression. Thus 'border thinking is the epistemology of the exteriority; that is, of the outside created from the inside' (Mignolo and Tlostanova 2006: 206). The border here is conceptualized in terms of both geographical distance from 'modern' places and epistemic difference from the Eurocentric centres of world power. Mignolo and Tlostanova write:

> Consider, on the one hand, knowledge in the modern and imperial European languages and – on the other hand – Russian, Arabic and Mandarin. The difference here is imperial. However, they are not just different. In the modern/colonial unconscious, they belong to different epistemic ranks. 'Modern' science, philosophy and the social sciences

are not grounded in Russian, Chinese and Arabic languages. That of course does not mean that there is no thinking going on or knowledge produced in Russian, Chinese and Arabic. It means, on the contrary, that in the global distribution of intellectual and scientific labour, knowledge produced in English, French or German does not need to take into account knowledge in Russian, Chinese and Arabic. (Mignolo and Tlostanova 2006: 214)

In this context, border thinking entails using alternative knowledge traditions and non-European languages of expression in order to reimagine theories of the social, the economic and the political. Examples of border thinking might include Islamic philosophical and scientific thought or First Nation epistemological traditions (Coburn 2016; Smith 2012). Examples of the enactment of border thinking might include the Haitian Revolution and the more contemporary World Social Forum (Santos 2008; Scott 2018; Trouillot 1995). According to decolonial theorists, these alternative perspectives introduce other cosmologies into the hegemonic discourse of western modernity which are not unwittingly committed to, or restrained by, its frame. Border thinking on themes related to international migration is already happening. Mignolo sites the location of border thinking in the Third World but, in acknowledging actually existing mobilities, he then charts 'its routes of dispersion travelled through migrants from the Third to the First World',which are then found in 'immigrant consciousness' (Mignolo 2011b: 274). Postcolonial intel-lectual Frantz Fanon then developed his immigrant consciousness at the point of migrating from Martinique to France (Fanon 2008 [1952]). Upon discovering that he was seen first and foremost as a 'negro' in France, he thus brought border thinking to France through the immigrant consciousness, encapsulated in the quote 'Oh, my body, make of me always a man who questions'. Equally, work on settler colonialism and within indigenous studies offers multiple challenging perspectives from the borders of colonial/modern thought which rethinks the power relations at stake in contexts of immigration (see chapter 4; see also Chatterjee 2019; Gonzales 2012; Jones 2009; Klooster 2013; Lugones 1992; Pulido 2018; Rodríguez 2014; Stanley et al. 2014). Whether such thought is transforming hegemonic ideas about international migration is then another question.

Rojas argues that the universalizing colonial logic of capitalist modernity 'eliminates entire life-worlds, declaring them non-credible alternatives' (Rojas 2016: 370). The universalizing logic is not equitable, however; modern reason is often thought of as superior to other systems of knowledge. Central to modernization is the distinction between culture and nature. Culture defined the subject that knows; nature defines the object to be known. Because nature is 'out there' and is knowable through reasoned examination, it must then be universal and equally accessible on the same terms, irrespective of the cultural background of the knower. As Reiter (2018: 7) points out, 'to think that the European way of explaining the world is somehow closer to the way the world really is is naive'. Such an assumption is culturally particular, and yet it is nevertheless universalizing. Against this universalizing project, one alternative – a pluriversal politics – offers, according to Rojas, 'a more just coexistence of worlds that exceeds what is possible under a colonial and capitalist logic' (Rojas 2016: 370). The pluriverse, then, is about recognizing that modern ways of understanding the world sit alongside other ways of understanding the world which are different, even incomprehensible, from a modern/colonial perspective (Seth 2013). These different ontologies and epistemologies do not exist in a hierarchy but in an 'ecology of knowledges' (Santos 2008), or an 'epistemological mosaic' (Connell 2018). Nevertheless, some of them may offer solutions to global problems, such as climate change or extreme inequality, which modernity lacks the tools to solve.

If border thinking and the pluriverse look towards the diversity of ways of imagining and understanding the world from different locations, Gurminder K. Bhambra's work on connected sociologies (2007, 2010, 2014), which is discussed further in chapter 4, is about drawing attention to the actual interconnectedness of the world over time. This is complementary to border thinking and the pluriverse, rather than necessarily at odds with it. Drawing on the work of Sanjay Subrahmanyam (1997), Bhambra is interested in overcoming the gap between general historical frameworks (which tend, even when critical, to be Eurocentric) and the many particular contexts and experiences that they then ignore. Subrahmanyam argued that the histories of different places are often analytically isolated from each other because of the way academic work happens, and he suggested that, through looking at the connections between places, deeper insights were gained. Rather than then looking at the diversity of particularity and relating it to European modernity in an implied or explicit hierarchy, or suggesting cultural relativism and reifying difference, Bhambra (inspired by Subrahmanyam) suggests that a focus on interconnectedness allows us to more adequately understand the world historically and contemporaneously. Focusing on interconnections, argues Bhambra (2010: 140), 'allows for the deconstruction of dominant narratives at the same time as being open to different perspectives, and seeks to reconcile them systematically'.

Historical examples of international interconnection abound, which, once acknowledged, make it difficult to contemplate topics such as democracy, human rights or nationhood without understanding these to have emerged from and in global interconnectedness (as opposed to from within the geographical space of Western Europe exclusively). But Bhambra's intention is not to simply argue for a reconstruction of how we understand history and its impact on the present. She goes further in arguing for connected sociologies, which in the present assume the world to be made up of a set of interconnections and influences, and within this context do not centre on particular locations such Europe or the West. In this sense, the South–South migration agenda, which is a burgeoning area of scholarship at the time of writing (Fiddian-Qasmiyeh 2015; Fiddian-Qasmiyeh and Daley 2019), might find theoretical inspiration in her interventions.

Conclusion

This chapter has described and discussed one of the most fundamental insights offered by post- and decolonial scholarship: the critique of the dominant discourse of modernity. It has explained how modernity can be understood as a way of thinking about the world in temporal and spatial terms, and how this framework then has far-reaching implications for the social sciences, including for migration researchers. The chapter has discussed Eurocentrism and the ways in which 'Europe' and 'the West' are symbolic geographies, containers of modernity, which shift over time and are not territorially delimited. After a detour into the 'migration and development' literature as an illustrative example of an area of migration studies that might benefit from being rethought in light of these insights on modernity and Eurocentrism, the chapter ended with a brief exploration of some proposals for overcoming Eurocentrism. Taking seriously the intellectual contributions to social scientific thought discussed in this chapter, we might strive to make our work more adequate to the task of understanding the world from different vantage points, plural as it is.

Having offered this important exposition on post- and decolonial thinking on time, space and modernity, the next chapter moves into a more specific engagement with the concept of race. Ideas of race, and ideologies and practices of racism, are deeply entangled with colonial histories and also migration histories. If migration studies is to take seriously the need to engage with past and present colonialisms, and their legacies and continuities, an engagement with race is essential. While migration studies scholars seem to have shied away from race as a concept, they can rest assured that others have been busy theorizing the social, economic, cultural and political through the lens of race for a very long time. We draw upon this deep and rich body of intellectual work to discuss how migration scholars can (indeed must) start to seriously engage with thinking on race without becoming trapped in essentialist and racist logics.

3

'Race' and Racism in International Migration

Introduction

The study of race and racism has been shaped by a diverse field of scholars, activists and social movements – often grounded in anti-colonial, anti-racist and decolonizing projects. The heterogeneity of approaches to race crisscrosses theoretical traditions – postcolonial, decolonial theory, critical race theory, indigenous studies, black studies and black, postcolonial and decolonial feminism, as well as queer-of-colour critique, have all developed sophisticated theoretical frameworks for understanding how race works as a social and social scientific category. What we learn from these schools of thought is that while understandings of race present it as shifting, contingent, localized and multivariate, it cannot be understood outside of histories of modern colonialism. Racism is a system, a mode of domination and a form of power. As a mode of domination, it persists despite scientific developments that have proven racial categories to be meaningless and racial hierarchies to be fabrications (although see Saini 2019). And yet ideas about different 'races' hold meaning for many people around the world, and of course racism is an enduring structural force in the contemporary social world. Recognizing that race is a fabrication does not mean that it does not have material consequences and shape political and economic structures and experiences. Nor does it mean that the histories and power of 'race' and racialization should be ignored.

Despite the breadth and depth of work on race and racism across the social sciences and humanities, theories of race and racism are remarkably absent from migration studies. Too often 'race' is not given analytical attention, nor is the political work that race *does* focused upon (although see de Genova 2018 and Tudor 2018, for example). As we argued in the last chapter, this is due in part to the history of social science knowledge claims which both underpin colonialism and obscure race as an organizing principle of modernity. Given migration studies' preoccupation with the movement of people from the Global South to the North, it is still surprising that even scholars researching exclusion or violence against those populations often do so without an analysis of colonial racism. In this way, inter-disciplinary debates on race have rarely made a serious impact on the way that migration is taught, theorized and spoken of. Where mobility and race are studied, it still remains largely ignored and under-cited (Rajaram 2018). This of course relates to the broader formation and forgetting of race across many areas of social scientific research, but it also relates to the specifics of migration studies.

This chapter aims to show the relevance of interdisciplinary work on race to the central questions of contemporary migration studies. It also serves a further purpose of highlighting and bringing together existing research on race from scholars working (often loosely) within migration studies. We thus seek to show how race as a concept is connected to colonialism, how colonial racism shaped mobilities in the past, and how racialization continues to shape migration and mobility in the present. The first half of the chapter focuses on the centrality of understandings of race to the shaping of the modern world through European colonialism. Here we demonstrate how ideas of race were bound to colonial rule and imperial capitalism and, as importantly, how systems of domination relied on the management of mobility globally. This is true of the multiple forms of European colonialism that existed from the mid-fifteenth century onwards from processes of territorial acquisition, war, enslavement, genocidal settler-colonial projects to the organization of indentured labour and later decolonization.

In the second half of the chapter, we explore how understandings of race must be understood as materializing logics which organize the stratification of human worth, dehumanizing violence and the perpetuation and justification of structural inequalities. Race is foregrounded here as a 'sociopolitical fact of domination' (De Genova 2018: 1770). In the penultimate section, we briefly explore some of Stuart Hall's writing on race and racism, focusing on his understanding of racism as having two registers – cultural and biological. This helps us in explaining how racism can be different in different places, how it changes over time, and how it has endured beyond the general popularity of scientific racism. In the final section of the chapter, we demonstrate in more detail how race informs the politics of mobility but also how an analytics of race helps us to understand migration in a more rigorous and historically grounded manner. We are better able to understand what underpins mobility, what structures responses to certain people moving and how people experience migration if we centre race in our analysis.

Empire and the invention of race

For more than 500 years, European colonial and imperial expansion fundamentally reshaped the organization of global social relations, economic (re)production, wealth, industrialization, human relationships with the natural world and, through the emergence of colonial scientific thought, how we know the world. European colonial projects, whilst localized and varied, were ostensibly premised on the subjugation – both material and symbolic – of the Americas, Africa and Asia and their peoples and cultures. Whilst too often narrated in western history as a series of benign 'discoveries', colonial expansion, territorial acquisition and accumulation were premised on dispossessive, genocidal and dehumanizing violence (Wolfe 2016). Warfare, disease and outright murder underpinned this process of invasion, territorial acquisition and extraction (Smith 2015). At the same time, the material extraction from colonization shaped the conditions for industrialization in Europe (Anievas and Nişancıoğlu 2015). Not only did the non-European world suffer violent turmoil, this involved the inclusion and subjugation of colonized subjects within an imperial capitalist system that was manufactured to benefit European colonizers (and later settler and allied capitalist regimes) and born out of the unfree labour and resources plundered from the 'new world' (Amin 1988; Federici 2004). This has continued long after the formal end of colonialism; it is embedded in the structural dynamics of today's global economy (Rodney 2018 [1972]; Wallerstein 1974). And these structures continue to be reimposed and sustained by imperial warfare, Afghanistan, Iraq and Libya being recent examples (see Bacchetta, Maira and Winant 2018).

What colonial expansion and violence did is reorganize global relations around European capitalist modes of exploitation, labour relations, private property and, with this, heterosexual relations of intimacy and reproduction (Robinson 1983; on reproduction, see Federici 2004; Lugones 2011). Central to this was the invention of race as a means of organizing and legitimizing colonialism (Goldberg 1993; Ndlovu-Gatsheni 2018a). Race was invented as a way of categorizing people in a taxonomy of humanity as more or less human (Fanon 1963; Wynter 2003). But race did not only justify colonialism after the fact. It also shaped the geographical and historical patterns of who was colonized and how people were treated and brought into colonial projects, for example as labourers, slaves or populations to be eradicated (Wolfe 2016).

The invention of race involved organizing human beings into a hierarchy connoting inferiority and superiority. This intensified in the eighteenth century, where physical traits, such as skin colour, took on a particular social meaning, alongside cultural traits and religion, to code people into this hierarchy. Through the emergence of scientific racism in the nineteenth century, it became possible to describe human beings in terms of ideas of racial 'stock' (and, when on the move, 'flows') – as eugenics sought to manage populations based on biological definitions of racial hierarchies (Kevles 1995). Race not only legitimated the subordination of non-Europeans but also provided a system of knowledge through which Europeans discovered their own 'superiority' and 'whiteness' (Cooper and Stoler 1997; Hall 2002). Of course, the language of 'stocks' and 'flows', which was central to eugenics, continues in the ordinary parlance of scientific demography (Saini 2019), which plays a not insignificant role in the field of migration studies (for example, see Castles, de Haas and Miller 2020; Piekut, Pryce and Van Gent 2019). Equally, it shapes the politics of whiteness and white nationalism that structures how European publics view immigration and how many scholars approach issues of migration and cultural difference. The phrase 'native stock' and 'migrant stock' are, therefore, still in common parlance (for a discussion of white nationalism in academia, see Holmwood 2019).

The work of Jamaican philosopher Sylvia Wynter (2003) calls for us to understand race, and the violence it propagates, not as an aberration of European modernity but instead produced through the revolution of Enlightenment thought. As we discussed in the last chapter, whilst the Enlightenment discovery of 'humanity' and the natural sciences is often viewed in western philosophy and history as the beginning of modern progress, understandings of race were central to such discoveries. As Da Silva (2007) argues, the idea of humanity, born out of the Enlightenment, actively relied on the denial of colonized people from this idea of common humanity. It was Europeans who possessed reason and history whilst lands primed for colonial conquest were viewed as 'without' history, as empty spaces (Vergara-Figueroa 2018) or merely places of 'savagery' and 'barbarism'. For Voltaire (1901: 240–1; see also Poliakov 1982), people racialized as black were heathens and imbeciles. For Locke (1988 [1689]), indigenous Americans were nothing but 'wild savage beasts'; for Rousseau, Aboriginal people were untouched by politics and history (Roberts 1997). The rational sciences of the Enlightenment would then go on to 'discover' the realities and objective evidence of racial categories and differences through the disciplines of biology, anthropology and phrenology. Such knowledge is far from rhetorical or symbolic. We should remember that when the French Revolution was made in the name of 'Liberty, Equality, Fraternity', black Africans enslaved by the French in the West Indies and in the Indian Ocean were actively denied such rights (Rodney 2018 [1972]: 89).

Processes of material conquest, accumulation, enslavement and the reorganization of work, labour and nature were central to the emergence of racial taxonomies because the subordination of colonized and colonizable populations, cultures and worlds needed to be legitimated and naturalized (Thiong'o 1986; Virdee 2019). This isn't to argue that colonialism and the invention of race produced social, cultural and human 'differences' or even notions of 'otherness' or 'strangers'. What race did as a process of categorization and relations of power was codify differences into hierarchies of humanity, which were then viewed as both 'natural' and 'scientific'. Non-somatic traits were steadily coded into classifications of who could be part of humanity and who was deficient, unworthy or in a state of infancy. As we discussed in the last chapter, people became placed in a temporality of modernity as either stuck in the past or progressing towards 'modernity' (as white and European). This temporality of development almost entirely approximated with those populations who were being colonized, or would be colonized, and slowly incorporated into a global system (Agathengelou and Killian 2016; Wolfe 2016).

Decolonial, black studies and Marxist scholars have long demonstrated how race interlocks with the emergence of capitalist social relations (see Quijano 2007; Robinson 1983). As Ndlovu-Gatsheni (2018a: 73) argues: '[racism] on a world scale emerged at a time that continents were being invented not only through cartography but also through the spreading of the exploitative and inhuman capitalist economic system across the human globe and the nascent unfolding of global colonial division of labour.' Here the surplus extraction of profit could be gained through the acquisition of territory (settler-colonial genocide) and/or enslavement, and it shaped the character of private property law and regimes of labour under capitalism (Kuppan 2018; on property, see Bhandar 2018). Violence and exploitative systems of enslavement and labour were produced which racial categories were developed to justify. However, decolonial scholars and historians tend to reject the economistic notion of race offered by some Marxists, which assumes race is a product of capitalist exploitation alone (Grosfoguel 2011; Quijano 2007; Walsh 2002). Jordan (1974), for example, demonstrates the longer legacy of anti-blackness that permeated English society and culture throughout the Middle Ages, from the 'blackened moor' to perceptions of the dangers of 'pagan heathens' (see also Heng 2018). It was commonly assumed that black people were 'devils made of flesh, who accepted neither God nor his commandments' (see also Van den Boogaart 1982). So rather than viewing race as invented for the sole legitimation of colonial projects, the extraction of profit or to divide the working class, it is more accurate to see how these older social relations were drawn upon and helped to shape the material function of race under different colonial projects. In his seminal book *Black Marxism*, Cedric Robinson (1983) complicated reductive readings of race when he argued that the racism and dehumanization of European colonialism drew upon the hierarchies and formations of slavery and regimes of dispossession within feudal Europe. These structures of difference were reformulated and intensified, Robinson argued, through the European enslavement of Africans and the political economy of the Atlantic slave trade. Here European ideas of inferior peoples were turned into absolute notions of racial difference which became central to the organization of capitalism (Kelley 2017; Tilley and Shilliam 2018).

For scholars such as Aníbal Quijano (2007), what changed with colonial expansion and capitalist social relations was a hardening and intensification (and eventually scientization) of European cultural schemas of physical and moral differences. This gave life and flesh to colonial power and the structuring of people into subordinate positions not only as 'labourers' but also as 'slaves' or as human waste which could be imprisoned, used or destroyed (see also Giroux 2008). Whilst race may have become 'scientific' by the nineteenth century, there is a long history that precedes this from the first encounter with indigenous people and the Spanish conquest of Moorish lands (Grosfoguel 2013). From the fifteenth century, Spanish and Portuguese explorers and missionaries debated the humanity of the indigenous peoples of the Americas (Grosfoguel 2013). Whilst wars of conquest took place within Europe, conquered people were viewed as 'enemies' who could be captured or assimilated. Grosfoguel argues that what changed with the conquests in the Americas is that the Spanish and Portuguese began to question the godliness and then humanity of indigenous people. It was not just a question of whether they could be converted to Christianity in this context, but a question of whether they were properly human at all (Gordon 2011; Rodriguez-Salgado 2008).

What we are illustrating here is that race was not just a series of prejudices; it became an organizing principle on a global scale through colonial encounters and was turned into a criterion of social classification for world populations and systems of labour (Robinson 1983). This meant that in the first place, new social identities were produced all over the world: 'whites' and 'Indians', 'Negroes', 'yellows', 'olives', using physiognomic traits of the peoples as external manifestations of their (apparent) 'racial' nature (see, for example, Buffon 1776; Knox 1850; Linnaeus 1964 [1735]). Racial schemas always privileged whiteness and Europeaness but were, and are, not propagated by white people or colonizers alone. Just as with ideas of modernity and notions of temporality that we discussed in the last chapter, some colonized peoples have historically bought into this schema of modernity and race. So, too, have many postcolonial states imbricated within the system of what hooks (2004: 17) calls white heteropatriarchal imperial capitalism (see also Fanon 1963; Mbembe 2001). Equally, it is important to recognize here that race became a *global system* of categorization through colonialism. Race was not only invented to rule colonies, it also shaped the organization of social relations, identities and systems of labour in European metropoles. European publics (particularly throughout the nineteenth century) began to imagine themselves as white and superior and this also structured class and gendered relations in the metropole (Hall 2002; Shilliam 2018).

Knowledge, modernity and huMan

In this section, we explore the work of scholars who emphasize how race is constituted within structures of knowledge. Decolonial scholars have been at the forefront of addressing the centrality of knowledge to systems of colonialism. Here colonialism – or, to be more precise, the continuity of colonialism conceptualized as 'coloniality' – rests on the imposition and normalization of western/European modes of thinking. In this approach, which we began exploring in the last chapter, we are shown that racial categories are a product of a wider civilizational structure where the (post)colonized world is placed outside of European conceptions of time and progress. From this perspective, European empires were just as much violent epistemic projects as they were ones of extraction and accumulation. For Thiong'o (1986), what gave imperialism power was the 'culture bomb' – that is, the annihilation and 'dismemberment' of indigenous ways of life, languages, the environment, heritage and self-capacity. Local systems of knowledge were subjugated and western categories, languages and aesthetics imposed (in part, through the removal of children from their parents to be placed in residential schools for cultural reprogramming), and with them norms of race, gender and sexuality (Lugones 2007).

What Enlightenment thought did was privilege European society as the home of modernity, rationality and objectivity – against this, other societies were 'discovered' as pre-modern, backward or savage. At first, Christian theology and then secularized humanism offered a 'hierarchy of superior and inferior knowledge and, thus, of superior and inferior people around the world' (Mignolo 2011a; see also Quijano 2000). For Mignolo (2011a), race is a historical–structural aspect of colonial/imperial difference. What maps people into racial categories is their relationship to colonial knowledge systems, and how colonial modes of science and progress deem certain populations to be more or less modern (superior/inferior). This is as true under contemporary schemes of 'development' (Escobar 2007; Rutazibwa 2018) as it was under high imperial categories of 'civilization'.

Here race is the outward expression of cultural and pathological underdevelopment as described by European thought. For example, consider (as discussed in the previous chapter) how Eurocentric linear notions of time and history plot different societies against the progress of industrialized Europe or America (Agathangelou and Killian 2016; Escobar 2007). This is more than a geographical distinction. Being from a pre-modern/underdeveloped/backward society is to be rendered more/less pre-modern/undeveloped/backward. Such a Eurocentric norm is also a judgement about civilizational worth, where those less modern are rendered less human.

This leads us to consider the relationship between race and the 'human' because it is with the advent of humanism that race as a naturalized idea connoting inferiority and superiority was consolidated (this is also discussed in chapter 5 in relation to the right to asylum). What was central to the European Enlightenment project was the discovery of 'man' as a universal category of 'all' human beings. And yet as we know, colonized and non-European peoples (and to a lesser extent European women and labourers) were immediately cast out of this universal category. Man was 'civilized', male, European and bourgeois. To Wolfe (2016), what was significant about this was that the discovery of a humanist and liberal version of Man accompanied the discovery of Man as the bearer of political *rights*. Wynter (2003) argues that this is significant because at various points the configuration of Man would allow for European women and all European men to be afforded rights, but it ultimately relied on a fundamental exclusion of colonized others who were cast as not only unable to bear rights but also not quite human or non-human (for more on liberalism and colonialism, see Bell 2016). She writes:

> It was to be the peoples of the militarily expropriated New World territories (i.e. Indians), as well as the enslaved peoples of Black Africa (i.e. Negroes), that were made to reoccupy the matrix slot of Otherness – to be made into the physical referent of the idea of the irrational/subrational Human Other to this first degodded (if still hybridly religio-secular) 'descriptive statement' of the human in history, as the descriptive statement that would be foundational to modernity. (Wynter 2003: 265)

Race is then the normalization of this exclusion and otherness from what Alexander Weheliye (2014) calls the huMan. Inferior races are those who are the irrational, savage remainder. If we think through this logic, it is not so much that colonized and enslaved peoples were dehumanized but that they were not accounted for within this conception of the human and the subject of political rights in the first place. Wynter (2003) and Da Silva (2007) push this further by arguing that this is more than an 'exclusion'; instead, the very possibility of the human relies on the racial subjugation of non-European and subalternized people for it to work. The colonial/European/ western conception of humanity only works because of its exclusion of inhuman others.

Grosfoguel, Oso and Christou (2015) describe the contemporary world through this legacy of the human. They argue that racisms are concerned with dividing people into those that can be recognized as socially and culturally human beings and those that are rendered sub- or inhuman. Drawing on Fanon (2008 [1952]), they argue that through colonial divisions of the world (modern/backward), there are 'zones of being' and 'zones of non-being', zones which create a fundamental dividing line between humans and non-humans. According to Wynter, it is people of African heritage who are most frequently demarcated in the zone of non-being, but Grosfoguel et al. (2015: 636) view this as more historically contingent: 'Depending on the different colonial histories in diverse regions of the world, the hierarchy of superiority/inferiority along the lines of the human can be constructed through diverse racial markers. Racism can be marked by color, ethnicity, language, culture and/or religion.'

So particular histories of colonial subjugation shape contemporary racisms which divide peoples into hierarchically organized racial groups. '[R]acialization occurs through the marking of bodies. Some bodies are racialized as superior and other bodies are racialized as inferior' (Grosfoguel 2016: 11). Significantly for our discussion, both Wynter and Grosfoguel and colleagues discuss racism as fundamentally about colonial ideas of hierarchical humanness in relation to mobility. For example, Wynter (2003: 261) argues that in our contemporary moment, the 'excluded and invisibilized' are 'defined at the global level by refugee/economic migrants stranded outside the gates of the rich countries' (see Mayblin 2017 for more on this).

Grosfoguel and colleagues (2015: 638) argue that contemporary borders differentiate people on the basis of prior racializations (into the human/non-human) but also show how rules around citizenship and immigration law work to produce new racial formations and new zones of non-being within the metropolitan North, as well as between the Global North/South (i.e. populations who are denied not only huMan rights but also recognition and personhood; for more on this, see de Noronha 2019, 2020). Grosfoguel and his team (2015: 640) suggest that 'the zone of being is the imperial world that includes populations oppressed by the imperial elites, while the zone of non-being is the colonial world with its non-western oppressed subjects'. This helps us recognize how movement from the Global North to the South can be viewed by northern publics as people moving across not just geographical space but also time. It equally helps us consider how the fact of mobility from South to North does very little to change global relations of race, as those migrants and minorities within the North continue to be viewed within the inferior zone of non-being and consequently as inferior. It also forces us to recognize that the function of race is reducible to questions about not just who is excluded, but also who is actively included and promoted in immigration regimes and how this relates to the shifting markers across zones of being and non-being.

Race, violence and slavery

To consider the interlinking of race, modernity and colonialism in more detail, we can consider the case of slavery and genocide in the Americas. In Blackburn's (2013) terms, this process of colonization was the 'crucible' of Euro-American modernity. For European explorers, the Americas were viewed as an empty land and wilderness, 'discovered' by Europeans. This cast indigenous First Nations people not as the rightful sovereigns of the land but instead as standing in the way of progress, development and 'Europeanisation' (Quijano 2007). Although colonial projects differed locally, indigenous peoples' existence was always ancillary to the colonial project, as evidenced in their genocidal destruction (Coulthard 2014; Wolfe 2016). For example, approximately 65 million inhabitants of what is now Latin America are thought to have been exterminated through war, murder and disease across the sixteenth century (Quijano 2007: 170).

From the sixteenth century, the colonization of South and then North America also relied on slave labour to fuel agricultural capitalism (which would become the plantation economy) and a system of global trade. The transatlantic slave trade relied on the capture of millions of Africans who were enslaved, coercively transported across the Atlantic to British, French, Portuguese and Spanish colonies, and converted into chattel, i.e. property, to be traded, put to work, sexually abused and often tortured and murdered. In the period between 1740 and 1781 alone, some 2.5 million African enslaved people were forced across the Middle Passage (Blackburn 2013). Such practices underpinned industrialization in key colonial metropoles such as Britain and France, as well as producing wealth for white settler plantation owners and their white labourers (see Blackburn 2013: 97–9). Capitalist modernity, then, was produced through both genocide and the enslavement of people who were made into the inferiors of Europeans (Robinson 1983).

Slavery not only extracted resources and profit for the Global North but, as Walter Rodney (2018 [1972]) has shown, slavery and colonialism in Africa directly *underdeveloped* the continent, and this structural legacy endures today (see chapter 2 for a discussion of the development discourse). Not only were resources stolen by colonizers but slavery actively depopulated many parts of sub-Saharan Africa (Andrews 2018). This process of what Harvey (2010) has called 'accumulation by dispossession' continues today. It is estimated that US$203 billion is still plundered from the African continent every year and that Africa makes a yearly net contribution to the rest of the world to the sum of US$41.3 billion (Global Justice 2017; see Hickel 2018 for more on global inequality and 'development').

Race is crucial to this arrangement. Ideas of racial inferiority facilitated the uprooting of indigenous peoples as well as the enslavement of Africans and slave trading. It shaped colonial extraction and the impoverishment of colonized populations. It is this relationship between race, destitution and violence that Mbembe develops with the concept of necropolitics (Mbembe 2003, discussed in more detail in chapter 5). What defined the historical experience of life under colonial rule was not the fostering of life or population (as in 'biopolitics') but the fostering of death (which equally fostered the life of populations racialized as white in Europe). To Mbembe, colonies or the zone of non-being were better thought of as 'death-worlds', rather than spaces for the promotion of life that we see in metropoles and settler populations. Equally, Wolfe (2016) argues that indigenous people were racialized in a way that meant they were not considered 'developable' either as part of settler societies or as free or coerced labour. They were merely 'savages', not included in the Christian universe of God and humanity (see Wynter 2003 for a comparable argument). In this way, it would be a mistake to see race as equated to labour exploitation or the window dressing of material extraction. If this was only about labour, extraction of profit and exploitation, then why enslave, hunt and punish African people? As Wilderson (2010) asks, why did slave gangs not hunt the banks of the River Thames or the Seine?

Black studies scholars (for example, Gordon 1999; Sexton 2008; Sharpe 2016; Wilderson 2010) have been particularly adept at stressing the place of race in the crucible of European modernity running through to the biophysical and structural violence of racism in the present. To understand racism within this tradition is to recognize the way that racial hierarchies have been stratified around the power of anti-blackness, particularly within the context of the slave trade and the plantation economy. For many black studies scholars, anti-black racism is the structural principle that underpins all forms of racialization and it is through the violence of slavery that we need to understand the stratification of people into human/not-quite-human/inhuman. Consider here how W. E. B. Du Bois mapped this production of race:

> The word 'Negro' was used for the first time in world history to tie colour to race and blackness to slavery and degradation. The white race was pictured as 'pure' and superior; and the black race as dirty, stupid, and inevitably inferior; the yellow race as sharing, in deception and cowardice, much of this colour inferiority. Mixture of races was considered the prime cause of degradation and failure of civilization. (Du Bois 1965: 20)

Frank Wilderson (2010) further argues that the enslavement of African people marks the simultaneous birth of modern racism and modernity. As we mentioned above, rather than being defined by exploitation or profiteering alone, slavery worked on a symbolic and ontological level. The enslavement of black African bodies marked the discovery of the 'human' subject as the white master (or even white free labourer). It was this full person who was compared to the non-human black slave or surplus indigenous population. Karl Marx argued that the emergence of the modern economic system was the wage labourer who could buy bread with the exchange of his labour. However, Robbie Shilliam (2018) argues that what was a more significant marker of modernity was the ability of the wage labourer (and bourgeoisie), through the system of Atlantic slavery, to buy a person (see also Bledsoe and Wright 2019). It is this fundamental inequality and process of commodification and dehumanization that structures modern racism, Wilderson proposes.

In Wilderson's work, slavery was more than the extraction of profit; slavery was defined by the non-contingent punishment of bodies racialized as black (see also Sexton 2008; Spillers 1987). It is then anti-black violence that characterizes the afterlife of slavery. Here racialization must be understood as the conditions of violence, its character, shape and intensity and normalization (Kuppan 2018). This should be understood as making populations racialized as black susceptible to death, that is, either the shortening of biological life or creating environments of social death (Gordon 1999; Patterson 1982). It is also the absence of accountability and grievability of those deaths, whether at the population or individual level, that shows the ongoing effects of racialization and anti-blackness (Dillon 2012; Sharpe 2016; Weinbaum 2019; on grievability more widely, see Butler 2009). For example, consider here the death of people of African descent at the hands of the police in many countries including Brazil, Colombia and the United States (French 2013; Moncada 2010; Paoline, Gau and Terrill 2018; Vargas and Alves 2010; also Maynard 2017), which is often connected to high rates of incarceration of black populations (see Elliott-Cooper 2016; Rowe 2004).

In this reading, it is from the racialization of people as black that other forms of racial violence emanate (see Gilroy 2002a and Robinson 1983 for alternative accounts). Recognizing the corporeal violence of race, how it is directed at particular bodies, as a form of power, should shape how we analyse the relationship between migration (or mobility) and race. For example, in this view investigating anti-black racism should be central to how we understand how borders function to 'exclude' and to immobilize specific populations. However, it is only recently that anti-blackness is being recognized in scholarship as a structuring element of mobility (Browne 2015; Danewid 2017; Saucier and Woods 2014). Consider the thousands of drowned migrants crossing the Mediterranean Sea – this cannot only be understood as an accident nor as a means of restricting access to cheap labour. That the most dangerous stretch of sea crossings is that between North Africa and Southern Europe, the route for migrants mostly from sub-Saharan Africa, is significant precisely because this danger is entirely avoidable – created by the denial of visas, containment practices and carrier conditions and the extraterritorialization of the EU border in North Africa (see Lemberg-Pedersen 2019 on extraterritorial controls and links to histories of slavery). But as Saucier and Woods (2014) argue, the abandoning of migrants to the high seas, to death, to be unburied and un-mourned, should be understood as part of the ongoing dehumanization of black bodies in Europe and the Mediterranean basin. For them, this goes all the way back to slavery (Broeck and Saucier 2016; Danewid 2017; Saucier and Woods 2014).

Racism's two registers: biology and culture

As well as understanding racism through anti-blackness, beginning from the violence of enslavement as an entry point to contemporary racist violence, other scholars have explored how colonial racism has developed and changed over time to incorporate an increasingly nebulous set of indicators. British-Jamaican cultural theorist Stuart Hall's (Hall 2000; Hall and Morley 2019) work has been important in showing how racism has two registers: biology (or, rather, physical appearance) and culture. The balance between these two articulations of racist discourse shifts over time, showing both how flexible and adaptable racism is but also how it functions in banal everyday or more extremely violent ways. Hall saw race as internal to all social processes, not as a subcategory which could be either selectively focused upon or ignored in favour of class or gender. In this way, he worked on the whole social formation of society as racialized. So for Hall questions of migration, diaspora, identity or multiculturalism, to pick a few examples, could not be understood without starting from the position that the whole social formation within which these phenomena occur is racialized, and that this underlying racial framework emerged through the age of empire (Hall 1993).

Hall saw biological racism and cultural racism not as two separate forms of racism. Just as individual musical instruments can be played in multiple registers, racism is articulated in these distinct but connected discursive registers. He explains that 'biological racism privileges markers like skin colour, but those signifiers have always also been used, by discursive extension, to connote social and cultural differences' (Hall 2000: 223). The interdependence of these two 'registers' (biology and culture) gives 'race' (but also ethnicity) meaning in the social world in the forms of both racism and identity formation. While he analytically distinguishes these two registers of racism, Hall observes that often both are in play at the same time in any single racist discourse, and that they therefore feed each other. For example, in anti-Muslim racism (discussed further in chapter 6), cultural 'difference' is important, but it is also encoded on Muslim bodies racialized as Muslim (brown or black skin, beards, etc.). Muslims are thus multiply racialized on somatic (bodily) *and* cultural grounds, with cultural racism being focused particularly on their religious affiliation. Similar logics appear in anti-Semitic discourses which draw on both physical and cultural stereotypes, with a focus on the Jewish religion as binding the two (see also Hage 2017).

Importantly for Hall's emphasis on the contingent nature of racism in a given time and place, the precise configuration and articulation of the cultural and biological aspects of any racist discourse are context specific. Anti-blackness in Australia may be focused on Aboriginal communities and be articulated in terms of particular biological and cultural logics. Anti-blackness in Brazil, meanwhile, may draw on similar tropes, but the interplay between biology and culture, as well as the stereotypes or assumptions at play in each, will be different. These are both forms of racism; they are connected by similar logics, but they articulate themselves in different, context-specific ways. This insight can help us empirically both in conceptually connecting racisms across contexts, while acknowledging their local particularity, and in recognizing how racisms change over time within single countries (see also Goldberg 2009).

Some scholars have been arguing since the 1980s that biological racism has been in decline and cultural racism has risen in its place (Barker 1981; Modood and Werbner 1997). It is in this sense that claims that some societies are 'post-racial' (Bonilla-Silva 2015) have become plausible for some as the kinds of eugenicist racisms of the Nazi regime, or scientific racisms such as taxonomies of humanity, have fallen out of favour (although see Saini 2019). This has occurred as a result of scientific racism being debunked within the natural sciences. Barker (1981) called this 'the new cultural racism' and was in this sense seeking to argue that, despite increasingly focusing on culture, racism still endured. But Stuart Hall (in Hall and Morley 2019) refuted this, seeing it as a misconstrual of cultural and biological racism as separate rather than entwined: 'What seems more appropriate is an expanded conception of racism, which acknowledges the way in which in its discursive structure, biological racism and cultural differentialism are articulated and combine. These two "logics" are always present, though in different combinations and differently foregrounded in the different contexts and in relation to different subject populations' (Hall and Morley 2019: 111–12).

Hall's work, and his emphasis on thinking with cultural and biological racisms, is particularly useful for unpacking claims around everyday forms of racialization and its links to questions around nationhood and 'belonging', key research agendas in migration studies (see S. Hall 2017, but also Hall 1978, 1996a, 1996d; Hall et al. 1978). This is especially pertinent in our contemporary moment with the global rise of anti-immigration nationalism and right-wing populism. Hall argued – particularly in the context of immigration debates – that appeals to nationality and belonging can never be fully separated from racial signifiers (S. Hall 2017). Ideas of 'cultural difference' and 'ethnicity', which are often presented as 'race free' by proponents, are actually far from it. Instead for Hall, when claims to culture and belonging are used to justify the exclusion of others (such as 'migrants', 'aliens', or asylum seekers), this frequently relies upon ideas of racial difference, nature and 'blood and soil' (S. Hall 2017: 126). And this is because the historical experience of western colonization continues to essentialize human difference into binaries of 'civilization' and 'barbarianism' (S. Hall 2017: 121).

These are the tools of identity formation that are handed down through colonial modernity even in 'civic' or 'cultural' claims to nationality (particularly in Europe, but Hall hints at the global dimensions of this). He writes, 'we may speak here of the "ethnicization" of "race"', or physical appearance. But at the same time 'cultural difference has taken on a more violent, politicised, and oppositional meaning – which we might think of as the "racialisation" of ethnicity (e.g. "ethnic cleansing")' (Hall 2019). In this way, there are no appeals to nationality or belonging which can be made sense of to justify the exclusion of others which aren't at the same time inflected with racial thinking and claims to colonial markers of superiority and inferiority. Take for example contemporary nationalist discourses over who is a 'good migrant', who is a 'worthy' or contributing subject, who can claim asylum, who can integrate and who can't, and so on. And yet so much of the ideas, use of language and cultural practices of nationhood and nationalism are so ingrained and normalized, it can be difficult to see how these things work to reify racialized understandings, for example around appeals to white superiority and supremacy (Tyler 2013; on whiteness, see Bhambra 2017a; Meer 2019; Wekker 2016). Following Hall, it is because these understandings are so ingrained that the role of public critique and scholarship is to tease out how these ideas are reproduced and how they continue to structure the experiences of communities, whether 'majoritarian', 'minority' or 'migrants'.

Whilst Hall saw structures of identification and claims to belonging as reifying and remaking racialized categories of cultural and biological worth, he did not see all cultural identification as regressive. One of the important aspects of Hall's work is the attention that he draws to the reappropriation of the term 'black' as positive cultural identification. He writes that while 'black' has historically been a negative label, it has in many contexts been reclaimed. The term 'black' to Hall did not have to be a closed formation of identity – rooted in the violent exclusion of others – but could point to looser and more open forms of solidarity, political affiliation and cultural creativity. He pointed to the experience of anti-racist and anti-imperial social movements in Britain in the 1970s, for example, where the category of political blackness became a form of identity that could be inhabited by different social groups who experienced colonial racialization and oppression (S. Hall 2017: 99; see also Hall 1992. For other accounts of anti-racist and political blackness, see Nayaran 2019a, 2019b, 2020; Baker, Diawara and Lindeborg 1996). Whilst political blackness has since been disputed and no longer has the same political salience, Hall saw hope, potential and resistance in the emergence of 'new ethnicities' which challenged dominant claims to cultural homogeneity and fixed ideas of belonging (Hall 1991, 1992; S. Hall 2017). Whilst the term 'black' related to 'symbolic practices of racialized oppression', Hall asked if it reflected '*also* the signifiers of a new kind of ethnicized modernity, close to the cutting edge of a new iconography and a new semiotics that are redefining "the modern" itself?' (S. Hall 2017: 121). We return to these debates around the different registers of race in chapter 6 when we examine Islamophobia/anti-Muslim racism and the drivers and consequences of border security.

Race, movement and immigration

These broad-based discussions of colonialism and race are highly pertinent to the specificities of migration studies. To consider movement as somehow separate from race is to undervalue how the control of movement and construction of borders have historically been racialized and how this continues to shape our present. Empires were racial projects, and this was exemplified in the control of movement. This includes slavery and the management of indigenous peoples, which was primarily organized around movement. Who could move where, for what purpose and under what conditions was central to the organization of colonial rule and imperialism (Turner 2020). Consider, for instance, how the control of movement was a key tool in the suppression of indigenous populations under (settler) colonialism through enclosure, the imposition of European rules of private property and contractual law and the erection of boundaries of razor wire, reserves and systems of camps and categories of tribal membership (Bhandar 2018; Blomley 2008; Goldstein 2013; Smith 2015; Young 2001). This reflects broader patterns of European colonial expansion, invasion and territorial acquisition, extraction by colonizers and the dispossession of land and resources which forced countless millions to move, to urbanize and to be left destitute.

If 'globalization' is often cited as a causal factor in explaining contemporary mobility, we contend that globalization is the expansion of European colonial modernity and of the ideology and practices of extractive capitalism. When we talk of globalization, we then need to understand how it has been shaped by and persists to reorder histories of exploitation, domination and accumulation which underpinned European and then US empires. Being attuned to the continued social significance of race is to be attuned to the historical continuities and legacies of empire. Colonialism may have formally ended in many (but certainly not all) places, but the power structures that dominate global politics remain broadly unchanged from the heyday of European empires. In this way, we need to understand how contemporary mobility from the Global South – whether South to South or South to North – is already embedded in what Da Silva and Chakravartty (2012: 365) call the 'colonial and racial matrix of capitalist accumulation of land (conquest and settlement), exploitation of labour (slavery, indentured labour, forced migration)

[and] appropriation of resources' which has underpinned modernity. This is far more than prejudice, intolerance and explicit 'racism' towards people on the move (although these have an impact). An analytics of race, in this sense, helps us to understand how mobility and the treatment of migrants is connected across levels of the macro (global governance of migration, global wealth disparities), meso (border regimes, deportation, detention) and micro (intimate, everyday microaggressions) to the stratification of peoples. Drawing on Bhambra (2017b), it becomes vital to comprehend how what is labelled 'migration' is bound to the historical racialization of mobility.

Exploring the fundamental relationship between movement, colonialism and race, we might identify the slave trade as a period of sustained 'forced displacement'. Blackburn (2013) reminds us that between 1500 and 1820, African slaves forcibly moved to the 'New World' outnumbered the movement of Europeans four to one. This created networks of transportation and mobility that laced together the Atlantic economy with the Mediterranean and West Africa – from Lagos to Bristol to Charleston. Migration studies scholars tend to focus on the internal histories of Europe, such as the control of vagabonds in Europe, for a history of borders and immigration control (see Hass, Castles and Miller 2019 but also Anderson 2013; Vaughan Williams 2009). And yet, as Simone Browne (2015) powerfully demonstrates, slavery was itself a system of (im)mobility that shaped future projects of immigration (see Lemberg-Pedersen 2019 on these links; on passports in other colonial contexts, see Singha 2000).

Enslaved people were sorted and categorized at transatlantic ports, inspected and documented in a manner that preceded and shaped the invention of paper documentation and the passport (this is often eclipsed in other accounts; Torpey 2009). In the plantation economy, whether in the Caribbean or North America, enslaved people were unable to move off a master's property without a 'slave pass' which identified them as a white person's property. Slave hunters, wanted posters and branding all regulated movement around racial categories and limited free movement (i.e. escape). This was organized around explicit and often gratuitous racialized violence. In nineteenth-century Georgia, for example, any black person found without the correct documentation (a slave pass or evidence of free status) by a white person could be subject to lashings (Browne 2015).

When black people 'migrated' to the Americas, this was as chattel on slave ships. This is very different from how most white Europeans moved across empires. Christina Sharpe (2016) talks of the horrors of the ship's hold in the Middle Passage, the dehumanizing cramped conditions, people manacled, torn from kinship, family, community. Disease was rife. Enslaved people were frequently drowned, both accidentally and on purpose (Hartman 2007). Records show that captors often threw enslaved people overboard in stormy weather if the ship was overloaded or to avoid capture after the abolition of the slave trade. Whilst the movement of white settlers, migrants, labourers and traders across the Atlantic was fraught with danger, they were not subject to the same dehumanizing conditions, violence and death. Instead, the passage of European passengers was oriented towards the sustaining and protecting of their lives (as 'customers', 'settlers', 'citizens' or 'labourers'), even if class and gender continued to structure these experiences differently. Even in the case of Irish indentured labourers, these experiences were categorically different from the treatment of the enslaved (and/or indigenous populations) (see Rodgers 2007). Writing of the contemporary crisis of immobility in the Mediterranean, Saucier and Woods (2014) remind us that the drowning and avoidable deaths of people moving from Africa today has a historical precedent in the Middle Passage and Europe's organization of the slave trade (see also Lemberg-Pedersen 2019). We might equally consider here the ease in which westerners travel and leisure in the same spaces and sites that are deadly for thousands of people moving from the Middle East and North Africa today.

Further to these histories of mobility, it is important to recognize where immigration regimes and law came from. Whilst migration scholars often consider immigration law to be about the nation-state, this silences the more global and colonial history (see Vigneswaran 2020 for a comparable critique). Take, for instance, events under the British Empire. After the abolition of slavery (in 1833), capitalists and imperial authorities drew on indentured labourers as a means of filling the labour shortages in settler and European colonies. This resulted in another large-scale forced displacement, this time from India and China (Lowe 2015; Mongia 2018). Indentured labourers travelled under slave-like conditions and worked under contracts which often left them destitute. As Radhika Mongia (2018) argues, throughout the nineteenth century the control of indentured labourer would result in the establishment and centralization of many of the border practices we are familiar with today (see also Sharma 2017).

Port inspections (both departure and arrival) expanded in this period to monitor labourers for disease and for correct documentation. The role of border officials was created to track this movement in collaboration with law enforcement officers. Private companies, ticket sellers and ships' captains were also expected to monitor who was moving (Gutiérrez Rodríguez 2018). This equally drew upon, and reinforced, laws against 'vagabonds' that were drawn up in Europe but then experimented with in colonies (see Federici 2004: 64–72). In this context, colonial bordering was not only about 'containment' but also about forced mobility where indentured labourers could be viewed both as an economic necessity within the evolving dictates of imperial capitalism and as a social risk. For example, in settler colonies such as the United States, South Africa and Australia, the influx of 'Asian' labour was often viewed as a threat to the social–sexual order of white supremacy and white nationalism (Virdee 2018) – black and brown men were often viewed as sexual deviants preying on white women (McClintock 1995; Shah 2011). Even if all British subjects had a formal right to travel across the British Empire, this was shaped by contingent practices of control, emergent forms of border bureaucracy and informal forms of management. In this context, internal and external borders were created to control racialized labourers and 'racial threats' – in work camps, through pass systems, through imprisonment and deportation and in practices of disease control and quarantine (for more on this, see Turner 2020; on the camp as a colonial technology, see Weheliye 2014). Borders emerged to police movement across empire and were tied to questions over the settlement, rights and personhood of those moving subjects (Sharma 2017). In this way, borders were from their inception focused on the racialized character of movement, as well as the racialized composition of colonial and settler societies.

Settler-colonial states in the late 1800s began to formalize and institutionalize immigration and citizenship law more rigorously around race, inventing as they did new categories of personhood. The 1870 Chinese Act in the United States banned the movement of Chinese labourers. The global system of race that underpinned global capital was captured in white nationalist moves to control who could settle in particular countries. In the 1880s, Australian federal states began to erect the 'white-only' immigration policy that would later dominate the twentieth century up to 1968. This was because, as elites argued, 'Asians were not suited to the Australian way of life.' This was soon followed by South Africa, which drafted immigration law as it produced categories of race which would eventually underpin Apartheid (see also Dubow 1989). Ultimately, these moves reflect the transposition of the 'global colour line' into formal immigration policy within nation-states (Lake and Reynolds 2008). To push this further, Mongia (2018) argues that the very structure of citizenship so central to the 'modern' nation-state itself was invented to stratify the movement and rights of people across empires. Importantly, this was not solely a project of settler colonies; metropoles such as Britain, France and the Netherlands formalized the divisions of the colour line in their citizenship and immigration laws and in imperial practices of movement. This was institutionalized throughout the twentieth century in the growth of immigration laws within European states as well as in informal practices of exclusion in housing, labour market access, policing, etc. (see Gutiérrez Rodríguez 2018; Shah 2011). This culminated in moves to deny rights of citizenship and settlement to colonized citizens who were racialized as non-white and who were encouraged to move after formal decolonization (Bleich 2005; El-Enany 2020; Goodfellow 2019; Hansen 2000; Paul 1997; Vigneswaran 2020). Against the view that borders are a product of the nation-state – as a political project separate from or counter to European colonialism – borders and immigration law are better understood as formed by and central to the function of colonial and imperial projects.

Such processes have contemporary resonance. We might consider how contemporary systems of containment in visa policies, no-fly rules and refugee camps structure the (im)mobility of people globally and rework categories of 'race'. Border policies emerged to control a racialized conception of mobility through empire, institutionalized in citizenship and visa laws. At the same time, the structures of global capitalism are inherently shaped by colonial and racialized logics, and this continues to structure mobility. Considering the interlinking of (settler) colonialism to the contemporary politics of mobility, we are reminded here of the purposeful destitution of Palestinians by the Israeli settler state up to the present (Puar 2017; Salamanca et al. 2013), Palestinians make up one of the world's largest displaced populations (UNRWA 2019). Equally, consider how throughout the 1980s International Monetary Fund reforms such as 'structural adjustment' worked to marketize the economies, welfare and health-care systems of sub-Saharan states. Critical development scholars have shown how this led to huge population displacement and the production of a landless and workless global underclass (see Selwyn 2015). This is increasingly compounded by environmental racism (Pulido 2018), and the inequalities of climate change have created further dispossession, mass urbanization and international mobility which continue to structure the movement of millions (Davis 2006; Walia 2014). Yet these colonial and imperial dynamics that shape movement are all too often forgotten in migration studies. Where poverty, wealth and violence are considered as causing movement or forced migration, this is too often not historicized, and it ignores how this dispossession is shaped by forms of racialized capitalism that dictate patterns of uneven development or underdevelopment (for example, Flahaux and de Haas 2016).

We have previously suggested that race structures immobility, such as how anti-blackness leads to the abandonment of people crossing the Mediterranean to Europe. Further to this, Ida Danewid (2017) has argued that anti-blackness as (im)mobility is not only defined by violence against people racialized as black but that this also mutually structures whiteness. What frequently defines the politics of the 2015 'refugee crisis' in Europe is not only explicit claims to white supremacy (Gutiérrez Rodríguez 2018) but also the largely unnoticed praise of 'white innocence' and the 'kindness' of European peoples which is precipitated through a collective colonial amnesia (see also Ahmed 2012; Wekker 2016). Danewid points to how there is almost no recognition of the devastations of colonialism, contemporary imperial capitalism or warfare in explaining why so many people attempt to move to Europe today (Danewid 2017; de Genova 2018). This is true of progressive scholarship and public debate (see also Bhambra 2017b). On the other hand, the deaths of black and brown people in the Mediterranean Sea are far too often utilized as an 'event' or moment for Europeans to 'rediscover' their own humanity and generosity towards those 'less fortunate'. We can consider here how the death of the toddler Aylan Kurdi who drowned off a beach in Bodrum, Turkey in 2015 was immediately transformed into an act of 'soul searching' for European publics. It became an event of mass extolling of 'grief' – immediately used to question how a 'tolerant', 'free' and 'enlightened' people could allow this to happen (Ticktin 2017). Rather than an opportunity to confront the underlying causes of these deaths, the 'solution' from the EU was the announcement of new disembarkation platforms in North Africa, which would prevent the 'tragic loss of life' of thousands of people (see Lemberg-Pedersen 2019). What continues to be obscured here is the very real history of the structural dehumanization of racialized people at the heart of the European project – not just through formal imperialism – central to the foundation of EU integration and European citizenship (see Hansen and Jonsson 2014).

At the same time that race/racism allows for spectacular violence such as purposefully allowing people to drown in the Mediterranean, these forms of necropolitics (power directed at killing certain bodies) are also structural, done quietly and conducted through institutional processes and technical procedures which are far from 'exceptional' or overtly violent (see Lemberg-Pedersen 2019). And this is important to recognize as it speaks to the vast majority of migration studies research. Mayblin's (2019) work, for example, examines how the destitution of asylum seekers in the United Kingdom works as a form of racialized necropolitics – subjecting populations not to immediate and sudden violence but long-term abandonment and slowly unfolding social degradation. The point here is that racialized violence is not always spectacle but technocratic, structural and administrated – enacted, for example, through regimes of waiting (Mountz 2011a) in detention centres (Bhui 2016) and refugee camps (Davies and Isakjee 2018), housing and labour policies, resettlement schemes (Turner 2017), deportation mechanisms (De Noronha 2019), integration strategies and the inclusion/exclusions of the welfare state (Bhambra and Holmwood 2018) or in social work practice (Turner 2020). The mundanity of violence and its technicality don't stop it being arranged by understandings of race.

What we can learn from these examples, and the many more that litter colonial histories, is that race was not only invented as an organizing principle of colonialism but it also structured the very architecture of mobility, immigration law and citizenship (see also chapter 4). Immigration regimes worked to ground racial categories into laws around mobility, settlement and rights. This is not just a matter of the historical record. Recognizing this should change how we understand immigration regimes today because it means confronting how movement and the governance of movement are already deeply intermeshed with issues of race. As scholars of migration, we lose so much if we fail to explore both the impact of colonialism on the construction of modernity and how central race has been to the colonial project and the control of mobility.

To help consider the impact of these histories, we argue there are (at least) three ways we should think about migration and the importance of race and colonialism. The first point to highlight here is the structural and racialized conditions of movement. Colonialism shaped who could move, to where and under what conditions. It structured, for example, who was a 'passenger' on a ship versus who was captive as an enslaved person in the hold. Enforced mobility led (as it does today) to the destitution and dismemberment of communities and societies and the transformation of those societies. So we need to understand this when we explore why people move. At the same time, imperialism and colonialism also created and continue to create networks of people, trade and goods. European empires created lines of dependencies, economic as well and intimate relations of language, kinship and culture that were global in reach and are reinforced under today's global economy. In light of this, we need to understand how people continue to move along such 'imperial grooves' (De Noronha 2018). A basic example of this might be people travelling to the United Kingdom because they speak the imperial language of English or because of kinship ties (Fortier 2018). We thus need to ground any understanding of movement today in these historical and material linkages, structures and connections to make any sense of migration.

Speaking of this hidden history of slavery, empire and its contemporary resonance in Britain, the late Stuart Hall asked people to consider how 'I am the sugar at the bottom of the English cup of tea' (1991). What Hall was talking about was the often forgotten structures which underpin cultural, economic and political life in European societies like Britain – the hidden racial logics of colonialism and racialized capitalism, systems which connected the sugar plantations of Jamaica, the mono-cropping systems of tea in Africa, China and India to the commodity of tea and the cultural practice of tea drinking as 'quintessentially English'. To begin any study of migration after colonialism, especially in the Global North, we need therefore to begin with an understanding of how colonial histories and racialized structures of capitalism shaped and continue to shape who moves where and how. For example, how dispossession, inequality and the accumulation of wealth drained from the Global South and used to 'develop' the Global North shapes mobility today.

We might also reflect upon how the treatment of migrants is shaped by colonial amnesia which is also central to the r ization of white supremacy and mainstream forms of nationalism. This is replicated, for example, in the commonplace argument that Europe or individual nations have no responsibility for those moving to claim asylum or the logic that people moving from former colonies to European metropoles have no rights to settlement or 'belonging' (for more on this, see chapter 4).

The second point of significance is the material history of immigration regimes and borders. We need to understand how the tools used to police mobility that continue to expand and proliferate today were created and arranged to control racialized mobility. Borders and the emergence of immigration practices have, from their inception, been attuned to the active dehumanization, surveillance and control of particular colonized populations and people racialized as non-white. This was their express purpose. Borders are and always have been oriented towards blocking the movement of some and not others. But this is not merely an economic calculus (although of course who has wealth or value as a 'labourer' is always racialized under modern capitalism). As Saucier and Woods (2014) argue, bearing the legacies of slavery in mind, borders and the policing of borders are commonly oriented towards black immobility, the conditioning and regulating of those people racialized as non-white as the 'uncivilized'. This does not mean that borders are oriented towards merely stopping racialized mobility, but borders reproduce hierarchies of race by distinguishing who can move and who cannot, and they function as a great 'sorting mechanism' which creates ideas of worth, as well as replicating historical constructions (Achiume 2019). We thus need to start any study of borders and immigration with this historical present in mind.

The third point is that it is not only through policies, laws and violent bordering practices that we might observe the legacies of colonialism. It is also, as Stuart Hall so powerfully demonstrated across his life's work, through cultural products, discourses and practices. Media and other apparently banal cultural representations – which form the background to people's everyday lives – of people on the move, and the responses of host communities to them, are all saturated with historically grounded ideas, assumptions and connotations which establish difference as self-evident and natural. In this way, and as we discuss further in chapter 6, racism does not only invoke somatic traits but also nebulous ideas around cultural difference as essentialized distinctions between different people. Ideas of cultural difference are often also connected to particular territories where different cultures are seen to have supreme claims to be 'at home', casting others as 'out of place'. Religion has been a reoccurring means of making such racist distinctions from Catholicism in the case of Irish migrant communities to Islam in the case of Pakistani migrant communities. Everyday and naturalized claims to 'cultural difference' are imbued with logics of colonial civilizational 'difference' which often rework and emulate ideas about inferior and superior forms of culture, community and the worth of certain subjects and societies over others.

The vital point to take way from the discussion so far here is that neither race nor colonialism are things of the past but are structures of our contemporary moment, and this has particular salience for migration studies. The very construction of the notion of 'migration' and the political processes that are involved in making someone a 'migrant' (borders, immigration regimes, etc.) are fundamentally colonial. Equally, ideas about human worth and cultural difference that shape current debates about migration are fundamentally tied to the invention of race under empire.

Conclusion

In the first part of the chapter, we made the case that race was a fundamental invention of colonialism and a global system that continues to shape economies, societies and culture today. We explored how race emerged historically but made the explicit case that the control of mobility was central to the organization of racism and forms of colonial and imperial governance. The point here was to show that it should not be possible to talk about migration without talking about colonialism, race and racism. We outlined the two interrelated ways that frame the place of colonialism and race in migration studies. First, colonialism, dispossession and racialized inequalities underpin who moves, and the imperial grooves of trade, people and kinship shape where people move to. Second, immigration regimes came out of the longer history of controlling movement under European empire. In this context, immigration controls transposed ideas of race into the control of borders and the centralization of movement. We argue that these two interrelated points provide a vital starting point for any analysis of migration. In order to more appropriately understand the role that race and racism play in modern migration regimes, governance and experiences, we highlighted both how racial logics organize the management and experience of mobility globally, and how we can understand the cultural aspects of racism through Stuart Hall's writing on racism's two registers – culture and biology. This can help us understand the everyday and often banal reproduction of racial understandings of 'belonging', nationhood and culture which is so central to social discourses on migration and shapes the experiences of migrants themselves. This is of course a non-exhaustive account but it provides a series of ideas that we will return to as we move through the following chapters.

4

Putting Sovereignty, Citizenship and Migration in Dialogue with Past and Present Colonialisms

Introduction

Most questions of the international, from migration to law to politics, take the system of territorially sovereign states for granted. Mobility is, therefore, often understood within the confines of sovereignty, which determines citizenship and rights. Without a sovereign authority, citizenship and the privileges that it confers are meaningless but, equally, migrants become subject to that sovereign authority upon entry to a country. Who can enter a territory and who has rights upon entry are thus wrapped up with questions of sovereignty. When colonialism, whether historically or in the present, is made central to one's analysis of migration, then the naturalness or inevitability of sovereignty and citizenship come into sharp focus. While sovereignty is typically defined as 'authority over a territory occupied by a relatively fixed population, supposedly necessary to protect that territory and its citizens from external [and internal] threats' (Leigh and Weber 2018, cited in Nisancioglu 2019: 2), an engagement with colonial histories, and the colonial present, significantly complicates this definition. This is in part because the myth of equality between sovereign states is brought into question and in part because the sovereignty of settler-colonial states is directly challenged (Mathieu 2018; Moreton-Robinson 2007, 2015).

This chapter explores the relationship between ideas of migration, sovereignty and citizenship when set within the context of colonial histories and presents. It does this through an engagement with three very different areas of scholarship that have centred colonialism in relation to these issues. The chapter is thus divided into four sections. First, we explore Gurminder K. Bhambra's work on 'connected histories' as a framework which disrupts the methodologically nationalist and presentist assumptions which underpin many studies of migration, citizenship and belonging. Through a focus on interconnection, Bhambra's work opens up the possibility of transforming Eurocentric understandings of migration, sovereignty and citizenship which assume that 'modern' phenomena began in Europe and diffused outwards from there. Recognizing historical interconnection then opens up new ways of understanding the global today. Next, we explore E. Tendayi Achiume's thesis that migration, from the perspective of TWAIL, can be understood as a just act of decolonization *in itself*. Achiume's thesis here disrupts ideas of rightful access to citizenship, as well as national sovereignty to control borders. She rethinks sovereignty as collective self-determination within neo-colonial empire, thus detaching it from a bounded nation-state territory. The third section draws attention to work in indigenous studies and, without doing justice to this rich field of scholarship, highlights the vital questions that indigenous studies raises for migration studies. What does 'immigration' mean in a settler-colonial society where the sovereignty of the settler state is contested, for example? This disruptive intervention then leads into the final section of the chapter which discusses the idea of 'no borders'. While generally favoured in critical scholarship, to what extent would a no-borders agenda be consonant with an agenda which makes colonialism central to our analyses? Some of the issues and debates at stake are drawn out here.

Together, these interventions present modes of thinking about migration in the context of citizenship and sovereignty regimes which denaturalize their formation today. All of these perspectives take seriously the importance of colonialisms of various kinds in shaping the present, and concur that what results are racially grounded global inequalities and injustices. But between them there are contradictions and disconnections. This in part arises from the different modes of colonial relations that are foregrounded in the work of the scholars. Achiume, for example, is interested in the inequalities between citizens of former metropoles and former colonies, across what she conceptualizes as the First World/Third World divide. Scholars such as Aileen Moreton-Robinson (2007, 2015), Bonita Lawrence (2004; Lawrence and Dua 2005), and Eve Tuck (Tuck, Guess and Sultan 2014; Tuck and Yang 2012), working in indigenous (Fourth World) studies in settler-colonial contexts in the First World centre inequalities and injustices between settlers and indigenous peoples in those locations. These different emphases do not necessarily sit easily together, as the discussion on 'no borders' makes clear. It is not our intention to smooth over these differences here but to draw attention to the multiple possibilities raised by a commitment to centring colonialism, and then the subsequent importance of local contexts in making sense of them in place.

Connected histories, connected sociologies

Mains et al. (2013: 134) point out that 'for some time, the primary spatial narrative constructed in most migration literature has been the movement from "there" to "here" or from "here" to "there"'. These movements are then viewed as interesting objects of study in that they produce a series of impacts on origin and destination countries. This is a particular way of thinking about space and time. As Mains and colleagues point out, postcolonial scholarship disrupts this by extending the temporality of discussion into the colonial past, and then by necessarily drawing attention to the ways in which 'here' and 'there' have both been formed through interactions between the two over long time horizons. This is where sociologist Gurminder K. Bhambra's (2007, 2010, 2014) work on connected histories and connected sociologies becomes relevant in rethinking migration, sovereignty and citizenship.

Bhambra argues that the world should be considered as always-already global. Distinct 'civilizations' are often 'presented as bounded and as having separate and distinct histories and cultures prior to European contact' (2014: 143). Of course, it is implausible that non-European societies were sealed off from each other prior to their discovery by Europeans, but Bhambra suggests that this is often implied in representations of the past. This is an understanding of society based on the naturalized idea of state sovereignty over a fixed population. The naturalization of liberal conceptions of nation-state sovereignty is methodologically nationalist and has implications for how we think about migration and citizenship both historically and in the present. Bhambra relates this idea of separate bounded societies to the inherent Eurocentrism of the social sciences, which works to produce a nationalist history of the present and is formed through distinctions between units of analysis produced through classification. She suggests in her 2014 book *Connected Sociologies* that sociology has been focused since its inception on the European origins of global processes, rather than global processes as global, in and of themselves. This means not only are connections between societies often assumed to be precipitated by European 'discovery' but also that the global as an imaginary has long been understood in European terms.

Yet this Eurocentric imaginary of the global is not one that necessarily centres colonial histories. On the contrary, 'the process of colonialism, enslavement, dispossession and appropriation are rendered as mere "interaction", "dissemination" or "spread"' (2014: 146). Such inaccurate descriptions of what colonialism entailed mean that a proper reckoning with what colonialism *did* to the world, what it meant, means and does in the present, is elided. For Bhambra, 'to think sociology differently is to take connections as the basis of the histories which we acknowledge; to do sociology differently is to act on the basis of having recognised those connections' (2014: 5). This is not, then, about acknowledging particular histories and cultures which have been ignored by Eurocentric accounts, and then including them in, or adding them onto, dominant histories which centre Europe in the emergence of modernity. We should not be looking for non-European thinkers and episodes in history and making space for them if this has no bearing on how Europe then recounts its past.

Even postcolonial critique, she argues, 'has itself frequently focused on the specificity of what is omitted in the standard accounts', for example Indian histories, Arabic histories or indigenous histories, 'rather than their interconnected and related nature' (Bhambra 2010: 128). In other words, postcolonial interventions also fail to make connections 'integral to the processes previously represented as independent of them' (Bhambra 2010: 128). Instead, Bhambra argues that we should be deconstructing the 'standard narratives' of global history (which are based on the universalization of parochial European histories) and 'reconstructing *global* narratives on the basis of the empirical connections forged through histories of colonialism, enslavement, dispossession and appropriation' (Bhambra 2014: 5). Bhambra explains that 'no understanding remains unchanged by connection. To understand events through their connections is to acknowledge from the outset that addressing particular sets of connections leads to particular understandings which are put in question through choosing other sets of connections' (2014: 5).

Kerem Nisancioglu draws upon these histories in exploring the concept of sovereignty specifically. He writes:

> the orthodox account [of sovereignty] presents Europe as a unique world-making agent and a prime mover of history, where the innovation of modern sovereignty is first generated within its pristine boundaries and then 'diffused' elsewhere. This claim rests on a geo-historical abstraction whereby European states are viewed as self-propelling actors that are hermetically sealed from external – non-European – relations, histories, or influences. In this Eurocentric narrative, colonialism acts as a force through which already fashioned European norms are spread and universalised, but does not figure as a structural condition that (re)produces those norms. (Nisancioglu 2019: 5)

Colonialism demarcated the inside and the outside, the colonizer and the colonized, not seeing the latter as co-constitutive of the former, though of course it was. This endures: once sovereignty is extended to, or claimed by, formerly colonized states, sovereignty itself is seen to be a neutral force which has no particular colonial, racial or racist content.

By exploring sovereignty as something which was conceived in racial terms through colonial projects, Nisancioglu is able to then trouble the naturalized assumptions of the states system. That is, the assumption that the system of sovereign states is a resolution to historical contestation over borders and boundaries, which has now been solved. What he calls 'racial sovereignty' then analytically focuses on untangling the 'associative chains of authority–territory–population' and understanding them as 'distinctly racialized formations' (Nisancioglu 2019: 8). Drawing on (and theoretically developing) the work of Jordan Branch (2012), he explains that 'territorially defined sovereignty emerged as a novel way of articulating competing claims between European colonialists over the newly "discovered" lands of the Americas' (Nisancioglu 2019: 10). An underlying continuity, he writes, in the practice of racial sovereignty is colonial dispossession, the ongoing practice of which continues today, as will be discussed later in the chapter. Modern state sovereignty is not, then, an idea conceived of in Europe and diffused out later. Instead, it emerged through colonial activities and encounters and was subsequently taken to the metropoles. It depended on the idea of newly 'discovered' lands as empty spaces, a way of thinking which also endures today (Vergara-Figueroa 2018). Seeing colonial histories as connected, we are then able to see how contemporary claims to sovereignty are often made on implicitly racial grounds in terms of authority over a defined territory and population.

Bhambra's work has not been widely taken up within migration studies, but Daria Krivonos's (2019) study of young Russian speakers in Finland offers an excellent example of its potential for the field. This is less about sovereignty and more about migration, citizenship and the enduring resilience of colonial imaginaries of western civilization. Krivonos finds that young Russian speakers' imaginaries of the world, which lead them to migrate to Finland, involve understanding Finland to be part of the global 'West', which is also understood to be 'white'. Her research participants conceptualize themselves as aspiring 'westerners' and 'Europeans' through their migration practices, and Krivonos argues that this 'should be placed within the broader connected histories that enable the idea of "the West" and "Europe"' to take hold, through the production of other geographical locations as 'not western and not European' (2019: 22). The shifting symbolic geography of 'the West' and 'Europe' is aptly demonstrated in the Finnish context because it is not a place that has always been understood to be western, European or indeed white. But through pivoting west and joining the European Union, in the late twentieth century Finland became western, and also came to be generally understood as a 'white' nation (see also Keskinen 2019). In migrating to Finland, the Russian-speaking migrants in Krivonos's study also then identified themselves as modern and white in ways in which those who remained in Russia were not imagined to be.

Through this analysis, Krivonos and Näre (2019: 22) show how the post-socialist world is imbricated in 'relations of postcoloniality vis-à-vis the "West"'. In taking seriously histories of interconnection that have enabled the world to emerge as a global space, as Bhambra urges, Krivonos is moving beyond Cold War binaries of East/West often associated with a post-socialist analysis. Instead, she explores the historical, colonial interconnections which mean that in 2019 Russian speakers' imaginaries of the 'West' are embodied in the city of Helsinki. This is not done by ignoring post-socialism but, as discussed in chapter 2, through recognizing the 'Three Worlds' thesis

(First World: modern, democratic and capitalist; Second World: post-socialist; Third World: postcolonial) as a discourse of western modernity and therefore superiority which necessarily draws post-socialist spaces into relations of interconnection globally. When we look at the history of colonialism, socialism and capitalism, what we in fact find are connected histories (Bhambra 2014). Krivonos is therefore following Chari and Verdery's (2009) call to look 'between the posts' because post-socialism and postcolonialism are not limited to particular geographical spaces but are also historically emergent representations of space and time which have implications for knowledge and practice everywhere.

Krivonos draws on the work of postcolonial scholars (Alatas 2006; Hall 1996a; Hesse 2007; Said 1995 [1978]) to explain how the idea of 'the West' and its opposite ('the rest' in Hall's terms), emerged in the context of producing the colonial system. But while formal colonialism has ended in many (but certainly not all) places, the ideas, which we might articulate as coloniality, live on and are articulated in relation to shifting geographies and bodies. In Lisa Lowe's (2015: 8) terms, coloniality is not about binaries but power relations 'that operate through precisely spatialized and temporalized processes of both differentiation and connection'. Through thinking with historical interconnection, not least the floating ideational connections between places and peoples, Krivonos argues that it is in this context that 'young Russian speakers' imaginaries of "the West" as more modern and progressive spaces should be understood, embodied by Finland and the metropolitan area of Helsinki despite Finland's position on the edge of "the West"' (Krivonos 2019: 23). This of course has racial dimensions through which the impact of colonial ideas of racial hierarchy on post-socialist spaces can be seen. As Aniko Imre (2005, cited in Krivonos) has argued, whiteness has been both one of the most widely used means to assert 'Europeanness' in Central and East European nations at the same time as being the least recognized. Through such an analysis, we arrive at an enriched understanding of migratory practices, patterns and motivations.

In a similar vein, Catherine Baker (2018) explores the Yugoslav region as a space in which ethnicity and nationhood have been given primacy over ideas of 'race', because south-eastern Europe is understood to be outside of colonial circulations of ideational and population migration. Rather than allowing the Yugoslav region to be seen as a space apart from formal colonialism, and therefore also apart from colonial ideas of racial hierarchy or racially diverse migratory circulations historically, Baker centres interconnection in her analysis. She sees the Yugoslav region not as exceptional and apart but as interconnected with broader global processes. Exceptionalism, she argues, 'obscures the global pervasiveness of "race" as a structure of thought by implying that race is not relevant for understanding somewhere' (Baker 2018: 10). This might be because that place was not directly involved in European colonialism or was colonized itself, or because other powers are seen to have had a more significant impact on it (see Wekker 2016). But assuming exceptionalism involves, according to Baker, 'extricating these regions from globally connected historical analysis' as well as 'defining eastern Europe as a space where identities are defined by ethnicity rather than race' (Baker 2018: 10).

Baker draws attention to a number of quantitatively small migrations which nevertheless reveal underlying connections between world regions historically, and in doing so contest accounts of south-eastern Europe as a space apart from colonial circulations of people and ideas. One such example is Afro-Montenegrin/Afro-Albanian families in the Montenegrin town of Ulcinj. Such families are a legacy of Ulcinj's place as a node in the Eastern Mediterranean slave trade.

Some people who had been captured and enslaved in Sudan were taken along established routes to North African ports and then on to the port town of Ulcinj in south-eastern Europe. Baker explains how once (later) freed, some of these people married into local Albanian and Montenegrin families, which led to the founding of Ulcinj's small bi-racial community. These histories are evidence of 'a literal "Black Adriatic": that is, the Adriatic just like the Atlantic is indeed a direct site of African diasporic history' (Baker 2018: 74). But we only get at this by approaching the present as produced by historical interconnection, not separation. Thus the common-sense understanding of the former Yugoslavia as free of migration and outside the circulations of empire, where citizenship and nationhood are conceived of as white and mono-ethnic sovereign spaces, falls apart once we think about connections (see also Drnovšek Zorko 2019).

As these examples show, Bhambra's connected sociologies approach potentially disrupts how we understand both particular migrations themselves and the role of migrations in the transformation of the world, including taken-for-granted conceptions of citizenship, sovereignty and belonging. Through starting from the premise of interconnection between places over time, rather than separateness, we are able to get at the actual complexity of the world, at the same time as taking seriously the legacies of colonialism in the present. We would not see migration as a movement simply from A to B where A and B are completely separate entities, and on the assumption that people from A will be internally homogenous and will be seeking to integrate into equally homogenous society B. Instead, A and B would be understood as having long-standing interconnected histories which have led both societies to be internally diverse and to create commonalities and differences, inclusions and exclusions, hybridities and interdependencies between and across both over time.

Whether the studies discussed above, which are inspired by Bhambra's call for connected sociologies, then wholly meet the aspiration to move beyond Eurocentrism and transform our understanding of the global through a focus on interconnection is open to question. What is certain is that through working with this theoretical intervention, empirical studies may well contribute in the future to an understanding of the global which decentres Western Europe. Bhambra's own example (in her 2007 book *Rethinking Modernity*) of the Industrial Revolution being funded by the wealth acquired through colonialism and enslavement is now a classic example. This explores how the cotton for the English textile industry was picked by enslaved Africans working on Caribbean island plantations, how textile workers in the north of England worked with Indian-designed technologies and how the supremacy of Britain in the global textile industry was dependent upon the purposeful ruination of the industry in India. In telling this story, which draws on the migration of wealth, ideas and technologies *as well as* people, we start to realize how rarely transformative phenomena in the past were endogenous to particular places or devoid of migration-related processes.

Migration as decolonization

In part, what Bhambra is doing with connected sociologies is to demonstrate how important complex and internationally connected colonial histories were in the past in order to then show how important they are to the world in the present. This is also the starting point for E. Tendayi Achiume in her thesis, 'Migration as Decolonization'. Working within the tradition of TWAIL, Achiume is ambitiously seeking to supplant the 'international legal fiction and logic of formally independent, autonomous nation-states' (2019: 13) who then, on the basis of this fiction, have the right to exclude non-nationals. By centring colonial histories and their legacies in the present, she argues that our understanding of Third World migration to the First World will be transformed. This transformation will allow us then to see such migration as responding to the desire on the part of migrants not only for economic parity but also for political parity.

Achiume observes that the European empires were built upon white economic migration. The mobility of First World citizens was prioritized while the autonomous economic migration of Third World citizens of empire was curtailed. But as economic migrants moved out of Europe, resources flowed in the opposite direction, bringing prosperity to the metropolitan centres. For example, according to Catherine Hall and colleagues, who have undertaken detailed research on British wealth derived from the enslavement of people, 15–20 per cent of the wealth in Britain can be attributed to slavery in every decade of the nineteenth century (Hall et al. 2014). Bhambra (forthcoming), drawing on the work of Maddison (1971), explains how, under direct British rule, official transfers of funds ('home charges') from India to Britain were in the range of £40–50 million a year by the 1930s (in 2019, that would be the equivalent of between £2.5 billion and £3.2 billion annually). In other words, the exploitation of Third World peoples brought wealth to First World peoples, wealth which they continue to benefit from today (again, see Hall et al. 2014 on the extent of these legacies). Relatively unfettered colonial migration was supported by international law (Anghie 2008) and legal scholars have demonstrated international law's complicity in sustaining neo-colonial dynamics into the present (see Pahuja 2011). Formal decolonization, then, was a process of shifting power within a relationship towards a more equitable interconnection but not reaching the point of equality.

Achiume focuses on South–North economic migrants, those moving in her terms from the 'Third World' to the 'First World'. She observes that the term 'economic migrant' has taken on negative connotations and that South–North economic migrants are both viewed as voluntary migrants exercising their preferences for a 'better life', and this agency also means that they are met with suspicion, even as an unwanted invading force. But this presumption of agency, and the ability to exercise it, hides an underlying context of power relations which curtails mobilities and produces immobilities. She writes:

> Those who seek legal authorization even to visit the First World are faced with complex and often prohibitively expensive visa restrictions that notably do not apply to the international mobility of First World citizens. And those Third World migrants who dare risk their lives to migrate to First World countries without legal authorization are confronted with increasingly militarized border regimes, negotiated by First and Third World nation-states and which amount to multilateral projects for the regional containment of Third World persons beyond the First World. (Achiume 2019: 1515)

In short:

> First World citizens have far greater capacity for lawful international mobility relative to their Third World counterparts, even holding constant or setting aside questions of personal financial means ... and because of the persisting racial demographics that distinguish the First World from the Third – demographics that are a significant product of passports, national borders and other successful institutions partially originated as technologies of racialized exclusion – most whites enjoy dramatically greater rights to freedom of international movement than most non-whites. The reality is that the mortal cost of international mobility is largely a non-white problem. (Achiume 2019: 1530)

The hostile response of First World states to Third World migrants is possible because nation-states have the right to exclude outsiders as a matter of sovereign self-determination. Non-nationals are 'definitionally political strangers with no cognizable claims to shaping the trajectory of the respective nation-state, and certainly no say as to the terms of their admission and inclusion within that body' (Achiume 2019: 1515), excluding the exceptional case of refugees (at least in theory; see chapter 5). What Achiume is seeking to do in 'Migration as Decolonization' is completely rethink this logic. She suggests that histories of colonialism represent an 'invitation to interdependence' and, having built deep global interconnection, metropolitan postcolonial states cannot ethically now disavow that interdependency (see Amighetti and Nuti 2016; Mathieu 2018). Peoples around the world (across the First/Third World divide) remain politically and economically interconnected, but people in the

Third World remain largely subordinated in this relationship, what Achiume refers to as neo-colonial empire. Her argument is that Third World peoples are 'co-sovereign members of neo-colonial empire' and are therefore 'entitled to a say in the vehicles of effective collective self-determination within this empire' (Achiume 2019: 1520).

The upshot, for Achiume, is that because of their connected colonial histories and continuing neo-colonial relations, First World nation-states do not have a right to exclude Third World migrants. Rather, as co-sovereigns in neo-colonial empire, Third World citizens have ethical claims to inclusion in First World nation-states. Claims to inclusion and equality are based on Third World citizens' status 'as political insiders bound with First World persons to First World nation-states, and not on their fitting into whatever exemptions apply to political strangers such as refugees' (Achiume 2019: 1515; emphasis added). The regional containment of migrants on the continent of Africa 'is undergirded by a sovereignty discourse that justifies African exclusion from Europe as an incident of collective self-determination of European nations, which may rightfully be wielded against political strangers' (2019: 13). But through foregrounding persisting neo-colonial inter-connection, Achiume highlights the political ties that bind Africans to Europeans and suggests that, while this relationship currently subordinates Africans for the benefit of Europeans, that very subor-dination gives Africans a right to migrate to Europe. Indeed, because decolonization did not undo colonial subordination, Achiume argues that 'so-called economic migration may enact a process that enhances individual self-determination within neo-colonial empire … This personal pursuit of enhanced self-determination (and its assertion of political equality with First World citizens) is thus de-colonial; it is migration as decolonization' (2019: 1522).

Rethinking the concept of sovereignty is therefore central to Achiume's 'migration as decolonization' thesis. Sovereignty is usually seen as a collective project of territorially bounded national self-determination which casts non-nationals as political strangers (as in the liberal democratic view). Yet, as Nisancioglu (2019) points out, this view decisively ignores how colonial racism influenced conceptions of sovereignty as something to be possessed princi-pally by 'civilized' colonizing nations and to therefore be denied to 'uncivilized' peoples who were not seen as ready for self-government. Achiume wants to trouble this binary and to understand all involved in colonial relations as de facto co-sovereigns within empires. She suggests that we should think of nation-states as complexly (and messily) politically interconnected as a consequence of historical imperial projects and their legacies. Empires brought people together in (highly unequal) transnational political communities, she suggests, and these histories and their legacies mean that rather than being outside of the sovereign political community, Third World migrants have just claims to being included in that community.

But the crux of claims to continued co-sovereignty is based on the way that decolonization unfolded in the Third World. Decolonization was, for many, a project of seeking equality, in part through decolonized states gaining political control, but also control of their economies. On the eve of decolonization, there were a plethora of ideas about how these states could pursue these goals and what their future international relations with former colonizers might be (see, for example, Wilder 2015 on Aimé Césaire and Léopold Sédar Senghor's contributions to these discussions in the French colonial context). Unfortunately, Achiume argues that the Third World states were unable to write colonial advantage out of international law or out of the international order. Rather than gaining full economic and political sovereignty, decolonization involved a shift from colonial empire to neo-colonial empire, as noted above. A premise of Achiume's argument, then, is that the present era is defined by neo-colonial imperialism, even if formal colonial imperialism has been outlawed, and that this maintains colonial advantage into the present (Mamdani 1996).

Neo-colonial empire is the projection of political and economic power in the absence of formal colonial control. It thus prevents less powerful states from taking full control of their destinies, a point made powerfully by Walter Rodney (2018 [1972]), amongst others. The effect of neo-colonial empire is that though formerly colonized Third World states have formal sovereignty, in fact this is more accurately described as quasi-sovereignty. They have less power in international decision-making fora and are economically subordinate. These failures of formal decolonization therefore maintain the political association between Third and First World persons 'in a de facto political community of de facto co-sovereigns mutually instrumental to the prosperity of neocolonial empire' (Achiume 2019: 1547). It is in this situation of co-sovereignty that, Achiume argues, Third World persons should have access to the shared goods, including territorial access, of First World states.

This, of course, goes against most domestic and international law as well as general understandings of sovereignty as collective self-determination, and the right to exclude, amongst a territorially bounded political community. Nevertheless, Achiume argues that the historical and continuing subjection and exploitation of Third World peoples by the First World should allow the former to hold an equal stake in the demos of the latter. In more poetic terms, when it comes to sovereignty, 'the colonies are never outside of Europe, or more accurately Europe is never outside of its colonies' (Nisancioglu 2019: 9). This of course extraterritorializes the demos beyond nation-state borders, moving its boundaries to neo-colonial interconnection. In some cases, this would involve reinstating previous instantiations of citizenship. For example, British citizenship only existed before 1981 in the form of citizenship of the British Empire and then the Commonwealth; it was only in 1981 that it became tied to the territory of the United Kingdom as we now understand it (see Bhambra 2017a). Since much of the wealth and power of First World states hinges, for Achiume, on these past and present relations, until unequal relations cease, co-sovereignty will be essential to partially mitigate the ongoing impacts of neo-colonial empire on Third World states. Through acknowledging interconnection, subjugation and exploitation, then, Third World persons cannot be understood as political strangers to First World nation-states. They should be understood as political insiders.

In part, this co-sovereignty emerges from, as noted above, the failures of decolonization to deliver political equality. The capacity of Third World states to self-determine is diminished by neo-colonialism, and so in the absence of an end to neo-colonialism other actions must be pursued. What, then, does this co-sovereignty in neo-colonial empire mean for migration? It means that Third World persons should be able to freely move within neo-colonial empire – as they have previously been (legally) able to do. Achiume here takes decolonization down from the level of the political collective to the individual. She argues that in light of how badly neo-colonialism continues to fail Third World peoples, 'individuals among them can take actions that we should understand as de-colonial' (Achiume 2019: 1552). Decolonization, then, can be personal. It becomes personal when necessary structural changes are not forthcoming, and individual actions to self-determine through migration should thus be viewed as a matter of corrective distributive justice.

This argument offers a radically different lens for considering the claims to admission and inclusion of Third World migrants, particularly those who violate existing laws, to settle in First World territories, and particularly when they are motivated by the pursuit of 'a better life' within the context of persisting neo-colonial inequality. The argument is not that citizenship in this articulation would necessarily lead to equality, but that it would bring the possibility of increased equality to the fore. Nevertheless, there are many complexities to contend with. For example, would migration as decolonization apply to all Third World citizens? Achiume answers no, because not all Third World citizens are disadvantaged by neo-colonial empire. Then there is the question of which countries it might apply to – former colonies and metropoles only, or a wider scope of countries? Here she argues that neo-colonial empire is an expansive multilateral enterprise between First World nation-states who benefit from it as a collective, as well as needing to maintain it. For example: 'the power and benefit that France enjoys within the World Bank and the IMF and any other institution that sustains neo-colonial empire and Third World subordination, and France's status as an effective sovereign nation, incur de-colonial obligations vis-à-vis Zambians even though France never colonized Zambia' (Achiume 2019: 1562).

A further question arises in relation to settler-colonial states, colonial projects founded on the appropriation of land, subjugation and ethnocide of indigenous peoples. Achiume observes that for those indigenous (Fourth World) peoples that have citizenship of the First World states which have been founded on their lands, her argument might be moot (though one might counter that it may, for them, represent a further wave of colonialism which is morally unacceptable; see the discussion in the next section). She concludes that settler-colonial states are key beneficiaries of neo-colonial empire and that 'the higher comparative vulnerability to marginalization and subordination of a non-white Third World person willing to risk her life for an undocumented life in a First World nation-state, relative to that of a Fourth World person with formal First World citizenship status, underscores (if imperfectly so) the de-colonial value of citizenship' (Achiume 2019: 1562).

This is not a no-borders argument to the extent that it does not allow for free movement of everybody across any border. It especially does not offer First World persons the right, as co-sovereign members of neo-colonial empire, to migrate to the Third World. This is because neo-colonial empire already operates to their advantage; their migration project is not a decolonial move. As South African academic Ndlovu-Gatsheni (2018b) points out, Europeans and North Americans continue to travel visa-free to and between African countries (as tourists, investors and experts) while mobile black Africans continue to be subject to strict visa regimes within the continent of Africa and are pathologized and problematized within that context. But while he envisages a transnational pan-African citizenship as a liberatory postcolonial horizon in Africa, Achiume looks to South–North migration. Migration as decolonization is therefore about articulating a more just arrangement than exists at present, and to that extent Achiume argues forcefully that it is not utopian but pragmatically ameliorative. But at the same time as imagining more just arrangements, Achiume's thesis is also centrally about drawing out the importance of recognizing historical interconnection in the ways that we understand the present and imagine possible futures. In the next section, we discuss issues of indigenous sovereignty and immigration, and through that a series of complicating questions are potentially raised which might challenge migration as decolonization in settler-colonial contexts. But as it stands, what 'migration as decolonization' offers is a radical rethinking of the foundations of sovereignty and citizenship when understood as emergent of colonial relations.

Indigenous sovereignty and immigration

The whole question of 'borders' and the crossing of borders is entangled in colonial/modern regimes of power and colonial territorial appropriation and possession. For many people in the world, the creation of 'modern' nation-states carved up their lands and placed borders in the middle of their communities (Luna-Firebaugh 2002). It is for this reason that the work of indigenous scholars brings such an important and interesting set of questions to the study of migration. Indigenous peoples are extremely diverse, and while they share common struggles, the context in which they live – whether a white settler state in North America, a former colony in Africa or Asia or the northern margins of a European state – will greatly affect the nature of debates on migration, decolonization and ongoing struggles for self-determination within those communities and countries. This section focuses to a much greater extent on the settler-colonial contexts of Canada, the United States and Australia, not least because this is where the greatest quantity of English-language debate on indigenous issues and immigration has taken place. We do this to make a provocation to migration scholars working in these contexts, but do not mistake our silence on the full range of indigenous contexts, writings and lives as evidence that they do not exist (for other contexts see Hembrom 2017; Kapoor 2010).

Work in indigenous studies within the context of settler colonialism has particularly significant implications for migration studies, in part because so much research is undertaken within settler-colonial contexts without recognizing indigenous issues at all. But such work needs to be attentively listened to by migration scholars working in these contexts. Through such a process of listening, it is quite possible that migration studies as a field and mode of scholarship, particularly in settler-colonial states, would be rendered untenable as currently approached. This is because indigenous scholarship and struggles delegitimize the very basis of the sovereignty claims of settler-colonial states. In doing so, any questions of immigration to such states then need to be set within the context of settler colonialism and indigenous sovereignty which transform the basis of discussions around multiculturalism or immigrant integration, to pick two examples. Put simply, from the perspective of indigenous peoples, 'settler nations are not immigrant nations' (Tuck and Yang 2012: 7). Indeed, 'settlers are not immigrants. Immigrants are beholden to the Indigenous laws and epistemologies of the lands they migrate to' (Tuck and Yang 2012: 7). Settlers then illegitimately 'become the law, supplanting indigenous laws and epistemologies' (Tuck and Yang 2012: 7). Indigenous studies therefore introduces important complexities (political realities) which have huge implications for migration studies in settler-colonial contexts, and central to this are questions of sovereignty.

In light of ongoing struggles for decolonization which indigenous peoples are currently engaged in, and the problematic history of academic research in furthering settler-colonial projects of appropriation and dispossession (Chilisa 2012; Smith 2012), it would not be appropriate to suggest that non-indigenous migration studies scholars simply adopt indigenous perspectives as new analytic tools or concepts. However, this is a rich, and politically urgent, area of intellectual discussion that must be listened to by non-indigenous scholars because it is in listening that learning (and transformation) can potentially take place. What is at stake here is not just developing an understanding of the present as a legacy of colonial pasts but developing an understanding of the present as one of colonial occupation and ongoing struggles for literal decolonization. We sketch out some of the debates that emerge from the indigenous literature here as they pertain to the study of migration, and suggest questions that this raises for the study of migration, particularly in settler-colonial contexts. We do this as far as possible in the words of indigenous scholars, which is why this section is heavy on quotation, but as with all sections of this book, it is always best to go the original sources and read them fully than to take our summary at face value.

The first issue at stake here is indigenous sovereignty, and the denial of settler-colonial (and other) states and their non-indigenous citizens of that sovereignty. Aileen Moreton-Robinson (a Goenpul woman from Minjerribah, Quandamooka First Nation in Queensland, Australia) points out that the media coverage of world events in countries such as Australia, Britain, New Zealand, Canada and the United States pays no 'serious attention to the ongoing tension and conflict between nation-states and the indigenous sovereign nations which exist within them' (Moreton-Robinson 2007: 2). She understands the ongoing logic of settler-colonial sovereignty in terms of 'white possessive logics' which are operationalized 'within discourses to circulate sets of meanings about ownership of the nation, as part of common-sense knowledge, decision making, and socially produced conventions' (Moreton-Robinson 2015: xii). The maintenance of this common-sense knowledge nevertheless requires continual work and renewal, as she explains: 'It takes a great deal of work to maintain Canada, the United States, Hawai'i, New Zealand, and Australia as white possessions. The regulatory mechanisms of these nation-states are extremely busy reaffirming and reproducing this possessiveness through a process of perpetual Indigenous dispossession, ranging from the refusal of Indigenous sovereignty to overregulated piecemeal concessions' (2015: xi).

The status quo, then, 'continues to target them for legal and cultural extinction' (Lawrence and Dua 2005: 125). But the effort of maintaining the status quo renders settler colonialism itself, as an ongoing situation of territorial occupation, largely invisible to settlers. Despite those who benefit from it failing to perceive its presence and power, the settler-colonial state is of course highly visible to indigenous people:

> In our quotidian encounters, whether it is on the streets of Otago or Sydney, in the tourist shops in Vancouver or Waipahu, or sitting in a restaurant in New York, we experience ontologically the effects of white possession. These cities signify with every building and every street that this land is now possessed by others; signs of white possession are embedded everywhere in the landscape. The omnipresence of Indigenous sovereignties exists here too, but it is disavowed through the materiality of these significations, which are perceived as evidence of ownership by those who have taken possession. This is territory that has been marked by and through violence and race. (Moreton-Robinson 2015: xiii)

Moreton-Robinson argues that indigenous relations to the land now known as Australia both are 'incommensurate with those developed through capitalism' and colonialism, and 'they continue to unsettle white Australia's sense of belonging, which is inextricably tied to white possession and power' (2015: xx). The sense of belonging that Australian settlers today feel to the territory which they occupy is, for Moreton-Robinson, one rooted in connections to whiteness and Britishness, is deeply committed to colonization and is built on the disavowal of indigenous sovereignty. This goes back to the founding of the settler-colonial state of Australia, in which Captain James Cook declared the land uninhabited (see Olund 2002). In doing so, he 'willed away the sovereignty of Indigenous peoples by placing them in and of nature as propertyless subjects' (2015: xxii). As settler-colonial projects unfolded over the subsequent centuries across the globe, they actively sought to eradicate indigenous peoples, communities, identities and claims to the land through extermination, displacement or assimilation. The aim, according to Lawrence and Dua (2005: 121), 'is to ensure that Indigenous peoples ultimately disappear *as* peoples, so that settler nations can seamlessly take their place'.

As Lawrence and Dua (2005) point out in the Canadian context, generations of policies have been formulated 'with the goal of destroying our communities and fragmenting our identities'. This has partly been done by spatial segregation. As Cole Harris (2002: 265) explains in the Canadian context, the allocation of reserves for indigenous communities 'defined two primal spaces, one for

Native people and the other for virtually everyone else'. These spaces were then understood as the spatial 'juxtaposition of civilization and savagery' (2002: 268) whereby the confinement of indigenous peoples to reserves emptied other spaces for settlement. The implication then becomes that, in leaving 'their spaces', indigenous Canadians become de-indigenized. In this context, Mi'kmaw scholar Bonita Lawrence (2004) defines indigeneity in terms of mutually recognized group identity, rather than an essentialized heredity that can be bred, migrated or assimilated out. She describes in her article with Enakshi Dua how Aboriginals in Canada have

> struggled with our lack of knowledge about our heritage due to our parents' silence, the fact that our languages were beaten out of our grandparents' generation, that we may have been cut off from access to the land for generations, that we may know little of our own ceremonies, and that our Indigeneity is ultimately validated or denied by government cards that certify 'Indian' status (Lawrence and Dua 2005: 121; see also Lawrence 2004)

Through both essentializing indigenous culture, identity and heredity, and (having exterminated, displaced and assimilated) representing Indigeneity as something that is of the past and is dying out in the present, 'Indigenous peoples are reduced to small groups of racially and culturally defined and marginalized individuals in a sea of settlers' (Lawrence and Dua 2005: 121) who might be incorporated into multicultural projects as one minority amongst many. But what Kerem Nisancioglu (2019: 9) calls racial sovereignty is, as he points out, 'not absolute authority (as much as it might claim to be)'. Instead, 'racial sovereignty always encounters resistance: uprisings, revolutions, riots, escape and everyday struggle mark the "intolerable contradictions" of racial sovereignty' (2019: 9). Settler colonialism and Indigeneity, then, both endure despite each other (Kauanui 2016). Indigenous resistance itself reveals, as Wolfe and others argue, that settler colonialism is a structure, not a historical event (Nisancioglu 2019; Wolfe 2016; and Kauanui 2016, who offers a critical engagement). In the simplest terms, then, recognizing states such as Canada as settler colonial rather than immigrant, multiculturalism as a deeply problematic reconciliation of difference in this context of occupation, and the resistance that is occurring to racial sovereignty is a good starting point for migration researchers.

Central to this is indigenous sovereignty, which Moreton-Robinson explains,

> is embodied, it is ontological (our being) and epistemological (our way of knowing), and it is grounded within complex relations derived from the intersubstantiation of ancestral beings, humans and land. In this sense, our sovereignty is carried by the body and differs from Western constructions of sovereignty, which are predicated on the social contract model, the idea of a unified supreme authority, territorial integrity and individual rights. As embodied Indigenous sovereign subjects, we are contributing to current debates by reconfiguring and challenging dominant perspectives about Indigenous politics and sovereignty. (Moreton-Robinson 2007: 2)

Connection to the land or particular lands, Lawrence and Dua (2005) explain, is central to indigeneity. Many things are understood by diverse indigenous peoples, to emerge from the land, including language, memory and history. The upshot, they argue, is that 'the Canadian nation is still foreign to this land' (2005: 127).

Acknowledging indigenous sovereignty not only raises questions for long-standing white settler societies, or for the national imaginary of settler states as immigrant nations, but is also of significant import for other migrations to settler colonies. Nihiyow (Cree) lawyer Harold Johnson (2007) takes a different approach. He suggests that, according to relational Cree law, settlers have a treaty right to be on the land now called Canada because they were given permission by Cree elders at Treaty No. 6. Through this treaty, 'we became relatives', 'cousins'. Settlers were welcomed as two families living in the same space. He suggests that newcomers, then, are being welcomed into the settler family and are the responsibility of settlers:

> We are happy that many people from different parts of the world have come to live here. They are as welcome as you are ... To my family, the minorities are all members of your family. They are your responsibility. You adopted them through your ceremony of immigration and naturalisation. To the extent that they are your relatives through adoption, they are also our relatives, because you and I are related. (cited in Bhatia 2013: 57).

Johnson's powerful account, however, does not speak to the cases of undocumented workers who are not naturalized or offered citizenship, or those brought forcibly to a territory through enslavement (Bhatia 2013). Tuck and Yang argue:

> People of colour who enter/are brought into the settler colonial nation-state also enter the triad of relations between settler–native–slave. We are referring here to the colonial pathways that are usually described as 'immigration' and how the refugee/immigrant/migrant is invited to be a settler in some scenarios, given the appropriate investments in whiteness, or is made an illegal, criminal presence in other scenarios (Tuck and Yang 2012: 17).

Lawrence and Dua (2005) go further in arguing that 'Aboriginal people' cannot see themselves in anti-racism contexts because struggles for recognition and against racism more often than not fail to acknowledge indigenous presence and ongoing colonization. People of colour have also, they argue, participated in projects of settlement. They are settlers, even if they are marginalized by white settler nationalist projects while doing so. Their argument is that despite experiencing racism and marginalization, 'people of colour live on land that is appropriated and contested, where Aboriginal people are denied nationhood and access to their own lands' (Lawrence and Dua 2005: 134). The question, then, as Haig-Brown (2009) asks in the context of diaspora studies, is not only where do people of the diaspora come from, but where have they come to?

Sharma and Wright (2008–9) have questioned the description of the forced movement of enslaved Africans which led to the large African American presence in what is now known as the United States of America, *as* settler colonialism, which some of these arguments imply. They also challenge Lawrence and Dua's (2005) argument that indigenous nationalism is the solution to continued settler colonialism on the basis that essentialized claims to land are widely used to exclude racialized migrants and citizens across the world and that in doing the same indigenous peoples would be using the tools of their oppressors to establish their claims to territorial sovereignty as supreme. Ethnic boundaries are not natural borders, they argue, and migrants are not 'out of place', particularly within the context of connected histories discussed earlier (Bhambra 2014).

In a connected vein, Byrd (2011) argues against 'competing oppressions' between migrants and indigenous communities, which she argues 'reproduce colonialist discourses' (2011: xxvi), and in her own work she seeks to decentre 'the vertical interactions of colonizer and colonized' and re-centre 'the horizontal struggles among peoples with competing claims to historical oppressions' (2011: xxxiv). Drawing inspiration from Barbadian poet Kamau Braithwaite, she proposes the concept 'arrivant' to describe non-indigenous immigrants to settler-colonial contexts, who then experience colonially informed racial subjugation. This concept moves away from the indigenous/ non-indigenous binary, which has been an ongoing concern for indigenous scholars within the context of generations of intermarriage, assimilation and de-indigenization, and towards a structural critique of coloniality that centres a diverse and non-essentialized indigeneity in struggling against ongoing colonialisms of all kinds. In other words, 'there are no automatic solidarities between "Indians" and "Aliens", but instead these relationships must be formed, maintained, storied, and revisited' (Bhatia 2013: 45).

Eve Tuck, Allison Guess and Hannah Sultan (2014) have written about this in terms of 'tripled relationships' between indigenous peoples, Africans-made-into-chattel and white settlers as antagonisms. Their desire is then 'to supersede the conventions of settler colonialism and antiblackness toward another kind of futurity' (2014: 2). They explain that 'settler colonialism has attempted to reduce human relationships to land to relationships to property, making property "ownership" the primary vehicle to civil rights in most settler colonial nation-states', and part of this project in the US context was chattel slavery and the logic that 'black people must be kept landless' (2014: 3). While Tuck, Guess and Sultan acknowledge the 'complicity of *all* arrivants (including black enslaved people) in Indigenous erasure and dispossession', they also acknowledge 'the complicity of white people and nonwhite people (including Native people) in antiblackness' (2014: 3). Thus, they argue, 'settler colonialism fuses a set of (at least) tripled relationships between settlers/ settlement, chattel/enslavement, and Indigenous/erasure' (2014: 3). Here they echo Bhambra's (2014) call to account for all who are present on a territory in relation to histories of interconnection rather than competition. In looking beyond this status quo, they look to Joy James's writing on the 'henceforward'. That is, 'the time and space in which we can tumble into something that will be arranged differently, coded differently, so that our locations and labours are more than just who we are to the settler' (Tuck, Guess and Sultan 2014: 7).

Within these dialogues and debates, there has been an increasing interest in questions of indigenous migrations, particularly the migration of indigenous Mexicans to the United States of America. Borders now separate single, contiguous indigenous communities from the Maasi in East Africa to the Mayas in Central America. Such processes have divided indigenous communities between the administrative rules of different countries and, as Trujano (2008: 15) points out, 'some of these separated communities still move within their territory, now straddling an international border' (see also Rivera-Salgado 1999). He goes on, 'these movements are considered international migration, even when the communities have not stepped outside their own ancestral territories' (Trujano 2008: 15). While for some indigenous peoples such borders may present obstacles to challenging settler colonialism (as they must engage with two settler states, such as across the Canadian–US border; see Austin 1992), for others the states in which they find themselves may have been created by both colonial powers and decolonial movements for independence (such as in East Africa). In other instances, indigenous people migrate away from their traditional territories. In doing so, they may experience anti-immigrant racism from a settler state – denials of their indigenous identity having moved 'out of place' and thus severed the link to their ancestral lands – and anti-indigenous hostility from other migrants.

There is, nevertheless, a long history of migrations amongst indigenous peoples, including practices of nomadism, seasonal migration, as well as economic or physical displacement from traditional lands. Equally, the forced migration, displacement or uprooting of indigenous communities by environmental events, development projects and armed conflict also lead to indigenous migrations. The extent to which people's indigeneity is respected in such contexts, or even recorded in IDP or refugee management responses, is highly variable. As Carlos Yescas Angeles Trujano (2008) discusses in a report for the IOM, the urbanization of indigenous peoples through processes of rural–urban migrations can further raise important questions about the ability of indigenous people to maintain cultural traditions and secure their rights as they are seen as 'out of place'.

How can the presence of indigenous migrants to settler-colonial states be reconciled with debates discussed above around new arrivals (or arrivants), which seem to presume that arrivants will always be non-indigenous people? What do these migrations do to the sovereignty claims of existing indigenous communities whose own claims have been denied, ignored or waylaid? There are sizeable communities of indigenous peoples from the Mexican state of Oaxaca working within Californian labour markets in the United States who find themselves marginalized on multiple fronts, including from the state (as undocumented) and from local indigenous struggles against settler colonialism (Kearney 2000). They have responded, in part, by developing binational grassroots organizations and maintaining strong ties to their homelands and communities, including returning to them to take up leadership positions to defend their territories (Rivera-Salgado 1999). This practice stretches the political community of the Mexican state to include the indigenous diaspora and is facilitated by indigenous governance systems.

Indigenous rights are secured (the extent to which is contested) by International Labour Organization Conventions 10712 and 169.13. These offer recognition and protection to indigenous peoples who are seen to have integrated into non-indigenous societies, including through migration. It does this by defining indigeneity on the basis of self-identification, which means that non-indigenous authorities cannot (on paper) define the parameters of indigeneity and in doing so disqualify some people from claims to indigenous rights and protections. Within this context, then, indigenous migration would not be understood as settler colonialism. The fact of continued ongoing occupation of indigenous territories in settler-colonial states remains and will continue to trouble liberal discussions of immigrant incorporation as long as that occupation continues. Nevertheless, as Bhatia (2013) points out, an indigenous immigration policy, if past behaviour is anything to go by, would not focus on keeping racialized immigrants out but on corporations who threaten life and land. This suggests that the idea of indigenous hostility to indigenous migrants is something of a red herring.

What, then, do the perspectives of indigenous peoples do to the way that we conceptualize and understand migration? First, they centre colonialism as something that is ongoing in settler-colonial states, not as something that has been consigned to the past and might be thought of in terms of 'legacies'. Second, centring settler colonialism in those contexts where it exists raises vital questions about sovereignty and the assumptions of state sovereignty upon which studies of immigration may rest. This significantly complicates debates over immigrant settlement rights, integration and multiculturalism, raising questions which must be wrestled with (as Lawrence and Dua 2005 and Sharma and Wright 2008–9 amongst others have done), rather than ignored. Third, it also complicates decolonial projects (such as that of Achiume discussed earlier in this chapter), which might not always centre continued situations of colonialism in discussions of reparative justice vis-à-vis First World–Third World relations.

No borders?

The discussions in this chapter raise an interesting set of questions around borders and bordering, particularly progressive discussions around 'no borders'. Achiume observes that since bordering practices tend to disadvantage Third World migrants and are associated with violence and fatalities, particularly against and amongst migrants racialized as black and brown, some scholars have argued for 'no borders'. In a particularly well-cited piece, Bridget Anderson, Nandita Sharma and Cynthia Wright (2009) argue that because human rights are tied to citizenship, the rights of migrants are unprotected. Migration, they observe, 'is always already a problem: an aberrant form of behaviour in need of fixing', which consequently means that 'people's mobility is seen as only ever caused by crisis and as crisis producing' (2009: 9). They suggest that solutions which tweak the system of exclusionary citizenship regimes (such as making immigration controls more humane) fail to see that it is citizenship and border regimes themselves which uphold inequalities, usually in the service of capitalist aims:

> What distinguishes a No Borders politics from other immigrant-rights approaches is their refusal to settle for 'fairer' immigration laws (higher numbers, legal statuses, and so on). Within a No Borders politics, it is understood that the border-control practices of national states not only reflect people's unequal rights (e.g. whose movements are deemed to be legitimate and whose are not) but also produce this inequality. Thus, the signal demand is for every person to have the freedom to move and, in this era of massive dispossession and displacement, the concomitant freedom to not be moved (i.e. to stay). (Anderson, Sharma and Wright 2009: 11)

Since borders are pervasive in social life, 'no borders' is not just arguing against lines on maps, or controls at the entry point to a territory, it is arguing against the broader scope of border controls, including the differential rights held by different groups present in different spaces. There is a distinction here between no-borders activism on the political left, and neo-liberal no-borders calls on the political right. A neo-liberal (and neo-classical) economic perspective critiques border controls and migration restrictions because they obstruct the free circulation of labour and decrease productivity (Casey 2010; Riley 2008). Proponents are often seeking more labour to exploit, easier access to land and therefore the possibility of further dispossession. Open or no borders, in this view, would permit free cross-border mobility of labour, increase labour competition, remove privilege from protected labour and increase efficiency and productivity.

Anti-capitalist no-borders and open-borders arguments focus on how borders and bordering practices such as immigration controls and stratified rights regimes produce social inequalities and injustices (Alldred 2003; Brown 1992; Hayter 2001; Walters 2006). Very rarely do these arguments seriously engage with the colonial histories of territorial borders, citizenship regimes and sovereignty claims. For example, when Bauder (2014) explores the possibilities of open or no borders, he does this under the pragmatic assumption that conditions of nation-state territoriality and formal citizenship would remain in place but may be modified. A radical no-borders politics rejects this. It acknowledges that inequalities today are linked to inequalities in the past, and names the connections as colonial. From such a perspective, if successful, no borders would have a 'profound effect on all of our lives for it is part of a global reshaping of economies and societies in a way that is not compatible with capitalism, nationalism, or the mode of state-controlled belonging that is citizenship' (Anderson, Sharma and Wright 2009: 12). The world would be more equal, which means a likely drop in living standards for some, with an increase for others. This view is closer to Achiume's vision of migration as decolonization, though hers is selective in who is allowed to cross borders freely and who cannot.

Raising the issue of colonial histories, therefore, complicates such no-borders arguments. On the one hand, drawing attention to the histories of colonialism in the formation of modern ideas about territory, states and citizens centres the coloniality of border regimes. As Pam Alldred (2003: 153) indicates, 'anti-imperialist analysis refuses to be silent on the role of rich nations in creating the conflict from which people flee, and points out the significance of (European and) British colonialism in creating contemporary patterns of migration to places people identify as the mother country or speak the language of.'

In this view, then, no-borders arguments can be used to unsettle colonialist assumptions about the naturalness of borders and the erasure of the histories of appropriation of land on which contemporary border regimes are dependent (Fortier 2013; Papadopoulos, Stephenson and Tsianos 2008). No borders, in the view presented by Anderson, Sharma and Wright (2009), might be interpreted as decolonial. They observe that many borders were created in and through colonial activities, and that their ongoing maintenance is dependent upon leaving intact racist, colonial scripts around citizenships and belonging. In this view, 'subjects are constructed neither as migrants and non-migrants nor as citizens and non-citizens', potentially resetting the clock of colonial relations (Bauder 2014: 78). As Hiebert (2003) notes (though not from a post- or decolonial perspective), by removing the right of a nation-state to *exclude*, its right to *include* would also be nullified. This would also nullify the idea of the nation-state as currently articulated. Hiebert (2003) himself suggests that rather than transcending existing relations, inequalities would in fact be amplified by a borderless world. But we might imagine the possibility that it could lead to the creation of new communities, which would of course have emerged through historical processes of mobility and migration, but might transcend the racially hierarchical articulation of their relationships to each other in the future (see de Genova 2017).

Thinking with the perspectives presented in this chapter, and particularly the insights of indigenous studies, presents some challenges to this tentatively decolonial politics of no borders. Borders are themselves a product of colonial and imperial histories, systems of control and violence. Before the beginning of the twentieth century, it is not historically accurate to talk of state borders in the way we see them now. So it is not so much the case that the world was one of 'open borders' before the twentieth century, it was that mobility was facilitated, controlled and imagined differently. But as some postcolonial and indigenous authors have demonstrated, this also worked to the detriment of indigenous inhabitants of would-be colonized lands. Colonialism assumed that many places which were already inhabited were empty, and that those who lived there were not the sovereign occupants of the territory. The perception that there were no substantive material or symbolic borders (because there was no territorial citizenship through European-recognized systems of land ownership), then, led to genocide, dispossession, subjugation, enslavement and invasive settlement. As indigenous scholar Linda Tuhiwai Smith (2012: 222) explains, 'in each place, after figures such as Columbus and Cook had long departed, there came a vast array of military personnel, imperial administrators, priests, explorers, missionaries, colonial officials, artists, entrepreneurs and settlers, who cut a devastating swathe, and left a permanent wound, on the societies and communities who occupied the lands named and claimed under imperialism' (Smith 2012: 22).

Equally, in the context of former colonies, nation-building projects and the gaining of territorial sovereignty were an important part of anti-colonial struggles. Opening up borders would then potentially entail a reversing of the powers that these states have gained to, in principle, exclude their former colonizers from their territories. While in reality those who are most often excluded are people of colour from other formerly colonized states (see Ndlovu-Gatsheni 2018b), decolonization through territorial sovereignty has nevertheless brought an end to the forms of European state-led direct-rule projects of occupation of territory as *terra nullius* that were seen in the past (though this is of course contested).

Opening borders, then, would not offer a solution to inequality, particularly in settler-colonial contexts, as Lawrence and Dua explain:

> Borders in the Americas are European fictions, restricting Native peoples' passage and that of peoples of colour. However, to speak of ongoing borders without addressing Indigenous land loss and ongoing struggles to reclaim territories is to divide communities that are already marginalized from one another. The question that must be asked is how opening borders would affect Indigenous struggles aimed at reclaiming land and nationhood. (2005: 136)

From an indigenous perspective, then, borders are not 'good' straightforwardly, but in light of the harms brought by border crossing through colonial and settler colonialism, even more migration into those territories is not going to aid struggles for indigenous self-determination on their ancestral lands. An anti-colonial no-borders agenda therefore contains within it a set of serious contradictions in both settler-colonial and formerly colonized countries, though for different reasons (see Fortier 2013 on the settler-colonial context). As Hiebert (2003) warns, there is also a distinct risk that existing relations of inequality and exploitation would only be heightened. This, for indigenous scholars living in First World settler-colonial states, would centre around continued waves of settlers, including corporations, moving to occupy their lands. Meanwhile, open or no borders could potentially offer safety to others seeking to move around indigenous territories which currently straddle modern/colonial borders and would open up the possibility of safe migration of Third World citizens.

It is with this in mind that Achiume (2019) does not advocate open borders but instead argues for the mobility of Third World citizens who are disadvantaged within neo-colonial empire. In light of the discussions above relating to the ongoing struggles of indigenous peoples against settler colonialism, however, even migration as decolonization would not offer reparative justice to Fourth World citizens living in First World countries. This debate is, clearly, unresolved, but this section has briefly sketched some of the issues at stake and some of the as yet unreconciled tensions within post- and decolonial discussions on the future of borders.

Conclusion

This chapter has explored the relationship between ideas of migration, sovereignty and citizenship when set within the context of colonial histories and presents. We did this through an engagement with three very different areas of scholarship which have centred colonialism in relation to such issues: connected sociologies, migration as decolonization and indigenous studies. Gurminder K. Bhambra's work on 'connected histories' disrupts the methodologically nationalist and presentist assumptions which underpin many studies of migration, citizenship and belonging. Her call to focus on interconnection resonates with the work of E. Tendayi Achiume and scholars within indigenous studies in that the point is to engage in a serious reckoning with what colonialism did to the world, as well as what it means and does in the present. The point is not to just make space for a multiplicity of perspectives but to keep the whole the same, for example, to acknowledge indigenous struggles in the present as connected continuously to anti-colonial struggles for self-determination over several hundred years, but not to think anything fundamentally different about (for example) Canadian territorial sovereignty while doing so. On the contrary, the point is to ask what recognizing indigenous sovereignty claims does to how Canada as a state is understood, and what migration studies would look like in Canada if this were taken seriously.

Bhambra (2014: 5) explains that 'no understanding remains unchanged by connection'. She goes on, 'to understand events through their connections is to acknowledge from the outset that addressing particular sets of connections leads to particular understandings which are put in question through choosing other sets of connections' (2014: 5). Achiume's thesis that migration, from the perspective of TWAIL, can be understood as a just act of decolonization *in itself* takes that challenge seriously. She is asking us what it would mean for migration regimes internationally today if we really took seriously the legacies of colonialism. Achiume presents one possible answer: it would mean the recognition of co-sovereignty in neo-colonial empire and the free movement of peoples from Third World to First World states. This radical reimagining of sovereignty, claims to citizenship and rightful entry to a host state (one which Achiume insists is not utopian) challenges us to think in new ways beyond the confines of the exclusionary colonial/modern nation-state.

In the final section of the chapter, we discussed some of the issues that these perspectives raise for a 'no-borders' agenda. While generally favoured in critical scholarship, we asked to what extent a no-borders agenda could be seen to be compatible with an agenda which makes colonialism central to our analyses. What this section did, in part, was to illustrate how not all projects which are seeking to centre colonialism are in harmony with one another. The job of imagining decolonial futures is one fraught with disagreement and debate. All of these perspectives take seriously the importance of colonialisms of various kinds in shaping the present, and they concur that what results are racially grounded global inequalities and injustices. But between them there are obvious contradictions and incompatibilities. This in part arises from the different modes of colonial relations that are foregrounded in the work of the scholars. These different foci do not necessarily sit easily together – justice for some is rarely justice for all – but, as the discussion in the section on debates around immigration (or settlement) to settler-colonial territories demonstrated, that does not mean that there are not common themes, struggles and articulations of the underpinnings of common injustices. It was not our intention to smooth over or minimize these differences but to draw attention to the multiple possibilities raised by a commitment to centring colonialism and the subsequent importance of local contexts in making sense of them in place.

5

Deconstructing Forced Migration, Rethinking Asylum

Introduction

Many people migrate within or across borders out of choice, but many are also forced to do so. An international regime to cope with such people and give them recourse to rights in the absence of their own state's protection emerged in the twentieth century. Such rights were initially reserved for Europeans in spite of purportedly being for human beings in general. This reflects the colonial contexts from which the right to asylum emerged, and it was only as increasing numbers of countries started to gain independence from the colonial powers that the right to asylum was (in 1967) expanded to potentially include everybody. Research on involuntary migrations as an institutionalized area of study is a relatively recent phenomenon and has tended to be, even when critical, responsive to policy priorities in the Global North.

The field of refugee studies thus emerged in the 1980s in response to the growth in the number of people from the Global South seeking asylum in the Global North (Chimni 1998). In the 2000s, scholarly attention then moved to the broader category of 'forced migration'. Under the heading 'forced migration' come such categories as refugees, asylum seekers, internally displaced persons (IDPs), trafficked people and those displaced by development projects and natural disasters (Bloch and Dona 2018). This concept of 'forced migration' ostensibly aimed at greater inclusion (Turton 2003), particularly in the case of a perceived historical neglect of IDPs (Cohen and Deng 1998), but its arrival has not been without criticism. Some characterize forced migration studies as an unequal marriage of migration studies and refugee studies in which the latter loses its distinctiveness: 'refugees are not just involuntary migrants, but are by definition the victims of fundamental social disfranchisement and uniquely within the protective ambit of the international community' (Hathaway 2007: 349). The arrival of forced migration studies is, then, potentially double-edged in that it is part of a 'new humanitarian agenda which furthers the goals of hegemonic states' (Chimni 2009: 12). Indeed, it may be no coincidence that attention on IDPs coincided with the emergence of the non-entrée asylum regime and redoubled efforts to quarantine displaced people in the Third World (Chimni 2009).

As this brief discussion shows, forced migration is a broad theme, but it has also both been deeply shaped by colonial ways of dividing up the world and the people in it and has been conscientious in its silence on the legacies of colonialism. That is, until recently. As such, the chapter focuses on three key interventions on this theme which have sought to rethink forced migration and asylum from a postcolonial, decolonial, or TWAIL standpoint. The first section addresses colonial histories in relation to asylum as a human right in order to draw out some important reflections on the exclusivity and Eurocentrism of the category of 'man' and 'human'. This echoes the discussions around race and the category of the human in chapter 3. The next section focuses on a key intervention made by a single scholar, Aurora Vergara-Figueroa, whose work offers a new perspective on forced migration. We argue that her recent book *Afrodescendant Resistance to Deracination in Colombia: Massacre at Bellavista-Bojayá-Chocó* (2018) has made possibly the most important contribution to the theorizing of forced migration of at least the past decade, and we felt that it therefore warranted extended attention. The next section discusses the concept of 'necropolitics', first proposed by Achille Mbembe but recently taken up by numerous scholars seeking to understand the role of violence, suffering and death, particularly 'letting die', in migration governance. Together, these perspectives are very different ways of thinking about and approaching 'refugee' and 'forced migration' issues to those usually seen in textbooks on the subject.

Asylum is a human right: postcolonial and decolonial perspectives on 'man' and 'human'

The human rights framework as we know it today was devised in the middle of the twentieth century. It was based on the idea that there was a need for some legal constraints on (non-colonized) states' sovereignty in order to prevent a repeat of the atrocities committed in Nazi Germany. Refugee rights were an integral part of this because many of those who fled the Nazi regime found that once they had crossed an international border they had, in the words of Hannah Arendt, lost the right to have rights (Arendt 1951). That is because until this point rights, where people had them, were tied to citizenship, making the uprooted and stateless effectively without recourse to rights or justice. The Geneva Convention on the Status of Refugees was meant to rectify this. It enshrined the right to asylum in international law for those displaced in Europe prior to 1951. It was agreed at a United Nations conference on 25 July 1951 following three years of discussion.

Though the 1951 Convention is remembered as a key moment for refugees globally, and it was agreed at the United Nations, which is an international body, it only applied to those displaced *in Europe before 1951*. The amendment of the Convention with a new protocol in 1967 responded to this limitation, but it occurred because of increasingly vocal petitioning to the UN by newly decolonized countries, not because the powerful members of the UN had concerns about its geographical and temporal limitations (Holborn 1975). In the next sub-section, we address the ways in which the Convention can be construed as Eurocentric and the initial exclusions from it rooted in colonialism. But it is worth noting here that despite being the key pillar in the international refugee regime, those states that host the majority of the world's refugees tend not to be signatories to the Convention and Protocol. Meanwhile, those states that are signatories to the Convention tend to have implemented measures which limit its effectiveness (see Chimni 2009; Janmyr 2017).

The myth of difference and the silencing of colonialism

In recent decades, wealthy western states have introduced highly restrictive asylum regimes which effectively seek to prevent would-be asylum seekers from accessing the right to asylum. These measures include extraterritorial border controls, carrier sanctions, safe country lists, safe third-country rules, detention, dispersal, deport–ation, fast-tracking of applications, limitations on the Convention definition, limiting appeal rights and restricting economic and social rights (see Fitzgerald 2019). They also involve numerous coercive collaborations with sending and transit countries to facilitate the quarantining of potential asylum seekers outside of these wealthy countries (Achiume 2019; Chimni 1998). These measures were first implemented in response to increases (when compared to the 1980s) in the number of people applying for asylum in western countries in the late 1990s and early 2000s.

These dual phenomena – the increase in asylum applications and the punitive response by western states – have garnered a significant amount of academic attention. Most often they are seen as causally linked: restrictive measures were introduced because numbers of applications were 'at intolerably high levels' (Hansen 2003: 35). This assessment is founded on what legal scholar B. S. Chimni (1998) dubs the 'myth of difference'. Chimni argues that during the first four decades of the refugee regime, Cold War priorities dominated. Those seeking asylum in the West were assumed to be white, male, European and fleeing the Soviet Union. Whether they were fleeing because of individual persecution or mixed motives related to poverty and 'seeking a better life' was not a matter of interest. When, in the late 1980s and accelerating into the 1990s and 2000s, different cohorts of asylum seekers began to arrive, they were construed as 'new asylum seekers'. At this point 'the nature and character of refugee flows in the Third World were represented as being radically different from refugee flows in Europe since the end of the First World War' (Chimni 1998: 351). Third World refugees clashed sharply with the image of the 'normal' refugee described above, and this difference was seen by western states as diminishing their claims for asylum.

The arrival of these new refugees, the start of which roughly coincided with the end of the Cold War, thus led to a policy shift. This policy shift can be summed up as the dawn of the non-entrée regime. The refugee 'no longer possessed ideological or geopolitical value' (Chimni 1998: 351) and as such powerful states individually, and through the UN, shifted the policy agenda away from refuge (or the 'exilic bias', as Chimni terms it) towards a focus on repatriation as the ideal solution to the refugee challenge. So, while the shift occurred in the policy preferences of powerful western states, this had global implications. There was concurrently a change in emphasis amongst those seeking to make sense of population displacements away from the *international* contexts which precipitated them and towards an emphasis on the immediate contexts which existed in sending countries.

But this is not simply a policy shift. Chimni is also concerned with the ways in which academic scholarship has reinforced the myth of difference. He observes that 'there is constant reference in the [academic] literature to the enormous magnitude and the unprecedented nature of the contemporary crisis' (Chimni 1998: 356). For Chimni, then, both refugee studies, and the more recent rise of forced migration studies, have contributed to the legitimizing of the containment of refugees from the Global South outside of the Global North (Chimni 2009). In fact, these new refugees were not necessarily different in terms of the legitimacy of their claim to asylum under international law. What was different was that they were from the Global South, usually from former European colonies. Underpinning the analysis that restrictive measures are a rational response to unprecedented burden is a 'standard narrative' on refugee history (Mayblin 2017). This standard narrative is the accepted historical context to this policy regime, a story which is widely accepted and is generally seen to be uncontroversial.

Allowing for variations in individual accounts, the narrative goes as follows. The number of asylum seekers coming to western, or 'First World', countries today is *unprecedented* (Appleyard 2001; Bohmer and Shuman 2008; Gibney 2003; Hansen 2003; Jetten and Esses 2018; Joly 1996; Koser 2001; Loescher 1993; Spencer 1995; Zolberg, Suhrke and Aguayo 1989). Present-day asylum seekers are unprecedented not only in number; they are also different from previous cohorts in various ways, including the reasons for their flight and their countries of origin. This 'newness' is in contrast to two previous cohorts of refugees who are often depicted as prima facie refugees, the original and the genuine, who were unequivocally the intended subjects of the international refugee regime. These groups are those displaced within Europe as a result of the Second World War, along with Cold War refugees, again from within Europe, who fled communism in favour of the capitalist West. Other refugees in other parts of the world are not a part of this standard narrative (see Crisp 2003; Friedman and Kelin 2008; Goodwin-Gill 2001; Haddad 2008; Hansen 2003; Joly 2002; Keely 2001; Squire 2009).

Having established that the Refugee Convention was devised in response to European refugees following the Second World War, and that Cold War refugees were few in number and were clearly politically persecuted, the sudden presence of large numbers of non-European asylum seekers at the gates of Europe, or within European territories, at the close of the twentieth century becomes a logical explanation for a tightened policy regime. These new refugees are different, and there are a lot of them. They also come from poor countries, meaning that they implicitly blur the boundaries between economic migrants and refugees, casting doubt on their claim to have been persecuted (see Crawley and Skleparis 2018). While policies which seek to respond to these new and unprecedented refugees are likely to prevent genuine refugees from being able to access their human right to claim asylum, politicians might feel assured that many are not 'genuine' refugees.

But what has been dubbed the 'standard narrative' (Mayblin 2017) is dependent on a sanctioned ignorance (Spivak 1999) of the actual history of refugees in the world. Certainly, refugee studies has been repeatedly criticized for being ahistorical (Kushner 2006; see also Marfleet 2007) in part because of the sheer urgency of the humanitarian challenges facing refugees today. Within this context, a discussion of historical displacements may seem like an academic indulgence. But in the absence of a serious engagement with history, the standard narrative has gone largely uncontested. It provides a brief introductory context to many books and articles but is rarely questioned (Marfleet 2007 and Chimni 1998 are exceptions). But the status of the narrative described above as a generally accepted historical context has implications for how we critically respond to refugee regimes today. The problem is not that the narrative is untruthful, it is that it contains many silences that hide the partiality and parochialism of the account. There are four key silences worth mentioning here, which are discussed at greater length in the book *Asylum after Empire* (Mayblin 2017): silences around non-European refugees before the 1990s, silences around colonial exclusions from the refugee conventions, silences around the legacies of colonialism for mobility and immobility, and silences around the legacies of colonialism in ideas of asylum seekers as undesirable and excludable.

First, in terms of refugee history globally, it is striking that the standard narrative singles out Europe and European refugees. Neither displacements outside of Europe (often caused by colonial activities and struggles around decolonization) nor the reception of European refugees in former colonies are included. And yet there *were* non-European refugees in the world at the time of drafting the 1951 Convention, for example, those fleeing China between 1949 and 1950, those (totalling millions) displaced by the Korean War 1950–3, and those displaced during the Arab–Israeli conflict of 1948 (Palestinian refugees estimated at 700,000) (Chi-Kwan 2007; Sandler 1999). Fifteen million people were forcibly displaced during the partitioning of India to create the new state of Pakistan in 1947 in one of the largest migrations of the twentieth century. Both countries were represented at the UN at the time of drafting the 1951 Convention and both vocally argued for the refugee convention to include all refugees (Talbot and Singh 2009). And yet these, and other, refugee crises go unmentioned in the standard narrative.

Barber and Ripley (1988: 53), in a typical early example, suggest that in 1951 'the overwhelming majority of refugees were European'. But what scholars usually mean when they say that 'the overwhelming majority of refugees were European' in 1951 is that asylum seekers and refugees seeking sanctuary in wealthy western states were almost always European, but two vital pieces of information are missing from this representation. First, the refugee conventions only allowed Europeans to be considered refugees until 1967. Second, and most importantly, just because most refugees in Europe were European in the middle of the twentieth century, that does not mean that most refugees in the world were European until the 1990s. This is more of a slippage than an omission, but it is important because it allows for a whole host of assumptions about contemporary (non-European) asylum seekers to go unchallenged. Indeed, these types of slippages, which start from the parochial history of Europe and somehow end up representing a global history, have been paid significant attention by postcolonial and decolonial scholars. This practice is, in part, what the concept 'Eurocentrism' encapsulates (Amin 1988).

If refugees in the past are assumed to be European, and to have fled a particular time- and place-specific *European* conception of persecution and displacement, contemporary asylum seekers are then automatically different from previous cohorts. But looking beyond the specificities and familiarities (to western readers at least) of mid-twentieth-century European refugees, the evidence suggests that asylum seekers today are not so different. They are migrating not because of poverty but as a result of the same kinds of reasons as were Europeans in the 1930s and 1940s – the threat or experience of persecution. When we look at the numbers, we see that applications spike in the contemporary period when refugee-creating situations, such as wars, occur. Research on this topic has shown that poverty alone is not sufficient to compel someone to leave their home country and seek asylum in the West; war, violence and human rights abuses must also be present to explain flight (Neumayer 2005). This demonstrates that asylum is not the mechanism through which 'the denizens of the world's poorer countries could enter the West', as Gibney (2003: 145) has suggested, but rather a mechanism for seeking protection from a foreign state as in the past. Their difference is not in the legitimacy of their claim to persecution but in their national origins.

The second key silence within the standard narrative is around colonial exclusions from the refugee conventions. There were, as we noted above, millions of refugees outside of Europe at the time of drafting the refugee conventions, and yet non-European refugees were purposefully excluded from these conventions (Mayblin 2014, 2017). These exclusions were pushed by the colonial powers, the United States of America and all of the British Dominions (Canada, South Africa, Australia and New Zealand) apart from India. The exclusions occurred despite extensive and protracted resistance from the representatives of formerly colonized states at the UN negotiations. These included India, Pakistan and Afghanistan. For example, at a UN General Assembly meeting in 1949, the Pakistani representative pointed out that 'if the proposal before the Committee were adopted, Pakistan would have to share in financing the legal protection of an undefined number of refugees in Europe, while obtaining no benefits for the millions of refugees in its own country'. Indeed, 'there was no mention in any formal proposal of extending the protection of the new organization to all categories of refugees and he hoped that some concrete amendments would be submitted in order to allay his anxiety ... it should be possible for the United Nations to extend his services to cover all refugees' (UN General Assembly, 11 November 1949, cited in Mayblin 2014: 13).

The actual histories of the drafting of the 1951 Refugee Convention therefore give us a clear insight into the silences that occurred from the very birth of the right to asylum onwards, and they demonstrate that the exclusions were based on colonial ideas of human hierarchy.

As Antony Anghie (2008) has argued so convincingly in relation to international law more broadly, colonialism was central to the establishment of international law. This includes a variety of areas that have a direct impact on refugee-producing situations and the rights of those fleeing them. Colonialism was not simply 'an unfortunate episode that has long since been overcome by the heroic initiatives of decolonization that resulted in the emergence of colonial societies as independent, sovereign states' (Anghie 2008: 3). Rather, it was in fact central to the formation of international law in that in the first instance it provided a legal framework for colonial relations and, as Brenna Bhandar (2018) has recently argued, the formation of legal rules around private property, sovereignty and citizenship, for example. The standard narrative does not include this history; the popular framing of the birth of the right to asylum omits these contestations over inclusion and exclusion. This has implications for how we interpret the present moment because it means that efforts at excluding people who are seeking asylum from western host states today, rather than being recent and unusual, are entirely historically consistent. The change is that all human beings now have recourse to these rights and can attempt to make claims in relation to them.

The third of our four silences is around the legacies of colonialism for patterns of mobility and immobility. Because colonialism is absent from the standard narrative in the ways sketched out above, it then also becomes logical to leave unmentioned the legacies of colonialism for a range of contemporary phenomena, for example, in relation to refugee-producing situations, for destination-country choice and for ongoing practices of border control. Colonial practices involved restricting the mobility of colonized peoples and facilitating the mobility of the colonizers using a wide range of implicit and explicit economic, cultural and political enablers and disablers. One reading of the contemporary conjuncture is that globalization has created 'mobility gaps', or new regimes of mobility and immobility (Shamir 2005). But these gaps have a long history which we might pay more attention to. As the world has become seemingly more mobile through processes and practices related to what has come to be labelled 'globalization', it is easy to forget that these same mobilities and immobilities characterize the contemporary period. As the formerly colonized have become more mobile, legal and practical barriers have been developed to reinscribe that very immobility which characterized colonial subjugation.

As Wendy Brown (2010: 7–8) has observed, 'what we have come to call a globalized world harbours fundamental tensions between opening and barricading ... These tensions materialise as increasingly liberated borders, on the one hand, and the devotion of unprecedented funds, energies and technologies to border fortification, on the other.' This is, in part, about long-standing ideas of citizenship and belonging. Citizenship depends on controlling mobility in order to support the 'sedentarist ideology of the nation-state', an ideology which, according to Hagar Kotef, is repeatedly confronted with the reality of human mobility (Kotef 2015: 11). But once this image of stability and rootedness is established for particular groups of people who belong, it then facilitates their mobility elsewhere. At the same time, the mobility of others, who do not benefit from the rootedness of belonging, is constrained (Kotef 2015). Thus, while British citizens benefit from the mobility afforded by their privileged status as travellers and 'expats', this is contrasted against continued efforts to immobilize non-European, often racially marked, 'others' – immigrants and asylum seekers. As E. Tendayi Achiume (2019: 1515) explains, 'those Third World migrants who dare risk their lives to migrate to First World countries without legal authorization are confronted with increasingly militarized border regimes, negotiated by First and Third World nation-states and which amount to multilateral projects for the regional containment of Third World persons beyond the First World' (see chapter 4 for more on Achiume's work).

The technologies, the methods of containment and restriction, which are used in contemporary border regimes around the world, follow the very same patterns of mobility and immobility that began in the colonial period (Mongia 2018; Turner 2020). Until recently, the rise of cheap international air travel meant that asylum seekers could flee contexts of violence and persecution and get to stable, wealthy countries relatively easily, that is, assuming they had the financial means (which the vast majority did not). The introduction of carrier sanctions, an effort at containing refugees in regions of original displacement, means that people are either successfully immobilized or they risk their lives on hazardous land and sea crossings in order to circumvent such controls. Thus, while carrier sanctions are new, the rationale behind them is not new. And through a deeper engagement with colonial histories and their legacies, we might start to grasp some of these continuities.

The fourth silence facilitated by the standard narrative laid out by Mayblin (2017) is around the legacies of colonialism in ideas of people seeking asylum as undesirable and excludable. The exclusionary impulse behind the range of limitations that have been placed by states on access to the right to asylum is difficult to render knowable without reference to colonial histories of exclusion from the convention, based on assumptions of human hierarchy. How can we make sense of these exclusions without discussing ideas of 'us' and 'them' which are rooted in colonial history? As British cultural studies scholar Paul Gilroy (2003: 263) has so eloquently observed, 'Old, modern notions of racial difference appear once again to be active within the calculus that tacitly assigns differential value to lives lost according to their locations and supposed racial origins, or considers that some human bodies are more easily and appropriately humiliated, imprisoned, shackled, starved and destroyed than others.'

Gilroy argues that fine ethnic distinctions, often based on country of origin, 'effectively revive a colonial economy in which infra-humanity, measured against the benchmark of healthier imperial standards, diminishes human rights and can defer human recognition' (2003: 263). The non-entrée regime, which acts as a sorting mechanism allowing some to move freely whilst immobilizing others, is implicated in this practice described by Gilroy. Immobility and continental quarantining are not simply about non-movement; the means by which they are achieved involves restricting people's access to human rights, denying them human dignity, where for others it would unquestionably be granted. People who seek asylum, then, are rarely bestowed with the same level of humanity enjoyed by pale-skinned westerners.

Man and human as a colonial construct

Taking a second look at the myth of difference and the writing out of non-European refugees from the standard narrative are two ways in which we might begin to rethink refugee studies and to critique asylum policy. But it is also important to draw in to this discussion the insights on the spatial and temporal limitations of modernity from post- and decolonial studies that were addressed in chapter 2, as well as the colonial contexts which gave rise to the categories of 'man' and 'human' (discussed in chapter 3). Because, if we are going to fully comprehend contemporary exclusions from the right to asylum in historical perspective we need to understand the original scope of the 'human' in human rights, not to mention the entanglement of universal human rights with ideas of European modernity.

As we know, the right to asylum is a human right. Human rights are, in principle, the ultimate leveller, offering recourse to justice for every person in the world simply on the basis that they are a member of the human species. The grand declarations in UN human rights treaties suggest that the rights contained within them inhere in 'all'. But these aspirations are faced with the reality that states may legitimately differentiate in the protection of rights between citizens on the one hand and non-citizens on the other. They are also belied by actual histories of human rights in which the colonial powers went to great lengths to exclude colonized peoples and people of colour from access to the category of the universal 'human' (Mayblin 2017; Mignolo 2009). Man, therefore, is not a simple descriptive term referring to human beings; it is a historically narrow term which has only recently been used on an international scale to refer to all human beings. Therefore, rather than being viewed as a universal concept applicable to all, 'man' and 'human' should, from a postcolonial and decolonial perspective, be located historically and geographically (Bhambra and Shilliam 2008) .

Through the centuries of colonial exploration, exploitation and the uprooting and enslavement of Africans, European scientists and philosophers have embarked on a project of categorization of living things which inevitably involved rationalizing these extractive and violent encounters, as discussed in chapter 3. Trouillot (1995: 75) suggests that what we now call the Renaissance ushered in a new set of philosophical questions: What is beauty? What is order? What is the state? But also, and above all: What is Man? Many taxonomies for classifying human beings were developed which drew on a combination of prejudice and new 'scientific' methods. Initially, the central debate was over inclusion: were light-skinned European-origin peoples the only humans, and all other similar beings animals? Or were they all a part of the same species?

In these early battles over ideas, the idea of human hierarchy supportive of colonial enterprise won out. Man was primarily European and male: 'on this single point everyone who mattered agreed' (Trouillot 1995: 76). Once it had been settled, following Darwin, that all were human, taxonomies were developed to explain white superiority over others. Philosophical questions about the nature and specialness of humankind then perpetually rubbed up against practices of violence and domination which were extremely profitable. So, as Walter Mignolo has acknowledged, 'the figure of the colonized did not qualify for the "right of Man and of the citizen" ... The rights of man and of the citizen were not meant for black and enslaved people' (Mignolo 2011a: 239).

Sylvia Wynter deconstructs the western understanding of the category human as 'man' and points out that the history of 'man' as a concept has left many problematic legacies for people of colour today. She argues that '"man" is not the human, although it represents itself as if it were. It is a specific, local-cultural conception of the human, that of the Judeo-Christian West in its now purely secularised form' (Wynter 2003: 260). While the contemporary articulation of 'man' is secular, Wynter observes its Christian roots in medieval Europe and argues that the Christian/Other dichotomy was transformed into Man/Other over time as secular rationality became the dominant mode of thinking and understanding:

> in the wake of the West's reinvention of its True Christian Self in the transumed terms of the Rational Self of Man ... it was to be the peoples of the militarily expropriated New World territories (i.e. Indians), as well as the enslaved peoples of Black Africa (i.e. Negroes), that were made to reoccupy the matrix slot of Otherness – to be made into the physical referent of the idea of the irrational/subrational Human Other to this first degodded (if still hybridly religio-secular) 'descriptive statement' of the human in history, as the descriptive statement that would be foundational to modernity. (Wynter 2003: 265)

The rise of 'rational' racial science facilitated this shift in that it 'would enable the now globally expanding West to replace the earlier mortal/immortal, natural/supernatural, human/the ancestors, the gods/God distinction as the one on whose basis all human groups had millennially "grounded" their descriptive statement/prescriptive statements of what it is to be human, and to reground its secularizing own on a newly projected human/subhuman distinction instead' (Wynter 2003: 264).

For Wynter, then, this history demonstrates that 'Man' and 'human' are not synonyms. The former was civilized, the latter existed in a state of nature. Yet 'human rights' were for man, not for humanity. The struggle between 'Man' and 'human' is for Wynter the struggle of our time because it facilitates an exclusionary logic. She explains that the 'usually excluded and invisiblized' are 'defined at the global level by refugee/economic migrants stranded outside the gates of the rich countries' (2003: 261). Thus, when Franz Fanon wrote, 'you are making us [the colonized] into monstrosities; your humanism claims we are at one with the rest of humanity but your racist methods set us apart' (Fanon 2008 [1952]: 8), he was pointing to this fundamental contradiction. The 'other' to man is not therefore woman, it is those humans, the wretched of the earth in Fanon's (2008 [1952]) terms, who are negatively marked 'within the terms of man's self-conception, and its related understanding of what it is to be human' (Wynter 2000: 25). However, this otherness is, for Wynter, a present absence. It makes possible the western concept of the human in that man is defined by what he is not. The racially marked person, therefore, is 'the deviant other to being human within the terms of man' (Wynter 2000: 25). Despite this problematic history, 'man' as a concept is today not seen as the product of human actions and decisions but instead is popularly construed as a natural occurrence (Headley 2005).

When placed alongside Chimni, Mignolo and Trouillot, what these insights from Wynter's work give us is an account of the idea of 'humanity' as a historically emergent (not eternal), place-specific (not universal), colonially entangled concept. Equally, coloniality/modernity – the historical process through which the West became modern – has produced the situation that people seeking asylum find themselves in today because coloniality/modernity was a cultural project as well as a political and economic one, and as such entailed the constant reinforcement of the hierarchical ordering of the world's people through a variety of overt and covert means.

Refugees are often described as a 'modern' phenomenon. That is, it is modern in the sense of being one of the features (or residual categories) of the system of democratic nation-states which emerged after the French Revolution and with which came the idea of the rights of man and then human rights (Arendt 1951). This is important because the alignment of refugeehood with modern states (those which experienced the Enlightenment, adopted democracy, developed and subscribed to human rights and industrialized in the nineteenth century) means that those displaced people coming from the non-modern world are not then necessarily refugees; they are something apart. To be a refugee is to be modern within this context. The association between modernity and refugeehood has been widely acknowledged. However, the link between modernity and colonialism is less often acknowledged in relation to many topics, including refugees. Foregrounding these links draws our attention to the fact that the central dividing line in refugee studies, as well as the realpolitik of asylum policy, is between the modern and the traditional. That is, the division of the world is between the modern and the not-yet-modern, always spatially, culturally and economically excluded from full modernity or the ability to fully 'catch up'.

If refugee studies has not yet dealt with histories of colonialism, even though they are entangled with the concept of modernity which underpins so much scholarship in the field, neither have those who seek to explain hostility to asylum seekers as racism without engaging with coloniality/modernity.

Uprooting: deconstructing forced migration

The previous section explored critiques of refugee studies which draw attention to colonial histories in rethinking the present. Part of that involved looking at the colonial history of the category of 'man' and the 'human' in dialogue with the theory of coloniality developed in decolonial studies. This next section also draws on work from a broadly decolonial perspective, this time in challenging the recent move towards 'forced migration' as a favoured term over and above the legally restrictive 'refugee studies'. This critique, brought to English-language scholarship by Aurora Vergara-Figuera (2018) who draws on the work of Colombian theorist Santiago Arboleda, emerges from the question of what happens when geographically specific situations of displacement, or forced migration, are explored in the *longue durée* of colonial history and concomitant power relations. As noted in the introduction to this chapter, 'forced migration' is a concept which has risen to prominence in recent decades. Indeed, 'forced migration studies' is widely seen as having usurped 'refugee studies' as the cutting edge of the field. This shift allows for a larger number of displaced peoples to be considered, rather than just those understood as asylum seekers or refugees under international law. And yet the emergence of forced migration studies seems to mirror and support the interests of powerful states in that it has come just as projects of containment and non-entrée for refugees have intensified. In other words, forced migration disperses the focus (Chimni 2009; Hathaway 2007).

From the perspective of Third World approaches to international law, forced migration studies is best understood within the context of the entanglement of colonialism and imperialism with humanitarianism. Humanitarianism, from this perspective, is not only a project of helping to relieve suffering but also one of establishing a postcolonial imperial order (Nardin 2003). Since western humanitarianism grew up through colonial encounters, taking note of this history allows us to see the continuities (though that is not to suggest that humanitarianism is an exclusively western affair; see Fiddian-Qasmiyeh 2015 for a rigorous discussion). Colonial states veiled their 'dependence on the world outside by legitimating and naturalizing empire, ultimately representing it as at best nothing more than a burden and a terrible responsibility' (Dirks 2006: 332). This meant bearing this burden of relieving the suffering masses while simultaneously pursuing global political and economic projects which systematically produced that very suffering which it then naturalized and attributed to the deficiencies of the suffering societies.

Vergara-Figueroa (2018) develops this critique in arguing that forced migration and forced displacement are inadequate concepts for grasping the phenomena that they are meant to elucidate. These concepts may even contribute to the continued exploitation and pillage of the populations that they seek to protect, she argues. A fundamental problem is that the concept of forced migration is ahistorical. Indeed, most definitions of forced migration focus on an external force which induces displacement without requiring any consideration of the complexity of the historical, social or economic processes that have preceded the precise events that precipitate it. For Vergara-Figueroa, then, forced migration 'needs to be un-thought both epistemically and politically from a black feminist perspective' (2018: 2), using Quijano's (2000) concept of 'the coloniality of power' (discussed in chapter 2) as a tool of world-historical analysis.

Vergara-Figueroa's 2018 book, *Afrodescendant Resistance to Deracination in Colombia*, lays out a framework for doing just that. The book explores in detail the historical conjunctures that led to the 2002 massacre at Bellavista-Bojayá-Chocó and the population 'displacement' (reconceptualized as 'deracination') that resulted from it. Vergara-Figueroa observes that, following the typology offered by Forced Migration Online (FMO), Bellavista could be placed within all the categories of forced migration and its inhabitants could be placed amongst all of the types of forced migrants and internally displaced persons used by the international community. Yet the concept of forced migration offers nothing in terms of explaining the serial occurrence of similar events throughout the history of this region and 'offers no guidance for contributing to the social mobilization that could cause its overthrow' (2018: 15). Scholars who have looked at the Bellavista case acknowledge that violent events such as massacres and land evictions have led to 'forced migrations' of the people living on those lands. What most analyses fail to do, Vergara-Figueroa argues, is to historicize these events. She argues that 'describing violent events, such as massacres in isolation, as new incidents, obscures or limits the possibility of critical historical sociological theorizing' (2018: 4). Violent events which lead to 'displacement', then, need to be situated within the history of the territory in which they take place. At the very least, such historicizing may well uncover multiple and repeated displacements of the same communities over centuries.

Her book addresses the question of 'how the context of place-based ethno-territorial resistance and violence in the territories of the state of Choco enlightens alternative ways to comprehend experiences of "forced displacement/migration", and new cycles of diaspora of Afrodescendent populations' (2018: xxi). Vergara-Figueroa's guiding question is 'how do the spaces in which land dispossession occurs come into being?' (2018: xxvi). Why are these people being uprooted in this time and place is an obvious starting point for any analysis of 'forced migration', one that almost always brings in histories of racial and/or ethnic hierarchy, marginalization and colonialism.

Deracination is a concept which has emerged from Colombian debates on the forced migrations caused by the armed conflict in Colombia since 1996. It means uprooting from the ground and breaking communal relations. Scholars from a broad range of social science and humanities perspectives as well as community organizations have argued for a reorientation away from the concept of 'displacement' which, they argue, does not aid understanding of what is happening in Colombia. Instead, the concept of 'deracination' has been widely adopted amongst scholars and activists in Colombia since around 2002, though little of this work has been translated into English (Vergara-Figueroa 2018). Santiago Arboleda argues that forced migration/displacement is a euphemism for deracination and that we need to look back to the mass kidnapping of Africans as part of the triangular slave trade, and then trace the continuities of marginalization and land dispossession in the Afro-Colombian diaspora in Colombia, in order to make sense of deracination today. As Vergara-Figueroa explains, Arboleda argues that what is being labelled 'displacement' in Colombia should not be conceptualized as such because what is happening in the Pacific coast region is part of a much longer history of colonial domination.

Vergara-Figueroa adds to this work the suggestion that deracination is constitutive of coloniality/modernity. In doing so, she argues that deracination is a foundational concept 'encompassing the diasporas, exiles, holocausts, ethnic cleansings, and genocide that different societies have known through their histories' (2018: 17). This assertion is not new; a number of decolonial scholars have pointed to the link between coloniality/modernity and a range of incidences of genocide and displacement both within and outside of Europe (see Mignolo 2011a). However, while they argued that these disparately located incidences of systematic violence can be understood in terms of the coloniality of power, it is Vergara-Figueroa who has described these linked colonial/modern phenomena as deracination. What this gives us, then, is a sophisticated new conceptual framework for the analysis of phenomena previously named 'forced migration' but henceforth known as acts of deracination.

In researching acts of land dispossession, and the deracination (or uprooting) that they give rise to, one inevitably must pay attention to the historical processes which lie behind these acts. And yet as soon as one looks at these historical processes, the limitations of concepts associated with 'forced displacement' and 'forced migration' become apparent. Vergara-Figueroa argues that to label as 'migrants' people who are the victims of land dispossession, those left in locations vulnerable to climate change-induced natural disasters and those evicted from their homes to make way for development projects is a harmful proposition. This is because it focuses on their movement and not on the historically emergent socio-economic factors which have led them to becoming vulnerable to deracination. The lack of historicity in the concepts furthermore lends them limited usefulness in terms of offering liberation or transformation for people wrapped up in multi-generational cycles of land dispossession. Not only that, Vergara-Figueroa argues that the concepts actually reinforce racialization and marginalization. She writes: 'describing or at least outlining the histories behind the representations of the state of Choco, suggests an epistemic decolonial turn is needed to disentangle colonial continuities of domination, such as deracination' (2018: xxi) which the region faces today. The question then becomes, how did the area of population displacement (more adequately conceptualized as deracination) come into being as a site of repeated deracination over many generations?

Vergara-Figueroa does concede that the concept of 'forced migration' serves humanitarian functions and has 'been useful as a legal and political concept to formulate policies of temporal protection' (2018: 7). It is worth noting here that other scholars view even this practical support with suspicion in that it entails symbolic acts of white saviourism without doing anything to address the global conditions of unequal power which gave rise to the suffering (see Chimni 2009). Despite conceding the practical benefits of humanitarianism facilitated via the rubric of 'forced migration' or 'forced displacement', this is nevertheless of little use in 'comprehending the complex structural, institutional, and everyday dimensions of the phenomenon' (Vergara-Figueroa 2018: 7) or in promoting long-lasting transformations of the living conditions of those who have been uprooted, or those left behind. Vergara-Figueroa points out that 'decades have passed since national and international legal norms have been proposed, approved, and compiled to *diminish* the impact of this worldwide phenomenon', yet 'deep-seated improvements have been few … in the lives and regions of the victims of an historical continuum of pillage expressed in massacres, genocides, ethnic cleansings, and acts of land dispossession' (2018: 8). This is, in part, because it serves the geopolitics of hegemonic states, as Chimni (2009) has pointed out.

The example of 'failed states' aptly illustrates this argument. The indexing of 'state fragility' is often tied to the problem of 'forced migration', making solving state fragility or failure a policy goal for tackling forced migration. Such efforts, Vergara-Figueroa suggests, 'contribute to a new version of a civilizatory mission into spaces that in previous centuries have been emptied epistemologically and cartographically, to be portrayed, afterwards, as spaces for conquest and exploration' as well as, more recently, for 'development'. The deficiencies of these 'failed' spaces that forced migrants ('wounded by inequality') come from distracts from questions of the historical and contemporary role of these regions in the world economy. Instead, state fragility is linked to 'forced migration' and terrorism – both existential threats to the First World (Bilgin and Morton 2002).

Failed and fragile states, having got themselves into a mess, then need saving in order to prevent terrorists taking hold or forced migrants being produced. Their salvation involves the re-establishment of unequal economic relations within a global capitalist system which disproportionately benefits the First World, and through which centuries of land dispossession are rendered more, not less, likely (see also Sabaratnam 2017 on 'decolonizing intervention'). Vergara-Figueroa argues therefore that 'the conceptual framework of forced migration has been one of the most important contributions the field has produced to support the civilizing missions and the need to create aid programs to "help" the countries in which victims are located' (Vergara-Figueroa 2018: 15). Policies of 'helping' through either short-term humanitarian efforts or long-term 'development' programmes will ultimately renew the cycles of marginalization and land dispossession for future generations to deal with. But if, as researchers, we trace the connected histories between 'world-historical conjunctures of capitalist expansion, and world-historical patterns of social mobilization of different populations', we will observe the formation of historical emptied spaces, in which the inhabitants are seen variously over time as potential slaves, refugees and forced displaced people (Vergara-Figueroa 2018: 15). In short, violent land dispossession is best understood in relation to long-term historical processes, the erasure of which only reinforces racialization, marginalization and domination.

Digging down into the *longue durée* of acts of deracination can only enhance our understanding of the theoretical issues at stake in the field of (as it is currently formulated) forced migration. Our new key questions are therefore: '[W]ho are those called forced migrants? Where are they located? What are their socio-political, economic, cultural and religious histories? What makes them potential "forced migrants", as compared to other populations of classes, races, genders, sexualities, and locations?' (Vergara-Figueroa 2018: 10). Using this framework requires us to reverse the order of the actions and to think not in terms of what displacement induces, but of what it motivates, what it produces, 'where it comes from in both the current conjuncture as well as in its *longue durée*' (Vergara-Figueroa 2018: 17).

We need, therefore, to approach deracination as a set of multiple *processes*, not as a set of multiple *conditions* as in a forced migration approach. Make no mistake, this is complex work. Vergara-Figueroa approaches deracination in terms of three components of socio-historical analysis (power, knowledge and liberation), which each have four dimensions (history, representation, memory and mobilization). Furthermore, processes of deracination, according to Vergara-Figueroa, take place in three locations: the bodies, the cultures and the territories involved. In applying this framework to Bellavista, Vergara-Figueroa deploys new concepts: historical-emptied spaces and the routinization of erasure. She uses these as 'working concepts to explore the fundamental questions such as how the epistemic, geopolitical, and historical production of the state of Choco as a marginal territory lies behind the contemporary deracination of the Chocoan population' (Vergara-Figueroa 2018: xxi). Her study demonstrates how the representation of spaces as 'blank' or 'empty' has historically been reliant on the violence, extermination, genocide, ethnic cleansing and deracination of slavery and colonialism.

Necropolitics: governing the uprooted through death

Where Vergara-Figueroa (2018) refocuses the moment and location of 'forced migration' as 'deracination', the third conceptual contribution explored in this chapter, necropolitics, is concerned with responses in host states, primarily post-metropolitan states. Nevertheless, this section, again, draws out the need to take account of colonial histories and their legacies in seeking to understand the politics of asylum in the present. The title of the section borrows from Vicki Squire's (2017) interpretation of necropolitics in the Mediterranean Sea as 'governing migration through death'. Achille Mbembe first proposed the concept of necropolitics in an article in *Public Culture* in 2003. Necropolitics begins from a critique of Foucault, whose posthumously published lectures at the Collège de France in 1978 and 1979 on 'The Birth of Biopolitics' (Foucault, Davidson and Burchell 2008) have provided the basis for theoretical development on the topic of biopolitics in the years since, and so this section will begin from there.

Biopolitics refers to the management and administration of life. According to Foucault, biopolitics is a function of bio*power* (Foucault 1991 [1975]). This is a type of power that can be exerted by the state (here speaking of the 'modern' European state), which works together with the repressive actions of state power but is positive in that it enables life. What has been particularly inspiring for scholars who have taken up the concept of biopower is the idea of a subtly coercive power which is dependent on 'a closely meshed grid of material coercions rather than the physical existence of a sovereign' (Foucault 2003: 36). Biopower therefore has a positive influence over life and operates through dispersed networks. It is focused on 'propagation, births and mortality, the level of health, life expectancy and longevity, with all the conditions that can cause these to vary'. The state acts upon these things through a 'series of interventions and regulatory controls: a biopolitics of the population' (Foucault 1998 [1976]: 39). Thus, if discipline focuses on making individuals behave (Foucault 1991 [1975]), biopolitics manages populations through, for example, the provision of vaccinations or birth control.

State biopolitics acts upon a defined population that falls under the purview of a state, but in doing so it also, of course, excludes. Those who are excluded are not simply killed by (or in the name of) the sovereign, however; they are allowed to die in the name of prioritizing a clearly defined society of the deserving, or legitimate, populace. This shift is often described as a move from 'make die' to 'let die' (Lemke 2011) and is encapsulated in the concept of necropolitics proposed by Mbembe (2003). If biopolitics facilitates living, necropolitics is its darker underbelly; they are two sides of the same coin. Necropolitics is therefore connected to biopolitics in that individuals are not killed (punished) as *individuals* who have defied the sovereign, they are targeted because their existence is seen as detrimental to the wider population. Their death is beneficial to the true population, and their suffering is of little consequence to society as a whole. Mbembe (2003: 16) notes that 'race' is often the principle marker of modern subjectification, and within this context 'power (and not necessarily state power) continuously refers and appeals to exception, emergency, and a fictionalised notion of the enemy. It also labours to produce that same exception, emergency, and fictionalised enemy' in racial terms.

In sketching out his theory of biopolitics, Foucault of course had in mind 'modern' European states, and he was primarily exploring their treatment of populations within the metropolitan territories (Scott 1995). The populations of colonized states, or the actions of what were later dubbed 'Third World', then 'developing', states, were not his concern. It is for this reason that some scholars working from these locations have explored necropolitics as an entry point to understanding the techniques, practices, apparatuses and strategies used in the relations of domination in 'peripheral' states (Estévez 2013). This is because in some contexts it is the governing through death, rather than enabling life, that more accurately characterizes the political context of the past, and indeed the present.

For Mbembe, the structure of the plantation system, and its aftermath, 'manifests the emblematic and paradoxical figure of the state of exception' (Mbembe 2003: 21). As we discussed in chapter 2, enslaved people were 'kept alive but in a state of injury, in a phantomlike world of horrors and intense cruelty and profanity' (2003: 21). As others have observed (Said 1995 [1978]; Bhabha 2005 [1994]), colonial occupation involved the production of a whole host of cultural imaginaries. These imaginaries were not *just* cultural, however; they 'gave meaning to the enactment of differential rights to differing categories of people for different purposes within the same space' (2003: 21). In the context of colonialism, 'sovereignty means the capacity to define who matters and who does not, who is *disposable* and who is not' (2003: 27) and, ultimately, power works towards 'the creation of *death-worlds*, new and unique forms of social existence in which vast populations are subjected to conditions of life conferring upon them the status of *living dead*' (2003: 40).

Scholars have drawn on the concept of necropolitics in making sense of policies which focus on dealing with so-called 'irregular' migrants, including people who are seeking asylum. Whilst analysis of biopolitics and ideas of 'states of exceptions' have proliferated in critical border studies (Vaughan Williams 2009) and other literatures associated with migration, this work has not always engaged with the colonial question which Mbembe's work is attuned to (Biswas and Nair 2009; Howell and Richter-Montpetit 2018). One example of the way in which necropolitics entails states letting unwanted outsiders die is in creating the conditions of possibility for large-scale death by drowning in the Mediterranean Sea, or forms of abandonment in the Sonoran desert in Arizona, and making minimal efforts to prevent it. Such policies are aptly described as 'governing migration through death' (Squire 2017). Mbembe's conceptualization of necropolitics demands that we understand necropolitics as grounded in colonial histories. As we observed previously, the long history of colonialism and slavery, and particularly the drowning of enslaved people in the Mediterranean and beyond, are, from a decolonial perspective, fundamental to making sense of this contemporary 'let die' phenomenon. Marxist analyses often read border violence as a logical response to a contemporary transgression of the laws governing borders and migration. But the drowning of people of colour in the sea, both through making and letting die, are part of a much longer trajectory (Gilroy 1993; Saucier and Woods 2014) and in arguing as much we come to a similar starting point as Vergara-Figueroa: setting contemporary violence first and foremost within the context of historical patterns of killing, deracinating, drowning and dehumanizing (Saucier and Woods 2014).

This application of necropolitics to the Mediterranean and the US–Mexico border has a violent immediacy but Mbembe's necropolitics is slower, more dispersed, less dramatic. Though necropolitics is always an outcome of the 'normal' functioning of the liberal democratic state, we need perhaps to think of it in terms of a spectrum of temporality and visibility – from the fast, dramatic and visible to the slow, incremental and invisible or largely unseen (Berlant 2007). Moving further along this spectrum away from the 'fast' necropolitics of drownings in the Mediterranean is the slower violence of Europe's spontaneous migrant camps. The so-called 'jungle' camp near Calais in northern France has, for Davies, Isakjee and Dhesi (2017: 1268), become a 'concentrated visible symbol of the "apartheid" of migrant Others from the Global South, who survive in conditions far removed from the residences of normative French and EU citizens, living in their neat houses with kept gardens'. From this perspective, the abject conditions of the camp in its various incarnations might be viewed as deliberately produced as part of a broader policy of necropolitical abandonment within Europe. Rather than actively killing the migrants who find themselves in the camp, the French state keeps them 'alive but in a state of injury' (Mbembe 2003: 21). We could also extend this to other contexts such as Libyan detention centres which immobilize sub-Saharan migrants in overcrowded and squalid conditions. Suffering, then, is a political technology of control for those designated illegitimate and therefore outside of the purview of the biopolitical community. Conditions which might, in other contexts, be viewed as extreme and grotesque cruelties become politically acceptable in fulfilling the aims of exclusion. Equally, humanitarian care for migrants is often located adjacent to, and intertwined with, enforcement efforts, making it contingent on their rejection at the border (Walters 2010; Williams 2015).

Vitally, necropolitics, as an analytical concept, centralizes the 'distinctly colonial and racial logics that (re)produce and sustain the ongoing violence of borders' (Davies and Isakjee 2018: 2). In other words, those who are repeatedly cast outside of European political communities are not generalized 'others'. Their otherness is a legacy of the hierarchical racialized logics of colonialism. If necro-power is the power to let die, and this power has historically been wielded by colonial powers on the basis of the racial value placed on some lives over others, its preferred mode of operation is necropolitics. In this sense, we might think of necropolitics as a function of the more generalized 'coloniality of power' that decolonial scholars refer to (Quijano 2000; Wynter 2003). The fact that the occupants of Europe's informal camps are excluded from the liberal freedoms that are totemic of western values, as well as the material comforts associated with them, and that they have travelled almost exclusively from former European colonies, is significant. Our analyses of these phenomena cannot ignore the ways in which the camps and other sites of necropolitical governance make visible the 'layers of global and historical injustice' (Davies and Isakjee 2018: 3; for more on race/biopolitics, see Weheliye 2014). But the reach of this logic exceeds the geography of contemporary Europe and can be seen at work in the Middle East, South and Central America (as Vergara-Figueroa argues in relation to Colombia), Asia and Africa. Ideas of racial hierarchy born of empire, then, are highly resilient, and global, as other chapters of this book have shown.

Conclusion

This chapter has explored the ways in which contemporary displacements, forced migrations and uprootings, as well as refugee rights, can be conceptualized in relation to histories of colonialism and their legacies. It has drawn out themes developed through previous chapters relating to, for example, the continued resonance of hierarchical conceptions of human worth and extended them into areas not covered so far in the book, such as Afro-descendant deracination and necropolitics. Ultimately, what all of the different interventions through the chapter speak to is the historically contingent concept of 'man' and human, and how this has helped to structure various responses to refugees in the world. If what is at stake is the very right to have rights, as Hannah Arendt suggested, then we cannot understand uneven access to such rights without a strong sense of history. In the next chapter, we take up some of the ideas we have began to explore in this chapter and move the focus to security in the context of anti-Muslim racism and the 'war on terror'. This draws out common threads which have been woven across the chapters thus far but speaks specifically to those researching security, securitization, Islamic terrorism and Islamophobia.

6

Towards a Colonial Account of Security and Borders

Introduction

This chapter examines the relationship between security and borders as part of the colonial present. Since 9/11, an ever-increasing body of scholarship on migration, borders and citizenship has sought to understand how the global 'war on terror', and more broadly 'security', has restructured immigration regimes. Since 9/11 (but of course even much earlier; see Huysmans 2006; Walters 2008), a succession of 'terrorist' incidents, including attacks in London, Paris and Madrid, have intensified the restrictions on international migration and settlement in North America and Europe. The 'war on terror' has to some extent been fought through immigration policies (see Sharma 2006). This still remains the case in the second decade of the twenty-first century. It was attacks in Paris in 2016 that led to the suspension of the EU Schengen zone at the height of 'the refugee crisis' in Europe. If prevention of terrorism was a logic that guided the invasions of Afghanistan (2001) and Iraq (2003), immigration measures have followed this, with restrictions on mobility rationalized as a means of preventing further 'terrorism', 'criminality' and 'human trafficking' (Amoore 2006). States continue to expand border regimes in the name of security. This has taken the form of visa regimes, identity checks, body scanners, surveillance and data systems which seek to filter and distinguish imagined 'threats', just as 'cruddy' (Povinelli 2011: 13) and spectacular forms of violence are used to exclude and contain certain populations from crossing borders into northern states and the EU. This is bound up with changes to citizenship and naturalization, integration programmes within states and policing tactics, counter-terrorism strategies and the multiplication of 'anti-radicalization' programmes which explicitly target the 'Islamic terrorist'.

An ever-growing body of scholarship in migration studies, inter-national relations, sociology and political geography has analysed how the 'war on terror' marks a shift towards a closer alignment of security and borders. But there is a tendency in this existing scholarship to ignore the colonial histories that underpin the war on terror, borders and security, and the majority of this work is not only preoccupied with northern Euro-western states but is equally avowedly Eurocentric. Nevertheless, within and beyond these bodies of scholarship there have been many dissident accounts (for example, on security/'war on terror', see Inayatullah and Riley 2006; Kapoor 2018; Khalili 2013; Lloyd and Wolfe 2015; Perera and Razack 2014; Richter-Montepetit 2014; Shilliam 2008; Thobani 2007; on border/security, Browne 2015; De Genova 2018; Frowd 2018; Sharma 2006; Tudor 2018; Walia 2014). It is to these interventions on border security and the 'war on terror' that this chapter turns.

The chapter seeks to ask three broad questions: (1) how can we understand border security by making empire and colonialism central to our analysis? (2) how is border security related to racialized violence? And (3) what do the 'war on terror' and border security look like from the Global South and beyond Eurocentric theorizing? The chapter is organized around three sections: the first section sets the 'securitization' of borders in the Global North in its colonial context. It explores how border regimes have been shaped by and reproduce longer histories of colonial racialization. This racial-ization is often obscured by claims that border regimes, integration programmes and counter-terrorism strategies are about 'culture', not 'race'. To challenge this, we draw on work on the concepts of neo-imperialism, anti-black violence and racial capitalism to better understand the colonial logics of border security. Drawing on critical surveillance studies literature put forward by Simone Browne (2015), we also show how security is bound to colonial rule. This includes how, for example, security was a key organ of colonial and settler-colonial administrations and how policies today are a reworking of these strategies (Li 2018).

The second section aims to decentre the Global North in discus-sions of border security. To do this, we examine work on border security in the Global South. We examine three approaches to border security beyond the 'West': studies of the securitization of borders and 'offshoring' in North Africa; postcolonial and Marxist studies of border security in Palestine/Israel; and decolonial studies which challenge us to rethink the Eurocentric concepts of border security from within African scholarship. We reflect on how the geographical expansion of studies of border security in the Global South still tends to replicate Eurocentric knowledge production (from Europe and for Europe). What decolonial scholarship offers is a more comprehensive attempt to 'provincialize' Europe (Chakrabarty 2008).

In the final section, we consider how Franz Fanon's work on violence helps us rethink the political violence called 'terrorism' which is so central to the contemporary analysis of border security. We examine scholarship on Islamic resistance to challenge the association between Islam, 'extremism' and 'terrorism' and argue that Islamic resistance (*not* to be confused with organizations such as ISIS) has been part of broader decolonial struggles and liberatory social movements. By re-centring the analysis on communities who are the subject of surveillance and security and exploring what border security looks like from anti-colonial struggles, we argue that security appears less as a mode of managing disorder and more as a means of distributing biophysical violence and disorder (Besteman 2019). This distribution of violence is focused upon populations racialized as black and brown, and it continues forms of colonial expropriation.

Terrorism and race

In this section, we examine how Islamophobia has energized border security. Whilst 9/11 played an important part in intensifying border security, the 'war on terror' needs to be placed as part of the legacies of European and US empire and coloniality. Colonial logics continue to shape border security and, we can argue, continue to form part of broader patterns of racialized capitalism, colonial rule and warfare. To begin, we need to consider how the equation of Islam with terrorism forms part of broader schema of colonial racism and Orientalism.

Sherene Razack (2008; see also Perera and Razack 2014) has argued that what is called 'Islamophobia' is more suitably analysed as global anti-Muslim racism (Morgan and Poynting 2012). Whilst presented as an issue of 'culture' (liberal secularism versus religious community) or 'freedom of speech', Islamophobia reproduces and remakes processes of racialization (Hage 2017; Tyrer 2013). To unpack this construction, let us consider how terrorism has been equated with Islam. Razack (2008) argues that the apparent rise of 'religious terrorism' as 'new terrorism' locates terrorist ideology and the causes of political violence in Islamic theology, 'culture' and the minds and bodies of Muslims (see also Abbas 2012). According to Razack, this equivalence between Islam and terrorism relies on a 'culturalist' reading of terrorism and violence more broadly. In this commonplace narrative, the terrorist is not a product of political struggle or structures of neo-imperialism but instead is produced by a *cultural pathology*. That is, terrorism is a product of different (problematic) 'values' which are then essentialized as 'Islamic'. Think here of George W. Bush's instigation of the 'war on terror' where he argued this was a war for civilization and progress: 'Those who hate all civilization and culture and progress ... cannot be ignored, cannot be tolerated ... cannot be appeased. They must be fought' (cited in Brown 2008). Such a reading is not only reductionist but also racializing. Because terrorism is viewed as cultural, all Muslims come to be understood as complicit and potentially dangerous, i.e. as Islamic extremists or people who can be potentially 'radicalized' (Heath-Kelly 2013).

Anti-Muslim racism is part of the contemporary disavowal of race as a significant social force in liberal societies, or what Herman Gray and Anja Franck (2019) call 'postracial racism' (see also Bonilla-Silva 2003, 2015). This means that at the same time as implicitly bringing all Muslims under suspicion as potential terrorists through far-reaching policies which seek to act upon Muslim communities in general, liberal politicians and commentators discursively insist that the 'war on terror' is not a war on Islam as such but a war on 'Islamic extremism' or part of a broader war on criminality and disorder (see, for example, Cameron 2011). In doing so, they often distinguish 'good' from 'bad' Muslims based upon specific markers of 'progress' (Morsi 2017), such as denouncing all non-state violence and unconditionally embracing 'progressive' (liberal western capitalist) values.

Swati Parashar (2018: 121) argues that global anti-Muslim discourse in this context represents a 'militant form of Orientalism' (see Said 1995 [1978]) where Islamic 'difference' is construed as danger. Islamophobia therefore relies on colonial systems of representation to make it intelligible (Parashar 2018). Just as with older forms of anti-colonial rebellions, revolts and revolutions, 'terrorism' is presented as a problem of deviant and backward culture(s) which creates illegitimate and violent 'eruptions' and endangers 'civilization', i.e. the 'West' (Said 1995 [1978]). This allows for the comparison between 'Islam' and 'the West' as though the two are equivalent and mutually exclusive categories, which they are not. Sarah Marusek (2016) thus argues that we must see the 'othering' of Islam as structured by colonial ideas about enlightened and unenlightened peoples. Non-Christian religions are, here, understood to be inferior (Wynter 2003) at the same time as post-Christian secularism is viewed as a defining feature of liberalism. In this context, the expression of public and political acts of religion and spirituality is deemed a sign of irrationality and backwardness (Helliwell and Hindess 2011). Liberals (like the colonizers before them) *have* culture, while non-liberal societies (like colonized societies before them) are instead represented as being *defined by* their culture (Brown 2008; Browne 2010). This inferior/superior construction can be observed in the way that 'democracy', 'equality', 'rights' and 'freedom' are presented by politicians, policy makers and conservative and liberal scholars alike as anathema to Islam, Muslim communities and more broadly other non-white communities living in Europe. In this way, 'Islamic culture' and 'non-western' cultures are rendered not only inherently backward but also violent and active threats to 'civilization' which must be dealt with through warfare (at home and abroad) and through border security (Morsi 2017: 63–93).

Detailing how claims to liberal progress versus 'backward' culture is racialized, we might consider claims by state authorities, 'experts', scholars and mainstream media outlets that Muslim communities have a unique problem with gender inequality and LGBTQ+ rights. This is articulated, for example, in the banning of full face coverings in France, the Netherlands and Denmark on the basis of gender 'equality' (see Farris 2017; Sajed 2012), or in expert policy reports that argue that Muslim communities are 'self-segregating' (for example, in terms of housing, socializing and labour-market decisions) because of a need to protect patriarchal gender relations. Authors such as Puar (2007), Razack (2008) and Weber (2015) describe how debates on integration, segregation, patriarchy and LGBTQ+ rights in Muslim communities often reproduce imperial feminist claims of the nineteenth century that justified colonial expansion and violence based on the 'treatment' of 'brown women by brown men' (on Sati, see Spivak 1988). For example, the apparent resistance to LGBTQ+ western-style rights in Muslim communities and states has been taken as a sign of backwardness and holding 'terroristic' values (Puar 2007; Weber 2015; see also Cowen and Gilbert 2008; Manchandra 2015; Rao 2020). Here the 'Muslim terrorist' is not only a threat through violence but also through illiberal values. Border security thus aims not only to contain people outside of the West (through visa bans, fences and military-style surveillance) but also to govern communities within western states – through enforced integration and counter-terrorism (Hage 2017).

Anti-Muslim racism as 'bio-cultural'

Whilst it is important to recognize how 'culture' is bound up with colonial demarcations of race, Nisha Kapoor's (2018: 41) work helps us understand how anti-Muslim racism is 'bio-cultural' in the way it underpins border security. Kapoor argues that the cultural pathology of 'terrorism' is bound to biological and physical markers of population difference, presented as markers of racial inferiority. In this way, her work is resonant of Stuart Hall's (1996 [1980]) conceptualization of racism as having two registers: culture and biology. Ghassan Hage (2017: 4) similarly demonstrates how physical or cultural signifiers of Muslimness are fluid, contingent and often linked to colonial connections – linked to being 'Asian' in Britain, 'Turkish' in Germany, 'North African' in France and 'Arab' in the United States. In the wake of the 'war on terror', looking 'brown' or 'black' or having Middle Eastern heritage has been linked to following the Islamic faith (Puar and Rai 2002). Markers of religion are equally articulated through physical characteristics, such as growing a long beard or wearing particular types of religious clothing – the shalwar kameez or head scarf, for example (Kundnani 2008, 2014). Thus Hage (2017) reminds us that racism is inherently contradictory and inconsistent. That is its political power. He reminds us that 'both racists and the police, on the lookout for "Muslim terrorists", have killed or captured South Americans, Africans, Sikhs, Hindus, Greeks, Southern Italians and many others' (2017: 8). Within the discourse of new terrorism, these imagined signifiers of Muslimness are equated with the potential for 'terroristic' violence.

In different social contexts, these markers of Muslimness become a cultural pathology bound to the body. This is particularly acute when considering how borders work to racialize people by focusing on calculations of risk (see also de Noronha 2019). Surveillance systems, airport security checks, scanners, asylum interviews and visa applications all systematically work to recognize and prevent 'threats' which are bound up with the recognition of identities and physical attributes of the dangerous and 'threatening' (see Browne 2010; Gray and Franck 2019; Salter 2008). So in this context, looking 'like a Muslim' is to become hyper-visible and racialized as a type of danger and then subject to forms of disciplinary control – for example, invasive security checks, stop-and-search, police suspicion and imprisonment without charge (see also Ali and Whitham 2018). This compounding of 'looking Muslim' with danger equally becomes bound up with and energized by other figurations of racialized danger, for example, black and Asian 'gang' violence and criminality (Browne 2015; Kapoor 2018; Sharpe 2016). Thinking through anti-Muslimism as one form of bio-cultural racism is important because much of the work on border security and civil liberties tends to view the balance of freedom and security as lying at the heart of security practices and as affecting an unspecified *everyone* in equal measure, i.e. as authoritarian (see Balzacq and Carerra 2016; Dillon and Reid 2009; Evans 2010; and Howell and Richter-Montpetit 2018 for a critique). Instead, we need to understand that whilst appearing race neutral, security practices are structured and attuned to contingent forms of bio-cultural racism.

To recognize the differing strands of anti-Muslim racism is important because of how it relates to broader structures of race and immobility. A number of scholars have attempted to unpick the organizing logics of these modes of racialization and border security. We should remember after all that racism is contingent but it is not only about shifting modes of representation. Racism is material. It is bound up with the distribution of violence, the forwarding of powerful interests and the reproduction of systems of capitalist accumulation and white privilege (see Tilley and Shilliam 2018). So how should we understand the relationship between race and border security?

For Kapoor (2018), racialization and border security under the 'war on terror' must be understood as shaped by imperial interests and projects such as ongoing wars in the Middle East and North Africa. Kapoor argues that because terrorism is viewed as senseless violence, rather than proper/legitimate violence conducted by states (see Blakeley 2011), and 'pathological evil', this involves representing terrorists as 'monsters' (Puar and Rai 2002). Here extraordinary measures (such as torture, rendition, deprivation of citizenship) are needed to prevent, or capture, the 'monster' terrorists but also to police and pacify the communities that they are attached to through integration programmes, stop-and-search, visa bans and immigration rules (see Turner 2020: 134–79). To invoke Fanon, we must remember that colonialism rested on the back of turning the native into the 'quintessence of evil' (Fanon 1963: 40). Here the representation of terrorists parallels the representation of organized criminals and 'human traffickers' as racialized 'monsters' or as 'evil'. This works to legitimize imperial warfare, such as in the drone bombing of ISIS recruits and/or dissident citizens, as well as restrictive border practices in securing western and particularly American and British interests (Kapoor 2018).

In a related argument, Melanie Richter-Montpetit (2014) draws on black feminist scholarship to argue that we can only make sense of the violence of contemporary warfare and security in the context of histories of racism which make some people disposable and susceptible to violence (see also Gordon 1999; Hartman 1997). She reminds us how enslaved people racialized as black were historically subject to systematic terror and sexualized violence, and she then considers how anti-blackness is central to security today. Richter-Montpetit (2014) thus draws connections between anti-Muslimism and anti-black racism over time and in different geographical contexts. She does this through a focus on colonial logics. Thinking through the multiple legacies of anti-black racism and border security, we should note that the 'war on terror' has led to the intensification of militarized policing in white settler-colonial contexts such as the United States and the occupation of black communities by militarized policing such as in Ferguson, Missouri (which reproduce counter-insurgency practices experimented with in Iraq and Afghanistan; see Cowen and Lewis 2016). This equally links up with the expansion of carceral practices, such as the supermax prison industry that now houses more than 2.3 million black Americans (see NAACP 2020; see also Davis 2003; Gilmore 2007). It is significant, then, that the group most likely to be subject to surveillance practices in the United States is now black Muslims (Nessa 2018). Anti-Muslim racism thus feeds into and off anti-black racism.

David Lloyd and Patrick Wolfe (2015) take a different approach to race and border security by drawing on accounts of racialized capitalism. Lloyd and Wolfe demonstrate how the racialized logics of the 'war on terror', including increased surveillance and border security, must be read as part of moves to contain people who have (always) been peripheral to capitalist production, who form part of the 'disaffected and rebellious' or who will (have) never be(en) included in labour markets (see also Bledsoe and Wright 2019; Hall et al. 1978; Virdee 2019). Prem Kumar Rajaram (2018: 628) further argues that surplus populations have always been racialized: 'in the colony, labour evacuated "native" work of any inherent meaning or value', though of course others have argued that slavery and colonial labour have in fact been central to the development of capitalism (see Bhambra 2007). The result, for Rajaram (2018), was that 'colonised peoples had to translate their body power into "productive" labour, but many would be doomed to always fall short' (see also Bhattacharya 2018; Danewid 2020; Robinson 1983; Virdee 2019); Lloyd and Wolfe (2015) further argue that border security creates a pool of disposable and deportable labour (in the North and South) that capital relies upon to drive down wages and conditions (De Genova 2013). Anti-Muslim racism, for them, is one nodal point in the contemporary logics of racialized capitalism which, in this view, links up with the racialization of other populations. The 'war on terror' perpetuates the containment of those deemed surplus and valueless through border security.

Following these three different interventions, we can begin to place border security in its colonial context. The intensification and proliferation of border security after 9/11 can thus be understood in the context of the rearticulation of colonial distinctions between peoples internationally. Here anti-Muslim racism provides one important vector for building restrictive border regimes. Muslims are read as migrants and as antithetical to 'western culture' so then all migrants, asylum seekers and refugees are presented as a potential cultural danger to 'western' and 'civilized' states. Security practices (visa bans, surveillance, de-radicalization programmes) work upon demarcating and locating threats in the body of certain populations. This further normalizes the containment of people outside of the boundaries of the 'West' (Achiume 2019). Appeals to 'culture' and 'values', so central to the 'war on terror', equally create a shorthand for denying neo-colonial practices such as military interventions and imperial capitalist interests in the Middle East which are often the direct continuation of colonial occupation (Gregory 2004; Harvey 2003). This ultimately obscures how colonial interventions, proxy wars, occupation, structural inequality through racialized capitalism and environmental degradation force people to move in the first place (Turhan and Armiero 2017).

Colonial rule and security

Complementing these approaches to the shifting dynamics of colonial racism underpinning border security is the emergence of critical histories of security. What is often left under-examined in migration and security studies is how mechanisms and technologies of security were produced and experimented with in colonial contexts and how this is linked into modes of control today. In this context, Simone Browne's (2015) work provides an important retelling of the history of surveillance, security and mobility which can inspire further critical work. In *Dark Matters*, Browne (2015) shows how contemporary biometric technology emerged out of the categorization and bureaucratization mechanisms used to control colonized people, for example, as slaves, as criminals, as indentured labourers. Browne (2010, 2015) shows how biometric surveillance worked as a racialized technology of mobility control from its very inception (see also Kaplan 1995). For example, surveillance was central to the government of risk and the insuring of human cargo in the Middle Passage, just as plantation slavery fixated on capturing and identifying moving black bodies as property through branding, wanted posters and slave logbooks. All of these modes of control underpinned the later development of border security, such as passport technology and modern biometric identity capture (Singha 2000).

Such histories are important to explore. Whilst modern biometrics appear technical and thus 'race neutral', Browne (2010) shows us how technologies continue to operate through colonial demarcations of race. For example, face and body scanners used in airports use 'prototypical whiteness' as the norm against which other faces and bodies are made 'identifiable' and 'recognizable'. Such bodies are thus constituted as (ab)normal and/or risky, leading to their disproportionate surveillance. In these histories, we learn that the logic of surveillance, the rationale and knowledge of who to surveil on the basis of who is considered dangerous, is always already racialized. For Gregory (2013), this means recognizing that other security practices such as drones (which are increasingly used to police mobility and borders as well as to cross the borders of postcolonial states in the Middle East) are 'techno-cultural'. That is, they are imprinted with ideas regarding who is seen as probably innocent and who is seen as potentially dangerous.

Browne's and others' work is a call to produce more studies on the colonial histories of border security. Whilst fascinating work is being done on security practices, biometrics, technological advancement of border security such as drones (Schwartz 2018), satellite tracking (Distretti 2018), data collection (A. Hall 2017) and visuality (Obradović-Wochnik and Bird 2019; Tazzioli and Walters 2016), more needs to be done to excavate the longer colonial histories of these practices (Dixit 2014). Equally, it is needed to map out how security practices at 'the border' connect up with other areas of state control, from stop-and-search, detention, housing policy and control orders to systems of identification, categorization and interrogations (Danewid 2020; de Noronha 2020; Shabazz 2015).

Ultimately, what such historical investigations can and should push is, as noted above, how border security is always already riven with past exercises of colonial power, modelled on the governance of people racialized as inferior and non-human. Once we start to probe at these histories, we can begin to challenge the assumption that the global 'war on terror' is 'exceptional' (as so much of the common sense of work on 'securitization', for instance, has suggested). Instead, these emerging forms of security mark an intensification of long-running colonial and imperial strategies of containing the Third World outside of the First World and stepping up the draconian policing of 'internal colonies' (Cusicanqui 2012; Danewid 2020; Mbembe 2017; Turner 2018).

But, equally, our understanding of this carceral landscape is limited by only focusing on security *as domination*. Browne (2015) also shows that a fully critical account of border security must engage with counter-histories of resistance which have sought to humanize, decolonize and recover the personhood of the oppressed (see also James 1996; Lugones 2007), that is, struggles which stretch from anti-colonial resistance throughout the formal histories of empire, slave rebellions and revolts to contemporary struggles against border violence in the Mediterranean or Palestine, in the politics of Black

Lives Matter and indigenous sovereign activism (see Andrews 2018; Coulthard 2014; Davis 2016; Shilliam 2008; Gopal 2019; hooks 1992 for other accounts of struggle). These resistances articulate both the dehumanizing logics of border regimes and ways to imagine humanity beyond the colonial/modern 'man'/huMan. Without recognizing the ongoing dynamics of resistance, we fail to understand border security.

Towards a global account of security and borders

We have so far focused on border security in the Global North and teased out how we might understand border security as interconnected to coloniality/modernity in that part of the world. However, postcolonial and decolonial interventions are also oriented towards decentring Europe and the West more broadly as the site of knowledge and history (Chakrabarty 2008). Following this, in the next section we ask what border security and the 'war on terror' look like from the Global South and, as importantly, how different ways of theorizing these processes can begin to disturb the Eurocentric account of border security.

Pratt and Rezk (2019) have argued that even critical border studies scholars have often ignored regions beyond Europe, North America and Australia – part of a broader neglect of the southern perspectives and scholarship (see also Bilgin and Herz 2019; Frowd 2018). Where scholars have studied the more global character of border security, this work falls broadly into three perspectives, all of which address colonial themes in different ways:

1 Securitization in the Global South. These studies explore how securitization and militarization work beyond the confines of Europe and North America – 'bringing' new cases from the Global South into the frame of Euro-American scientific study.
2 Postcolonial and Marxist-influenced work that examines border security in the context of global colonial violence. This works within a tradition of western postcolonial and Marxist postcolonial theory that examines the specific continuities and interconnectedness of borders with racialized capitalism and coloniality.
3 Decolonial resistance. Rather than treating the Global South as a case study for Eurocentric science (which 1 and parts of 2

replicate), these studies aim to resist the Euro-western knowledge which prioritizes security through the state borders and also works to disturb the binaries around liberal secularism versus religion, democracy versus tyranny, modernity versus backwardness and so on that energize scholarship and praxis within the 'war on terror'.

We outline the different debates central to these bodies of work below and indicate how they can help us rethink border security.

Securitization in the Global South

The first body of work responds to the expansion of border security beyond Europe and North America and is attuned to the way that mobility is managed at the global level and reflects how the global 'war on terror' has ostensibly been fought in the Global South (for example, Gaibazzi, Dünnwald and Bellagamba 2017; Hammerstad 2014). This relates to the expansion of international organizations such as IOM and UNHCR (Hammerstad 2014) in the regulation of mobility, the offshoring of borders by the EU into north and sub-Saharan Africa, the entanglement of development with border practices, as well as the advancement of military aims through the regulation of mobility and the tracking of transnational crime (for example, see Evans and Duffield 2011). This also responds to concerns regarding how postcolonial states have become sites for experiments in security governance (Abrahamsen 2018; Amar 2013).

Much of this work is detailed and empirically grounded. Scholars are also increasingly seeking to provide re-theorizations of borders by examining how border security works outside Europe and the United States (for a good example, see Frowd 2018). This push to explore how border security works beyond Euro-America has led to a focus on how the 'war on terror' and restrictive border policies emerge in countries that border the EU and the United States or in 'sender' states. Examining the process of 'offshoring' borders has been a particularly rich strand of research in this context, exploring how northern states enact border security through the expansion and deterritorialization of borders throughout North Africa, the Middle East (EU), Mexico and Central America (US), Indonesia and Papua New Guinea (Australia) (see McNevin 2014; Mountz 2011b).

In Bialasiewicz's (2012) analysis of offshoring, she shows how the 2011 Italy–Libya agreement expanded a network of carceral practices to violently disrupt the movement of people from sub-Saharan Africa (into Libya and then to Italy/Europe) (see also Segre, Yimer and Biadene 2008). Through practices of offshoring, European border security has become networked across North Africa from Libya, Algeria, Tunisia and Morocco through sub-Saharan Africa and into Sudan. The expansion of border security involves European security authorities training coastguard and police across North Africa and organizing forced removals and detention centres at a distance which the EU ultimately uses to 'deter' people crossing into Europe.

Julien Brachet (2016) similarly explores how international organizations such as the IOM work as a conduit for European migration policies in North Africa, whilst rhetorically professing to be concerned with 'humanitarianism' and migrant welfare (on humanitarian borders, see Fassin 2011; Perkowski 2018; Walters 2010). Brachet shows how under appeals to security the IOM has become central to a global system of surveillance where any migration in and through sub-Saharan Africa is deemed a potential threat to Europe (see also Frowd and Sandor 2018). Here mobility is made knowable and controllable in relation to European interests and concerns – even if the movement of people across borders in the Sahara is oriented towards cultural, political and economic relations *in excess* and separate from Europe. Brachet demonstrates how IOM and EU policy creates further conditions for racialized violence within Africa as well, for example, in police and paramilitary brutality towards black migrants, workers and refugees in Libya (see the Tajoura detention centre massacre in 2019). This reminds us that colonial racial hierarchies are reproduced not only by people racialized as white but through the multiplicities of anti-black racism which is sustained by border security – for example by North African Arabs towards black sub-Saharan Africans.

This type of work provides necessary and vital accounts of how border violence is expanded and proliferated at the shifting frontier of 'EUrope' (see also Stierl 2017). As the expansion of border security is intensified across Africa and Asia (Buur, Jensen and Stepputat 2007), for example in Nigeria, Eritrea and Indonesia or in the occupation and violence enacted on Muslim communities by the Chinese state in Xinjiang, we need accounts of the reach of these mechanisms and the violence done by border security globally. And yet, perhaps surprisingly in this context, there is still only tentative recognition of the imperial and colonial legacies and dynamics at play in work that examines securitization and militarization of borders in the Global South. The explicit recognition of either contemporary imperialism, the structure of racialized global capitalism or colonial war is still rare (with the exception of nods to past colonial histories, Frowd 2018; or racialization, see Brachet 2016). This is compounded with the orientation of this work which focuses on how mobility effects the 'West' (even when it is concerned with violence done to migrants). For example, the study of mobility in sub-Saharan Africa all too frequently becomes reduced to the question of what this tells us about security borders in the Global North or the effectiveness of regimes of governance in the region (Obi 2010; Zanker 2019).

This has serious implications for scholars seeking to challenge Euro-/American-centric accounts. The risk is that the Global South becomes a site to better understand the dynamics and proliferation of the US 'war on terror' and European border security for the objective of making better policy and development strategies or to guide 'migration management'. By focusing solely on how border security has proliferated in the Global South (separate from imperial and colonial histories), studies can reproduce colonial and racist assumptions that represent the non-European world as over-securitized or militarized (see Baaz and Verweijen 2018), that is, as a space of abnormal politics and exceptional danger, i.e. reduced to hyper-violent border zones (Amar 2013; Howell and Richter-Montpetit 2020; for a different account of security; Bilgin and Morton 2002 on 'failed states'). Expanding the geographical reach of border security beyond the Global North can also become a means of theorizing *for* Europe (Hönke and Müller 2012). Whilst expanding the geographical area of study for migration scholars in western academies, this does not disturb Eurocentric and/or racist knowledge production. As Shilliam and Pham (2016) remind us, all colonial knowledge must follow routes which travel back to the imperial centre. When studies of border security merely expand the geographical remit of studies, the imperial centre remains the structural location of theory, knowledge and humanity (see Bhambra 2014).

Postcolonial borders (in Palestine)

As we noted above, the second set of approaches to border security in the Global South are influenced by postcolonial and Marxist theory. Here we turn to work that argues border security in postcolonial states is conditioned and sustained by imperial, colonial and settler projects (for example, see Mahmud 2010; Pradella and Taghdisi Rad 2017; Sharp 2011). In the context of sub-Saharan Africa, for example, bordering and enclosure extended from the inception of the slave trade, through periods of formal colonization in the nineteenth century into neo-imperial interventions and systems of dependency within the world order (Ndlovu-Gatsheni 2013; Ndlovu-Gatsheni and Ojakorotu 2010; Wallerstein 1974). This structures how postcolonial states function alongside the changing dynamics of extraction and accumulation under contemporary (neo-)liberalism (Bledsoe and Wright 2019; Cross 2013; Hesketh 2017; Mezzadra 2011; Salem 2020; Tilley 2020). In fact, as we discussed in more detail in chapter 3, according to Ndlovu-Gatsheni and Ojakorotu (2016) the very organizing principle of citizenship that underpins territorial claims to sovereignty (and border control) can be understood as a Eurocentric (as noted in chapter 4) part of an ongoing colonial mandate, even if it was strategically useful in anti-colonial struggles (see Salem 2018 for more on this; on citizenship and colonialism, see Hindess 2005). Invoking Fanon (1963: 31), it is pertinent to remember that 'the colonial world is a world divided into compartments', of which racialized sovereignty is one postcolonial ingredient.

Some of the best examples of a postcolonial account of border security can be found in studies of mobility and security in Palestine, even as this context continues to receive minimal attention in mainstream migration studies. The Israeli occupation of Palestine continues to be organized around the control of movement, not only the containment of one of the world's largest populations of refugees through the erection of physical borders (although see Busbridge 2013) but also through different speeds of movement, the control of urban space and legal regimes of property ownership (Bhandar 2018; Griffiths and Repo 2018; Kotef 2015; Weizman 2007).

Movement is always racialized in the settler-colonial context (Wolfe 2006) but Hagar Kotef (2015) shows how border security is particularly central to the Israeli settler-colonial project (and to liberalism more broadly). Under the logics of Israeli occupation which runs from management to elimination, Palestinians have been rendered uncivilized by how their presence on the land, in labour and mobility is deemed unruly and savage (Bhandar 2018; Tawil-Souri 2012). Thus bordering practices such as checkpoints, walls, barriers, fences, different transportation systems, differentiated systems of rights and surveillance systems are all central to the violence of occupation. Significantly for how we think about border security, since 9/11 and in recent bombardments of Gaza, the Israeli settler project has become more closely bound to the wider geopolitics of the 'war on terror' (Puar 2017). This means that any political resistance (including the actions of Hamas but also day-to-day civilian protest) can be legitimated and violently suppressed as 'terrorism' (Charett 2019; Khalili 2007). Critical studies of the occupation keenly show border security is reformed and reimagined in Palestine and shaped by local and global processes of settler colonialism, regimes of racialized labour and dispossession (Seidel 2017), which meet up with the geopolitical and economic interests of the United States and European allies.

And yet, as postcolonial scholars of Palestine insist, border security in this context is not only the manifestation of violent occupation. Sharri Plonski (2018) argues that we should instead view borders as materialized 'sites of struggle' which shape (settler) colonialism. She argues that borderscapes 'evolve as members of these communities engage the state', for example, in battles for recognition of their land rights and in 'specific acts of negation, resilience, refusal and negotiation' (2018: 1351) against the settler state, legal categories of citizenship and liberal concepts of property ownership (Shamir 1996). In this view, we should consider borders as modes of power, which only form through resistance, even if resistance is the 'crossing' of a border or the enduring presence of people demanding a right to move and work (see also Salaita 2016; Seidel 2017; Tabar 2017).

Here we can see how postcolonial scholarship on Palestine/Israel provides vital lessons for how we study security and borders beyond Euro-America. This work situates mobility in the context of the local and global dynamic of contemporary imperialism and settler coloni-alism, which resonates with other studies of mobility, borders and also indigeneity (Coulthard 2014; see Davis 2016 for more on global forms of solidarity). Occupation rests on the supposedly excep-tional denial of Palestinian rights but it is also exemplary of a more global condition in which border regimes and colonially mandated schemes of race and dispossession work on and through movement. Importantly, this type of connected work is not wholly oriented towards producing knowledge on how mobility affects Euro-America. Through being attuned to the local and global patterns of (settler) colonialism, Palestine is connected to other sites of border violence in both the Global North and South. To Eyal Weizman (2003: 195), the West Bank is an interconnected site of global urban security: 'The West Bank can be seen as an extreme model – perhaps a laboratory – of a territorial and urban conflict that can take place in other places. Globalization takes the periphery straight to the centre; the frontier between the First and Third worlds starts running through the middle of World cities.'

Techniques crafted for control and urban warfare in Palestine are used in border security elsewhere (and vice versa). Palestine becomes one source of policing and bordering technologies that migrate and connect up with, through international chains of capital and production, other global border sites: for example, in urban policing projects, from the destruction of favelas to the spatialization of Indian reservations, from the histories of plantation economies to border surveillance systems, to integration and social engineering strategies (see Gahman and Hjalmarson 2019 for similar connections). In this way, we can begin to tie together border security across Palestine, policing in Johannesberg or Ferguson, slum clearances in Rio de Janeiro, reservation controls in Manitoba, surveillance at the Greek–Turkish border, Danish integration strategies and 'ghetto' clearances (see Davis 2016 on solidarity across these spaces). Thinking through connections between different border security sites is different to comparing like for like. Instead, this is a recognition of the local and global dimension of struggles and the intertwined character of border security and its colonial racialized characteristics (for a comparable analysis, see Danewid 2020; Li 2019). As Goldberg (2009: 253) argues, such an approach can help us understand that 'racist arrangements anywhere – in any place – depend, to a smaller or larger degree, on racist practice almost everywhere else'.

What this shows us is that border security in the Global South is related to global patterns of dehumanizing violence which are linked to concrete material interests of security companies and postcolonial, metropolitan, imperial states, and are conditioned by longer histories of colonial racialization, dispossession and accumulation. In this context, we should remember that the 'war on terror' continues to be fought in the Global South, whether in the form of 'shock and awe' (Iraq), colonial occupation (Iraq and Afghanistan), regime change (Syria and Libya), drone war (Pakistan, Libya, Syria, Yemen and Somalia) or clandestine special ops (Afghanistan and Somalia), or in the production and then policing of refugee populations. Border security remains embedded as part of these broader strategies of violence and control which connects violence going on in the North and South. But this is not a passive account. We can conceive borders as sites of struggle and resistance and as technologies that connect places and struggles, which are often 'peripheralized' (Palestine, Mauritius, Sudan), to centres of power (the United States, Europe, China) (see Barkawi 2016 for an elaboration on this perspective).

Decolonizing borders

Scholarship that recognizes the centrality of colonial violence to bordering is vital. However, decolonizing border security also means being attuned to work which questions what non-Eurocentric analysis of border security might (not) look like, and then asking how different accounts of world order understand the political violence of, for example, the 'war on terror'. How are borders reconsidered in these traditions? This means challenging the very concepts through which most social scientific approaches to border security start (even those exploring and expanding geographical boundaries beyond Europe, or in critical variants of postcolonial and Marxist theory). In our third account of border security in the Global South, we explore decolonial accounts of border security through African scholarship before, in our last section, turning to examine how we also need to challenge the 'common-sense' equivalence between Islam/terrorism/religious conservativism.

Southern African scholars such as Achille Mbembe (2018) and Ndlovu-Gatsheni (2018b) have produced extensive academic and political work explicitly addressing the decolonization of borders. This fundamentally challenges the way border security focuses on the containment of racialized bodies and the abandonment and punishment of people racialized as non-white through the contemporary 'carceral landscape'. For Mbembe (2018), we need to begin any challenge to border security by refusing the liberal conceptions of freedom and mobility which dominate the discussion of borders and migration, as well as the horizon of the political. A decolonial approach to borders, for Mbembe, thus demands denaturalizing the nation-state, sovereignty and liberal capitalism as the reference through which we understand politics.

Unpacking this, Mbembe (2018) warns us not to look to a liberal Kantian cosmopolitanism for decolonial futures, nor a 'no borders' politics often professed by the liberal left in solidarity with migrants (as we discussed in the last chapter). This is because, as Kotef (2015) argues, liberalism is inherently contradictory when it comes to mobility. In the western liberal canon, order and freedom are central to political subjectivity, as is sovereignty as political authority. Because of this, excessive or unruly mobility is often configured as a security risk (i.e. a challenge to order) which demands management. Even in a universalized cosmopolitan model, liberalism can only offer 'managed mobility' as a solution to this problem of freedom and order (see also Ansems de Vries et al. 2017; Calhoun 2002; Gaztambide-Fernández 2012). And, as we have seen, 'managed mobility' and the focus on security in liberal states imagines that the movement of the world's poor and racialized is threatening, and that this threat can be domesticated, pacified through liberal reform (i.e. integration, multiculturalism, counter-terrorism) or expelled (visa, borders, deportation) (for more on liberalism and colonialism, see Bell 2016; Losurdo 2011).

Against this, Mbembe (2018) and Ndlovu-Gatsheni (2018b) offer interrelated ways to begin to challenge how we analyse border security. This begins by tracing the coloniality of modern border security but pushes to exceed this critique by focusing on how border struggles can (and do) draw on other political possibilities and ways of being in the world. To do this, both authors suggest that we should examine the lived reality of traditions, sensibility and convivialities of movement and struggles in Africa which are in excess of a liberal/sovereign conception of mobility. For example, Mbembe shows how movement was central to Equatorial African cosmogonies. Rejecting the statist concept of 'security', which rests on a conception of territorial order and the individual subject of rights, these cosmogonies are based on flows, networks and the distribution and intensity of movement 'between places and things'. Rather than mobility being the antithesis of order (i.e. a risk or danger), mobility is instead *survival*: 'the primordial principle of spatial organisation was continuous movement. And this is also still part of present-day culture. To stop is to run risks. You have to be on the move constantly', Mbembe (2018) argues. To base a political project on movement as survival is antithetical to the colonial cartography of borders as security.

Ndlovu-Gatsheni (2018b), drawing on Mbembe, equally traces how mobility in Africa occurs irrespective of (post)colonial borders. Against Third World nationalist accounts that focus on sovereignty, he argues that nationalist borders are a continuity of empire. Even if Third World borders were initially forged through necessary and vital anti-colonial struggles, they continue the conservative politics of a world system defined by racialized capitalism and border security (for different accounts of Third World nationalism, see Sajed and Seidel 2019; Salem 2018). These boundaries of nationhood, citizenship and free market economics are counterproductive of a more radical imaginary of pan-Africanism and revolutionary solidarity. Against this, Ndlovu-Gatsheni offers three principles for understanding mobility 'otherwise': multiplicity (the hybridity and plurality of African thought), circulation (everything being on the move), and composition (communal agency in relation to others).

From within these traditions, he argues for the need to expand 'a transnational ideology of solidarity amenable to pan-African citizenship as a form of horizontal African comradeship' (2018b: 27). We should recall here that pan-Africanism is a liberatory philosophy developed during anti-colonial and black power struggles. Pan-Africanism rests on a reconception of sovereignty, personhood and security which aims at unifying both people in Africa subject to the violence of imperialism and colonization and the global African diaspora under one political project (for key thinkers and activists, see Marcus Garvey, Walter Rodney, Kwame Ture and Malcolm X; on Garveyism and sovereignty, see Shilliam 2006; for a critique of pan-Africanism, see Andrews 2018). Pan-Africanism offers the forging of unity beyond the boundaries of African states for the objective of overthrowing colonial systems and knowledge. Ndlovu-Gatsheni (2018b) argues that this is a vital project to resist the criminalization of African bodies under contemporary global border security. Pan-African citizenship seeks to actively dismantle the border system financed and policed by northern states as well as the postcolonial border regimes of African states which ultimately still privilege the movement of white bodies (as travellers, experts, entrepreneurs) 'over fellow Africans' (Ndlovu-Gatsheni 2018b).

These powerful interventions offer us political traditions that are both shaped by, but in excess of, colonial modernity. They are firmly rooted in traditions of thought which aim at recovering humanity through movement (for other comparable accounts, see Santos 2014; Shilliam 2015). Whilst humanist and cosmopolitan in orientation, these perspectives refuse to claim a universalized knowledge or to speak from anywhere. In the case of Mbembe and Ndlovu-Gatsheni, they speak from Africa *for* Africa and the African diaspora. This is not a model or a theorization for Europe. It refuses to collapse all knowledge into knowledge for Europe. Working with a different political ontology based on movement as survival (as Mbembe gives us) demonstrates how the very notion of border security is actually a deeply ethnocentric concept born out of the identity politics of white European anxiety.

Political violence and terror

We began this chapter by outlining the centrality of the 'war on terror' to the politics of border security. In this last section, we return to this theme by exploring scholarship which rethinks the categories of terrorism and political violence and, particularly, the vilification of Islam. It is perhaps obvious at this stage that security is premised on a colonial/statist view of the world. Security, as James Eastwood (2018) has argued, is (much like borders) both a practice and a concept of the (colonial settler) state. Equally, it is worth reiterating that security as it has been conceived is racialized through colonial claims to human worth and value (Agathangelou and Killian 2016; Bilgen 2016). Because security is always premised on the security of some at the expense of the insecurity of others, it has replicated patterns of colonial power where colonized (including indigenous) people have been cast as dangers to white supremacy, imperialism, capital accumulation and 'world order'. To preserve order as the status quo is always to preserve the privilege – material and symbolic – of those states and populations who have gained most from the violence of colonialism and imperial racialized capitalism (Mills 1997, 2015). This is the context into which terrorism emerges as a contemporary threat (see Parashar 2019).

Eurocentric accounts of security, even critical accounts, often start by outlining the parameters within which violence is viewed as legitimate (Thobani 2007). The state is thus usually understood as the bearer of legitimate violence against terrorism (see Blakeley 2011). But from the perspective of colonized and indigenous populations, this story of legitimate violence is instead a story of oppression and dispossession, potentially both in the form of the (post)colonial administration or settler state (see Razack 2002). Violence, we should remember, was the *raison d'être* and technology of the colonial state (Fanon 1963). For Fanon, rather than the bringer of order (as in the white/settler/European account), the security apparatus of the colonial state, the 'policeman and soldier', is 'the bringer of violence into the home and mind of the native' (Fanon 1963: 31). In light of this, security is merely the justification for disorder and violence conducted on the body of colonized peoples. As Fanon reminds us, it is the sheer naked force of 'bayonets and cannons' that creates the conditions for the dispossession and exploitation of colonized peoples, lands and resources.

Alongside this account of colonial security, Fanon argues that because of the violent nature of colonialism, decolonization itself had to be a violent act because it involved turning the existing order of things 'upside down': 'The native who decides to put the programme into practice, and to become its moving force, is ready for violence at all times. From birth, it is clear to him that this narrow world, strewn with prohibitions, can only be called into question by absolute violence' (1963: 31).

Decolonization, for Fanon, whether enacted through armed conflict or not, had to be violent because it was revolutionary. This was a very different sort of political violence than that which organizes the status quo and the colonial order of things (such as border security) because it involved putting the native first, upending the idea of 'who comes last comes first' (Fanon 1963: 31).

Thinking through the violence of (de)colonization with Fanon means asking very different questions about the nature of border security and the 'war on terror'. The colonial order of things is perpetuated in part through the vast technology of border security. It is colonial war, imperial interventions, the demands of capitalist accumulation and inequality that continue to force so many peoples from their homes and communities in the Global South as refugees and migrants. This is at the same time as borders work to contain and expel people who make up the world's displaced (Walia 2014).

In this context, Islamic terrorism should be viewed within a history of colonial struggles.

From this perspective, it is the (neo-)colonial architecture of the world, including centuries of colonial intervention, occupation, warfare, bloodshed, extraction and dispossession in the Middle East and Africa, that produced al-Qaeda, ISIS and al-Shabaab (see Ingiriis 2018). We should remember that what is labelled 'Islamist' political violence is oriented not towards theological ends as such but distinctly political and territorial claims regarding the removal of imperial and colonial occupation and intervention in the Middle East and North Africa (see Elden 2009 for more on this). Border security can thus never be the 'solution' to this political violence labelled 'terrorism' because it is part of the system that caused it. Border security here looks like systematic disorder and colonial violence (whether conducted by former imperial states or not).

However, drawing on Fanon to understand the conditions of 'terroristic' violence is not the same as saying that al-Qaeda and ISIS are 'liberatory' or revolutionary or truly decolonial. They are distinctly neither of those things. As Agathangelou (2010) insists, this force of political violence is counter-revolutionary in that it doesn't aim to turn societies upside down. For example, organizations such as ISIS and al-Shabaab sustain heteropatriarchal capitalism often at the end of the barrel of a gun. Instead of a liberatory violence, this form of violence is actually the mirror image of the modernist colonial state that it attempts to destroy or take over (Agathangelou 2010). In the case of ISIS, the fascist cleansing of Syria and Iraq was precisely a process of state building (Ahram 2019), mirroring the ethnic cleansing and genocide of settler colonialism that preceded it. And whilst professing the 'liberation' of Muslims and the building of a 'homeland', this has so often been conducted by murdering, purging and bombing more Muslims than any other group. This form of violence remains a product of fascistic oppression. According to Howard Caygill (2013), it represents 'a world of alienation (in all senses of the word) created by colonial violence, an abstract violence that provokes responses which initiate a mutually destructive escalation' (Caygill 2013: 101).

Marusek's work on Islam and resistance is a useful resource in light of these discussions. She suggests that what the liberal secular and Eurocentric perspective on 'savage violence' as 'terrorism' fails to understand is the more radical and progressive possibility of liberatory violence and struggle. Religious movements and non-secular forms of politics have been central to this. In the context of even well-meaning liberal and 'critical' work, Islam is (and Muslims are) still often presented as something to be tolerated or viewed as merely 'culturally alien' (if not necessary inferior). But as Marusek (2016) shows, terrorism is used as a label to actively delegitimize the work of liberation and anti-imperial movements across the Middle East (Hezbollah, Hamas and Interpal, among others; see also Saeidi 2018a). 'Terrorism' in this context is an instrumental label which can transform resistance movements into merely the perpetrators of 'hatred and intolerance' and justify their eradication.

Instead, Marusek shows how 'Islamic resistance' has been central to anti-colonial/imperial struggles over the Middle East, in Lebanon, Egypt and Palestine, but we can also add to this the United States (Gomez 2005; Rashid 2013), Latin America (Rosa 2018) and Europe. Anti-colonial variants of Islamic thought and practice have been historically oriented towards a politics of social justice. For instance, Marusek traces how this social theology has been reinterpreted through readings of Fanon, Marx, Césaire and Sartre in different historical moments. Equally, Islamic thought has influenced key revolutionary figures such as Malcolm X (Gomez 2005). In the context of Shi'a activism, Marusek argues that thinkers and clerics over the course of the twentieth century 'historicised Islam by viewing religion through a lens that reflects and responds to modern-day structures of oppression' (Marusek 2016: 27; see also Saeidi 2018b). What Marusek calls Islamic resistance are radical and transformative Islamic movements. These traditions can be found in organizations from the Muslim Brotherhood and Hezbollah to the Nation of Islam (see Pratt and Rezk 2019 on the Muslim brotherhood). We are not here saying that such groups represent perfectly developed forms of liberatory politics. Instead, there are elements of more radical and progressive traditions within these groups and, much like the way that social movements in the Global North are approached and studied as complex heterogeneous assemblages (from their inception), it is important to treat social movements outside of Euro-America as also inherently complex and produced through multiple and often competing social forces.

Whilst Islamic resistance is oriented towards localized struggles, these are internationalist projects which seek to affirm the *Ummah* (a worldly Muslim community) through solidarities and connections with a global Muslim diaspora (Daulatzai 2012). Whilst often used as a means for western scholars and governments to pose the inextricable alienness of Muslim communities (see Koopmans and Schaeffer 2016; Van Ginkel and Entenmann 2016), much like pan-Africanism, this diasporic solidarity challenges the arrangement of the nation-state sovereignty as *the* form of political authority. Islam is shaped by conservative and resistant movements, multiplicity and complexities which are historically located in the geopolitics of Muslim diasporas. However, Islamic resistance offers radical ways of being human (see also Sheikh 2016). It offers sensibilities, convivialities, forms of rationality, collective mobilization and spirituality through '[a] distinct view of human behaviour that posits an alternative method of thinking about the human being; his or her place in the natural order; his or her conduct towards others; his or her place in society; the ordering of his or her material needs. And the management of politics' (Crooke 2009: 29, cited in Marusek 2016: 96).

In concrete terms, Islamic resistance is articulated through participation in liberatory movements and campaigns of social justice at different scales of community membership and through the articulation of anti-colonial and anti-capitalist political and cultural projects (also see Sheikh 2016). We can see historical examples of this in the rebellions led by enslaved African Muslim clerics in Bahía (Brazil) in the nineteenth century (Rosa 2018), or in the influence of black radicals in revolutionary struggles in 1960s America (Daulatzai 2012), or in the influence of Hezbollah in Lebanon. For example, the United States still treats Hezbollah as a 'terrorist' organization. And yet whilst the organization is a paramilitary force in Lebanon and beyond, it is also an embedded social movement which provides material resources, food, water, infrastructure, health care and schooling to oppressed and abandoned communities. It played a significant role in the reconstruction of Southern Beirut after the civil war in Lebanon and the 2006 war with Israel (Marusek 2016: 89–123). Liberatory violence in this context is not only about the destruction of occupying colonial forces but, in the context of Islamic resistance, this provides people with forms of cultural and social empowerment, collective mobilizations, creativity, poetics and material survival in the face of imperial and settler-colonial violence (see also Saeidi and Vafa 2019).

Such resistance is echoed in the work of diasporic organizations working across the Global North and South in the countering of white supremacy, in anti-racist mobilization and in social justice projects. Islamic resistance thus plays a key role in wider decolonial struggles (see also Bayat 2010). It also plays a distinct role in experiments in the construction of what Agathangelou calls 'an alternative international whose locus is the tabula rasa, that is, the dis-investment from and the changing of the whole social colonial structure from the bottom up' (Agathangelou 2016: 102–3).

What has this got to do with migration studies? What we want to point out in this final section are other ways of thinking about security and political violence that challenge the fundamental assumptions on which dominant accounts of border security and ways of viewing *and* researching the world are based. It is not enough to only explore the continuities of colonial or imperial power and the racialization central to contemporary borders. We also need to dismantle the claims to superior and naturalized knowledge that this rests on and show the continuous and long-term emergence of alternatives. In light of the 'war on terror' and the power of anti-Muslim racism, it becomes important to demonstrate the dehumanization of communities through discourses of 'new terrorism' and insecurity but also to think Islam otherwise. By examining decolonial scholars, we have shown how colonial borders are being rethought and challenged in Africa through different political imaginaries and cosmogonies that defy liberal constructions of freedom/security/movement. By examining the work of scholars of political violence, we have shown that we need to rethink how security and particularly (counter-)terrorism are conceptualized. We can treat terrorism as a racialized geopolitical discourse but also one that obscures important developments in decolonial politics such as in Islamic resistance. This demonstrates the importance of work which challenges the Eurocentric and clearly racist depiction of Islam as terror/danger/evil. But this also challenges the liberal construction of Islam as traditional and conservative against a secular 'progressive' modernity. Thinking about border security differently opens up new worlds beyond our current neo-liberal carceral landscape.

Conclusions

What we have shown in this chapter is the colonial character of border security. In doing this, we have also tried to place work on migration, integration, social cohesion and, jointly, securitization and militarization in a different light. This urges us to rethink the historical conditions under which questions of integration, segregation and cultural difference have emerged. It also draws attention to the absence of engagement with postcolonial (and even less so decolonial) thought in the analysis of securitizations under the 'war on terror'.

To approach border security differently, i.e. rather than as a necessity or something to ameliorate or to critique through a return to 'normal' politics, we sought to examine work that unpacks the colonial histories of border security. This began by thinking through the role of race, colonial power and rule in the 'war on terror'. We showed how Islamophobia is better considered as anti-Muslim racism, rejecting the simplistic construction of Islamophobia as prejudice against values or 'ideas'. Anti-Muslim racism is bio-cultural, resuscitating colonial and Orientalist imaginaries of backward/pre-modern social structures of gender, sexuality or religion. Scholars of anti-Muslim racism have been keen to show how this underpins immigration regimes, particularly in the 'West', as well as the intensification of authoritarian governance (surveillance, policing, extradition, etc.). But anti-Muslim racism is also geopolitical and conditioned by the shifting dynamics of racialized capitalism as well as older histories of dehumanization. An analysis of race, whiteness and coloniality must shape investigations into border security from the beginning, and we need to explore how local struggles and sites of 'security' are networked into broader global trends of colonial racism.

Drawing upon Simone Browne's work, we then considered how to rethink work on securitization and militarization of borders by being attuned to the institutional histories of borders and technologies of surveillance. One way of approaching border security is through tracing where these logics, practices and ways of doing security have emerged from and what this means for the management of particular populations today. But central to all of this must be a fundamental rejection of the idea that we can return to a 'normal liberal politics' when borders were less violent. The very architecture of borders and security has always been a racist imperial project in the context of northern metropoles and settler-colonial states, a project that contains the Third World in a state of inequality.

Whilst the first part of the chapter considered border security in the Global North, we turned in the second half to work that has attempted to decentre Euro-America as the site of theory/knowledge production. We examined work that has expanded the remit of studies of borders, particularly by tracing the practices of offshoring European borders into neighbouring states and regions such as North Africa and the complex character of borders in postcolonial states which are often shaped by colonially mandated border practices and European ideas of national sovereignty. Whilst this work is often vital and necessary, we suggested that lessons could be drawn from scholars who have used a more explicit postcolonial and Marxist lens to understand borders in the Global South – namely, in the context of border security in Palestine. We suggested that this work reveals particularities about Palestine/Israel but also connections with other sites of border security and resistance which demand further study.

In the continued refrain to 'provincialize' Europe, in terms of both geographical study and the production of Eurocentric knowledge (Chakrabarty 2008; also Santos 2014), we turned to consider how decolonial scholars have thought border security differently. We explored how African scholars have rethought the politics of borders, freedom and mobility on the continent with the express aim of decriminalizing and revolutionizing borders and citizenship. This reimagines pan-Africanism as a humanizing force against colonial bordering and security.

In the last section, we examined how we might rethink the equivalences between Islam and terrorism which dominate in the West. Reflecting on Fanon's work on violence, we examined how political violence can be revolutionary. We used the example of Islamic resistance to explore how Islam is not only a conservative and/or dangerous religion but also a political theology of oppression that is embedded in ongoing decolonial struggles over material resources, survival and personhood. We do this not to legitimize all organizations that might come under this concept but to complicate dominant understandings of Islam and to treat Islamic resistance (not to be confused by the fascist violence of ISIS and al-Qaeda) as a complex and heterogeneous international practice and an embedded social movement. Just as social movements are treated as complex arrays of social forces and competing traditions – conservative, progressive, regressive, radical – in Euro-American contexts, we need to treat Islamic movements in a connected fashion and remain indebted to the colonial struggles and alternative systems of knowledge they rest upon.

So on one hand, postcolonial/decolonial interventions give us the tools to analyse border security differently; on the other, they urge us to lay down these concepts and their Eurocentric baggage altogether.

7

Gender, Sexuality, Colonialism ... and Migration

Introduction

Gender and sexuality have become increasingly prominent concepts and research agendas in some quarters of migration studies. This reflects the emergent influence of feminist theory, and to a much lesser extent queer theory, across the social sciences, and the wider acceptance – even by conservative academics – that gender and sexuality 'matter'. Without overstating this influence, migration scholars have found institutional space to study how gender and sexuality shape migrants' experience of mobility (Bennet and Thomas 2013; Bhabha 2004; Freedman 2007; see also IMISCOE 2019), how migration policies work to reproduce discrimination based on gender (Buckley-Zistel and Krause 2017; Crawley 2011; Freedman 2007; Lutz 2004; Nayak 2015); and how states have used and abused the inclusion of LGBTQ+ rights in asylum regimes (Ferreira 2018; Hertoghs and Schinkel 2018; Lewis 2013, 2019; Luibhéid 2018; Nayak 2015: 137–69). This builds on long-standing work from feminists who have studied questions of mobility, transnationalism and migration (Fournon and Glick-Schiller 2001; Lutz, Phoenix and Yuval Davis 1995; Morokvasic 1991). Increasingly, lived experiences, family migration and issues of social reproduction have become validated areas of research influenced by the refusal to separate public/private spheres and following the axiom that the personal is political (Erel and Acik 2020; Gerver and Millar 2013; Kilkey, Merla and Baldassar 2018; Kofman and Raghuram 2015; Kraler et al. 2011). More critical variants of this work have begun to explore how gender and sexuality work as forms of power to organize systems of mobility both locally and globally (Johnson 2011; Lewis 2019; Luibhéid 2013; Luibhéid and Chavez forthcoming).

With the growing influence of feminist and queer theory across the field in mind, this chapter aims to take up and expand interest in gender and sexuality in migration studies by arguing that migration scholars interested in gender and sexuality (as well as feminist scholarship on migration and mobility) need to engage more seriously with the role of colonial modernity and race/racism in contemporary systems of oppression. This is particularly important with scholarship in migration studies because of the field's historical amnesia over questions of colonialism and race (for some recent exceptions, see Boulila 2019; Camiscioli 2009; Keskinen and Andreassen 2017; Laskar, Johansson and Mulinari 2016; Michel 2015) and, as we have argued throughout this book, because of the analytical necessity of engaging with work in postcolonial and decolonial theory which exposes how ongoing systems of colonial power structure how mobility is experienced and managed. Whilst attempts to embrace work on 'intersectionality' have begun to offer some useful insights to migration scholars, we propose that analysis of intersectionality, along with many variants of feminism and queer theory, do not go far enough to challenge the hegemony of white feminism and the historical subjugation of colonial critique within the field. Instead, we suggest an engagement with decolonial feminism, queer-of-colour critiques and different traditions within black feminism. Taking this engagement seriously provides vital insights into how gender and sexuality were central to the way in which colonial rule was established and continues today. To do this, we will focus on the work of Maria Lugones, Hortense Spillers and Roderick Ferguson. We use their work to explore the ways in which we can rethink how systems of mobility are gendered, sexualized and racialized through colonialism. But we also use their work to ask how the very concepts of gender and sexuality are themselves derived from colonial systems of knowledge and dispossession. This has important implications for the questions we ask about migration and the analytical concepts (and research methods) that scholars use to study social phenomena.

The chapter begins with a brief engagement with the 'turn' towards gender and sexuality in migration studies and the popularity of intersectionality as a way of understanding multiple systems of oppression. After outlining the benefits and limitations of intersectionality as a theory/methodology, we suggest that three authors' work and three key concepts can help us to understand further how gender and sexuality work within coloniality: Maria Lugones and the concept of the 'coloniality of gender', Hortense Spillers and the concept of 'ungendering', and Roderick Ferguson and the concept of 'taxonomies of perversion'.

Each scholar speaks to different but interrelated traditions within postcolonial and decolonial feminism, black feminism and queer-of-colour critiques. In doing so, they represent radical departures for how we think about interconnected questions of gender, intimacy, sexuality and, importantly, their deep connection to racialized violence and the imposition of colonial and imperial rule. What is so instructive about these authors' work is that they challenge us to start by understanding that the struggle against patriarchal society (and more specifically heteropatriarchal society – the dominance and 'superiority' of both men and heterosexual gender and sexual relations) – is at once a struggle against imperial racialized capitalism and colonial dispossession. This is increasingly important in a world where claims to protect 'women's' and 'LGBTQ+' rights are being used by states to justify racist and imperial policies (see Farris 2017; Luibhéid 2018; Puar 2007). After introducing the three thinkers, we outline how thinking with the coloniality of gender, with ungendering and with taxonomies of perversion helps us understand key elements of contemporary regimes of mobility – from issues of gender-based violence, to integration strategies, to human trafficking.

Gender and sexuality in migration studies

As we began to outline above, studies of migration are increasingly engaging with questions of gender and sexuality. This is partly down to the disciplinary arrangements of research within universities. As Mügge and de Jong (2013) argue, whilst gender studies has been largely shaped by feminist social movements working towards issues of social justice, migration studies has developed (context-specific) arrangements with the state, policy makers and international funders that shape which kinds of work are privileged and reproduced (see, for example, Ruhs, Tamas and Palme 2019). Recent incorporations of questions of gender in migration studies tend to reflect the mainstreaming of some elements of feminist research into the social science (and to a lesser extent queer theory). For example, research has explored how female migrants specifically navigate the experiences of migration differently – as 'mothers', 'wives', 'dependants' and so on (Kilkey, Merla and Baldasser 2018; Ryan 2011; Sigad and Eisikovits 2014), and LGBTQ+ rights scholars have explored how experiences of migration or asylum are related to occupying the position of a sexual minority (Chavez 2011; Kahn et al. 2018; Picq and Thiel 2015). The expansion of this work also reflects changing priorities within international organizations and donor states to focus on women's rights, especially in the context of increasing focus on gender-based and sexual violence (Obradovic 2015; UNHCR 2019). We might call these approaches *gender and sexuality as identity* (influenced as they are by liberal and radical feminist positions and work on LGBTQ+ rights). In this context, we shouldn't assume that all studies that talk about gender or sexuality are necessarily drawing on critical feminist or queer theorizing. Many studies in mainstream migration studies simply use gender or sexuality as one variable amongst many to understand migration (see Hyndman 2010 for a critique of the absence of explicitly feminist work in migration/refugee studies).

Within contemporary scholarship there are also studies that clearly start with an understanding of gender and sexuality as systems of differentiation, that is, how gender and sexuality relate to patriarchal and heteronormative power. Such studies tend to be more keenly influenced by Marxist and post-structuralist feminism. When these approaches are used to study migration, the focus tends to be on the ways in which borders, policies, institutions, economic systems and states are themselves gendered and sexualized (Barabantseva, Ní Mhurchú and Peterson 2019; Cantu 2009; D'Aoust 2013; de Jong, Koevoets and van Leeuwen 2014; Lewis 2019). This research is more keenly attuned to the ways that powerful social and political structures work to constitute certain bodies as gendered (masculine/feminine) and sexualized (heterosexual/homosexual) within wider fields of capitalist social reproduction. Such structures reproduce political, economic and cultural hierarchies of superiority/inferiority (man/woman, straight/gay, etc.). Work in this vein has, for example, examined how family migration policies work to differentiate people based on heteropatriarchal assumptions about gender relations or ideal models of monogamous relationships, kinship and sexual intimacy (D'Aoust 2017; Peterson 2020; Turner 2015). In this way,

systems of bordering are explored that maintain binary constructions of man/woman, straight/gay and so forth which migrants have
to perform and inhabit (Lewis 2014; White 2014). These types of
studies can still be interested in how different people are subject to
different experiences of mobility, based upon gender and sexuality.
But the emphasis is on how structures work to subject people to
systems of categorization and in turn *make* people into gendered and
sexualized subjects (Berlant 2007; Butler 1990). We might call this
gender and sexuality as power. This work has been productive and
it is important to recognize that some of the most pressing critiques
within this wider body of theorizing, especially regarding queer
theorists' work on the instability of gender and sexualized binaries,
have still rarely translated into significant work in migration studies
(although see Luibheid and Chavez forthcoming).

Despite these emergent bodies of work, the problem with both
gender and sexuality as identity and as *power* is that gender and
sexuality (with this and patriarchy and heteronormativity) have been
broadly conceived of as separate from other systems of domination,
including the organization of colonialism and race/racism. However,
Third World, postcolonial and black feminists have a long tradition
of critiquing the whiteness of western feminism and queer theory.
In her seminal account 'Under Western Eyes', Chandra Mohanty
(1988) called out western feminism for its inability to see or hear
Third World and colonized women's experiences and knowledge.
This also fed into the critique of western/white feminists' complicity
with imperial and colonial projects of racism. What was so powerful
about this critique and others like it (Carby 1982; Davis 1981; Lorde
1984; Moraga and Anzaldúa 1984) was that they mirrored and drew
upon similar calls made by social movements and women's organizations across the twentieth century and throughout decolonization to
recognize the overlapping of oppression under colonial rule (Spivak
1988). From this perspective, the political and social position of
'women' could only be occupied by a white, western, 'cis'-gender
woman, with women racialized as non-white occupying a position of
passivity and disempowerment (Mohanty 1988).

More recently, queer-of-colour critiques have complicated the
self-identified radicalism and progressivism of queer theorists and
activists by emphasizing the way that queer scholarship focuses on
white middle-class subjecthood which silences black and indigenous
experiences (Haritaworn 2008). In this context, these charges of race

blindness and colonial amnesia have only relatively recently been taken seriously by western feminist and queer scholars and, even then, not in large numbers (see Richter-Montpetit 2018 for a more comprehensive overview regarding queer theory). If taking postcolonial and Third World feminist critiques seriously has been neglected in most branches of western feminism and queer theory, then this critique has barely translated into studies of migration (although, for exceptions, see Hyndman and Giles 2016; Tudor 2018; Ahmed 2000).

Intersectionality

One response to calls to take race seriously has been the adoption and development of 'intersectionality' into western academic research. This has had an emergent if liminal impact in migration studies (Bonjour and Duyvendak 2018; de Jong 2013; Erel, Haritaworn and Gutiérrez Rodríguez 2011). It is fair to say that when migration scholars engage with gender, sexuality, intimacy and so on alongside race, this tends to focus on the analytical potential of intersectionality. Intersectionality was originally devised by the black feminist and legal scholar Kimberlé Crenshaw (1989), building on the work by the Combahee River Collective (1983 [1977]). Intersectional analysis aimed to recognize the complexity and multiplicity of oppressions in a world saturated by patriarchy, misogyny, homophobia, wealth inequality and racism. Intersectionality calls attention to the complex positionality of people within these often-overlapping oppressions. In doing so, this work highlights how, for example, black women and queer women of colour, in particular, were subject to multiple forms of oppressions simultaneously and how this was missed by social movements focused only on racial equality (civil rights) or social inequality and class (trade unions) (see Hill Collins and Bilge 2016; Lorde 1984). Thus, as the now famous Combahee River Collective (1983 [1977]) statement argued, 'racial, sexual, heterosexual, and class oppression ... are interlocking'.

Given the potential of this type of critique, why is it that we are not advocating in this chapter for a more enhanced engagement with intersectionality? There is certainly a profound power in the original ethos of Crenshaw and other black feminists working on intersectionality (see, for example, Hill Collins and Bilge 2016) that we would like to see engaged with more rigorously across the social sciences. However, what critiques of this approach have pointed out is that intersectionality has become 'co-opted' and 'whitened' by broad academic use and take-up by policy makers and institutional authorities (see Bilge 2013; Dahmoon 2011; Lewis 2013). This has co-opted the radicalism of the earlier forms of intersectional analysis. What critics point to is that intersectionality too often descends into an ahistoricism regarding the organization of oppression and violence (Puar 2007), especially by omitting the role of colonial modernity in the creation of these global systems of oppression and the way that (settler) colonialism plays an active role in today's struggles (Arvin, Tuck and Morrill 2013).

Equally, when this approach has been applied in the social sciences (mostly in western academies), and this is true of migration studies, the intersection of gender, sexuality, race and class are too often run together as if they are equivalences – as if they are the same kinds of difference. According to Gail Lewis (2013), this can often lead to the omission of race as an analytical category (see also Dhamoon 2011; Erel et al. 2011). This is what critics argue leads to the whitening of intersectionality (Bilge 2013). This is not just the take-up of intersectionality by white academics (although that may indeed contribute to the problem). The problem is also that people racialized as white (and thus privileged and not exposed to colonial violence in the same way) can claim or be assigned differences – as gendered, sexualized, classed subjects – which erase the global working of race and coloniality. In the context of the power of western academic research, which has consistently failed to take race and especially colonial racism seriously, along with arguments in Europe and the United States that material 'class analysis' has been overtaken by 'identity politics' (Fraser 2000), we can see how this risks producing further profound silences and omissions on race and anti-racist work (see also Kerner 2017).

This does not mean rejecting intersectionality as an approach. But instead we suggest that we are better able to appreciate the intersection of oppressions by exploring traditions of decolonial, queer-of-colour and black feminist scholarship that put colonialism, white supremacy and race front and centre of their analysis (see, for example, how intersectionality is considered in de Jong, Icaza and Rutazibwa 2019). In light of this, we argue that, in studying these traditions and key thinkers, we gain a better grasp of how gender and sexuality are central not only to colonialism but also to how race was constructed under colonialism. Rather than mutually exclusive processes which 'intersect', we show how race, gender and sexuality have always already been bound together and, thus, how contemporary regimes of mobility continued to be shaped by gender and sexuality. In the next section, we outline three different ways of reconceptualizing the role of gender and sexuality by examining (amongst others) the work of Maria Lugones, Hortense Spillers and Roderick Ferguson. Throughout, we tie these debates back to questions relevant to migration scholars and to issues of migration, borders and mobility.

Decolonial feminism: the coloniality of gender

Decolonial feminism is a movement that takes as its starting point that gender and sexuality are central aspects of what Partha Chatterjee (1993) and later Walter Mignolo (2000) call the 'colonial difference' – the hierarchization of people as human/not-quite-human/non-human. Decolonial feminists argue that western feminists tend to start with the assumption that gender – the binary construction of men/women – is a universal condition which plays out differently depending on local contexts (illustrated in concepts such as 'global patriarchy'). This has then been expanded and intensified by modern forces of capitalism and colonialism, where gendered social positions have increasingly hardened so that people perceive apparent differences between men and women as 'natural' (for a recent account of this, see Enloe 2017; also Mies 1999). However, what decolonial feminists argue is that what such an account does is 'veil the ways in which non-"white" colonized women were subjected and disempowered' (Lugones 2007: 188). Decolonial feminists invert the assumption that we need to start an analysis of gender with global patriarchy by instead starting with the uneven structuring of the world through colonialism and imperialism. They propose that gender and sexuality are not universal aspects of all cultures trans-historically and trans-globally, but in fact western systems of categorization have been imposed (in a heterogeneous and non-linear way) and universalized onto different communities through colonialism.

Maria Lugones's theory of the 'coloniality of gender' has been central to the development of decolonial feminism. The focus of Lugones's early work on the coloniality of gender (Lugones 2007) was to re-theorize coloniality and colonial difference by integrating scholarship on gender and race from Third World and women-of-colour feminist scholars. This project is inspired by a larger commitment to social justice. As Lugones explains, exploring the coloniality of gender is to help 'understand the indifference that men, but, more importantly to our struggles, men who have been racialized as inferior, exhibit to the systematic violence inflicted upon women of colour' (Lugones 2007: 188). What Lugones presents in her work is an account of how, rather than ancillary to colonization, gender was central to colonial power and the violence enacted through categories of race (including, we would argue, borders and the control of mobility).

To understand this, we first need to reconsider what gender is. In western science and even in critical decolonial theories (such as Mignolo's and Quijano's), Lugones argues that sex (on which social categories of gender are often understood to be based) is still approached as a biological category. Against this, she reminds us how gender and sex are in fact historical categories, produced within particular regimes of Eurocentric capitalist social relations. 'Gender does not need to organize social arrangements, including social sexual arrangements,' she argues. '[G]ender arrangements need not be either heterosexual or patriarchal' (Lugones 2007: 190). This is instead a 'matter of history'. To illustrate the historicity of gender, Lugones refers to the naturalized assumption that there are two sexes on which gendered categories are 'based'. To question this, she refers to the existence of intersexed individuals (1–4% of the world's population, according to Greenberg 2002) who have some characteristics traditionally associated with both male and female. That intersexed people are assigned a binary sex through law, and are often subject to medical interventions to make them appear male or female, reveals that social categories and law continue to play a fundamental role in producing people as binary sexed (male/female) as well as gendered (man/woman). Rather than a biological 'fact', argues Lugones, law and medical practice impose *a sex* onto people whose bodies are *intersexed*.

Whilst this account appears to share common ground with feminist and queer accounts of gender (see Butler 1990), what Lugones goes on to show is how binary constructs of sex and gender were part of a global colonial system which produced dispossession and violence. For example, sexual and gender binaries were imposed on indigenous communities through colonialization and were used as a means of racializing indigenous people as inferior to Europeans. If being either male or female, man or woman, were naturalized and viewed as *normal* in European social relations, these categories of gender didn't always fit when it came to the 'dark side of coloniality' (Lugones 2007: 195, 2008). That is, gender functioned differently in the treatment and representation of indigenous, colonized and enslaved peoples (Lugones's 'dark side'). Lugones argues that Europeans viewed the different intimate, kinship and social relations, and sexual and gendered structures, of indigenous groups as a sign of their inferiority. Through colonization, non-European people were instead categorized as 'abnormal' and 'deviant' for not following European heteropatriarchal relations of hierarchies of gender, domesticity, reproductive family and the division of labour (for more on domesticity and race, see Bhandar 2018: 57–61; Turner 2020; Virdee 2019).

Lugones (2007: 195) argues that the 'sexual fears of colonizers led them to imagine the indigenous people of the Americas as hermaphrodites or intersexed, with large penises and breasts with flowing milk'. Likewise, we might consider the exhibiting of the 'Hottentot Venus', Saartjie Baartman, across European metropoles in the late nineteenth century. Baartmann was presented as an example of oversexualized black native bodies with her 'dark complexion' and 'large protruding buttocks' (Mendez 2015). She was, according to Mendez (2015: 48), an example of the 'sexual difference not just between men/women, but a non-normative/excessive sexuality which was used by pseudo-scientists to locate the human/racial differences between "Europeans" and "blacks" in the material and biological body'. Baartmann was not just gendered; the fixation on her sexuality and gender worked to reify and produce racist ideas of the human/non-human. Racial difference was inscribed through ideals of gendered and sexual conformity (for a key debate on theories of race and gender in this context, see Gilman 1985 and Magubane 2001).

What is important to recognize here is that, in Lugones's account, the 'discovery' and imaginary of peoples with different regimes of gender and sex and social organization were central to the system of racialization and dehumanization that structured colonization. Gender wasn't only something that intersected with race but was bound to the very material encounters and systems of knowledge through which race was made and organized. Again, this wasn't only an issue of representation. Systems of gender and heterosexuality were intertwined with the justification of material conquest, dispos-session and genocidal violence. Trexler (1995) argues that the Spanish and Portuguese used indigenous peoples' different systems of gender/sexuality to legitimize the conquest of the Americas. Equally, Anne McClintock's (1995) work reminds us that central to the invasion of colonized lands was the imaginary that those lands and peoples were undomesticated and 'empty' (Vergara-Figueroa 2018. In such empty space, indigenous peoples merely lived in an inferior state of sexual barbarism and immature eroticism (see also Said 1995 [1978]). In this context, the presence of non-binary forms of gender and complex forms of kinship and intimacy 'of darker peoples', rather than Christian marriage and heterosexuality, was used to demonstrate the ungodly 'savagery' of these communities and with it their claim to land, resources and even life (a practice that Rifkin 2015 argues continues in settler-colonial states to this day).

What the coloniality of gender gets at is how racialization takes place through the system of gender – where people are viewed as inferior, deviant or non-human for not practising or inhabiting categories of European heteropatriarchy (heterosexuality, patriarchal lineage, domesticity, private property, nuclear families, the division of labour, private/public etc). But Lugones is also interested in demonstrating how the colonial system of gender was imposed and continues to be imposed on colonized peoples to differing degrees. She shows how colonization was a fundamental reorganization of social relations *into* the system of gender. The consequence of this imposition of Eurocentric and Christian ideas around gender and sex was that it appeared universal when in fact it was parochial. To make this point, Lugones connects to and draws upon Third World, women of colour and Afro-feminist scholarship which has produced vital knowledge of colonial systems of gender of restructured indigenous societies across different geographic locations.

The Nigerian feminist Oyèrónkẹ́ Oyěwùmí has produced detailed accounts of how the Yoruba society (living in what is present-day Nigeria) practised modes of identification and social relations which were not organized around binary and hierarchical forms of gender (cited in Lugones 2007: 196). Instead, the greatest effect of coloni-zation, Oyěwùmí argues, was the imposition of a system of gender that essentially created a category of 'women' as inferior within every aspect of life and through bureaucratic and legal mechanisms created a feminine/masculine division of private/public and a division of social reproduction and labour. This point is illustrated by other thinkers. Ifi Amadiume's work *Male Daughters, Female Husband* (1989) shows how pre-colonial West African societies were based on matriarchal social structures. In a different context, Paula Gunn Allen (1992 [1986]) has argued that many indigenous American tribes were also matriarchal, with accounts of third genders and an egalitarian notion of what we now call 'homosexuality' and other non-normative intimacies and kinships. Arunima (1995) has evidenced how the social relations of the Nair people of Kerala were matrilineal, with different cosmological understanding of the relations between bodies and the natural environment until these modes of living were coercively reimagined through missionary work, colonial administrators and then the modernizing project of the postcolonial Indian state (see also Devika 2005; Gopinath 2007). The imposition of gender was thus a project of colonialism. Whilst colonizers viewed indigenous systems of social relations as 'savage' and inferior, the imposition of gender, through legal, pedagogical and coercive means, was also key to the false 'developmental' promise of liberal colonialism. This position, highly influenced by nineteenth-century anthropology (see Stoking 1995), was that the emulation of European forms of domesticity and intimacy by colonized people was a sign of 'progress' towards modernity (see Weber 2015).

By drawing upon this body of work, Lugones's coloniality of gender produces a vital framework through which we can inquire into the historical bonding together of race, gender and sexuality through colonialism. It equally provides a powerful correction to accounts which view gender and patriarchy as universal and to ahistorical accounts of intersectionality. This forces us to interrogate the very concepts of gender and sexuality that are often viewed as vital for critical feminist analysis. The coloniality of gender also provides vital tools for exploring questions of border regimes, mobility and the movement of migrants and refugees. Rather than starting with the line of questioning that assumes that understandings of gender are universal, and that gender can work as a critical category, we need to begin with gender and sexuality as colonial categories. Furthermore, we need to again appreciate that colonialism is not 'past' but is relived in the experiences of gendered systems of domination and violence (Arvin, Tuck, and Morrill 2013).

Take the example of asylum policies, gender and sexual violence. A study interested in the role of gender in mobility might ask, for example, how are men or women affected differently by policies on asylum? As per the *gender as identity* line of research discussed above. Or, it might ask, how are policies on asylum gendered? As per the *gender as power* line of research discussed above. Following a decolonial feminist approach, we could instead begin by asking how are colonial categories of gender reproduced and systematized in migration policies? Following the example of asylum policy, we could then ask how do asylum policies, or policies on forced migration that centre on issues of sexual violence (for instance), work to silence or devalue colonial violence – colonial violence that may in fact shape the historical conditions of sexual violence and knowledge systems which surround research on it? Too often in studies of gender-based violence and forced migration, the focus is on women in the Global South in, for example, refugees camps, where their experiences of violence are reduced to questions of the exceptionalism of war, or being subject to violence is viewed as a product of their vulnerability and/or the 'cultural' context. Central to this are recycled representational systems of passive women racialized as non-white which risks reproducing elements of a 'white saviour complex' (see UNHCR 2019) and equally obscure the complexities of colonial histories.

Against the over-representation of victimhood and exceptional 'cultural' circumstance, following decolonial feminism means centring the experience of oppression and the struggles of colonized women as a cornerstone of research (see, for example, Icaza and Vázquez 2016). For example, Vergara-Figueroa's (2018) work (discussed at length in chapter 5) shows how the experience of Afro-descendant women in Colombia, subjected to violence by government and FARC rebels, is intertwined with longer histories of dispossession and deracination. In her case study, these women's experiences of being subject to uneven forms of violence and uprooting in Colombia and forced migration are presented as not separate from but in fact underpinned by longer histories of treatment by the Colombian state, international organizations, missionaries, mining companies and colonizers who converged in their interests to clear them from their land and subjected them to forced labour and poverty. Their experience of gendered violence – as women with gendered duties of care, dependencies, lost incomes, households, partners, relatives – can only be understood, Vergara-Figueroa argues, in the context of the spectacular and 'cruddy' (Povinelli 2011) forms of coercion across history and the afterlife of slavery, the destruction of homes, the evisceration of their rights to food and labour and to work the land all the way up to recent military bombardments that destroyed their villages. In the spirit of intersectional critique here, we thus need to point to the intersection of oppressions in such a case, the interlocking of race, gender, class and sexuality. But going further than this, with decolonial feminism, we need to be aware of how these oppressions (and knowledge of them) are continually shaped by coloniality (see also Zaragocin 2019). In the context of women's experiences of deracination, then, we need to consider how they experience gendered violence which is bound to the colonial system of gender.

Considering how our categories of gender are always already interlinked and structured by colonial power also demands that we interrogate the analytical categories we are using in our analysis and how this is used by states and other powerful actors. For example, as discourses of sexual violence become increasingly used by inter-national organizations and states to discuss refugee vulnerability, how does this work to reify particular experiences and bodies as gendered around binaries of man/woman which are as colonial as they are patriarchal? How, for example, do debates on transphobia and trans-refugees and migrants build on and develop histories of colonial racism where women of colour were historically denied the rights of 'womanhood' and with it access to humanity (see Weerawardhana 2018)? How might the pledges of liberal states to include sexual orientation as a category of persecution reproduce Eurocentric and western ideas of LGBTQ+ rights? Or, considering who is excluded and silenced from producing knowledge on gender and migration, how might debates about indigenous community and sovereignty contribute to our understanding of gendered violence (see Mack and Na'puti 2019)? As the colonial system of gender structures masculinity and femininity, we equally need to interrogate how masculinity functions in the context of the global control of mobility. And how, for example, this builds on and interplays with the racial hierarchies of white supremacy (see, for example, Gahman 2020). These are a few examples of the research questions that can be enhanced by an engagement with decolonial feminism.

However, thinking through the research implications of decolonial feminism, we should also be uneasy about considering decolonial feminism as a new 'tool' to employ in scholarship. First, it is not only an analytical position but a powerful activist social movement and a commitment to social justice. Decolonial feminism is concerned with historicizing gender as part of coloniality but it is also about creating conditions to reimagine gendered relations and being together otherwise (Mendoza 2016). It is about centring different lived experiences of those subject to the colonial oppressions and the colonial system of gender in order to think about knowledge differently and to support coalitions for resistance (including, as Lugones sets out, between both men and women who have been subject to colonial violence) (Icaza and Vázquez 2016).

This is to recognize, as de Jong, Icaza and Rutazibwa (2019) argue, that Lugones's work is 'not only a feminist critique of decolonial thought but also a decolonial critique of feminist thought' (2019: 11). The project of decolonial feminism refuses to be subsumed and merely recognized within the hegemonic project of white western feminism (Arvin, Tuck and Morrill 2013; Lugones 2011: 755). This also goes beyond demonstrating how concepts of 'gender' and 'women', so central to western feminism, are colonial categories. Lugones stresses the need to sustain and foster alternative modes of non-hierarchical and egalitarian ways of living together within decolonial resistance and struggles. This is not about finding an 'authentic' way of living free of colonialism and 'western' influence and beyond the colonial system of gender. It is about forging a critical praxis that creates the conditions for a constant interrogation of systems of power and domination (see also Anzaldúa 1987).

This can be productive for considering how resistance and calls to be otherwise are always embedded in regimes of colonial power. We might consider here how 'borderlands' are not only spaces of evisceration and despair but also sites of hybridity and resistance (Mack and Na'puti 2019) for the play and survival of different modes of desire, intimacy and kinship (Anzaldúa 1987). Likewise, this requires us to question easy calls for global solidarity within feminist movements and no-border movements with this (see chapter 4 on sovereignty and citizenship). Whilst many white feminists like to imagine a 'global sisterhood' (Narain 2004) which needs emancipation, decolonial feminists push at these categories of solidarity by reminding us that, 'while "gender" reveals the ways in which free "Women" were subordinated in relation to free "Men," it obscures the ways in which those same free "Women" were partially empowered in relation to enslaved males, females, and everything in between' (Mendez 2015: 45; Wynter 1990: 360–3). Rather than dismissing solidarity outright, instead decolonial feminism is focused on building solidarity in ways that centre the experience of those subject to dispossession and the violence of colonialism globally (rather than being 'included' or 'recognized' by white/northern feminist movements).

Ungendering and anti-blackness

Hortense Spillers' work provides another powerful intervention into how we study gender, sexuality and intimacy after colonialism. Spillers' work speaks to many of the connected themes highlighted by the projects of decolonial feminism but does so through the traditions of black studies and black feminism. At the heart of Spillers' work is a familiar ambivalence and 'critical relationship' to feminism, or perhaps more explicitly to hegemonic (white) feminism (see Spillers et al. 2007). This perspective recognizes that this feminism has not only largely ignored the experience of black women but has also been actively complicit in the violent suffering of black communities. To get at the relationship between race and gender, Spillers' work centres an exploration of gender around an account of histories of embodied violence and anti-blackness.

In what is perhaps her most influential text, 'Mama's Baby, Papa's Maybe', Spillers (1987) centres the history and afterlife of slavery in her account of gender and sexuality. Spillers' argument is that gender is historically contingent. If feminist accounts of gender are created through a focus on white womanhood, then centring our account of gender on the figure of the enslaved women transforms how Spillers understands violence, race and patriarchy. In intersectional accounts of gender and race, these two forms of power are considered as interlocking and intensifying each other. So, for example, violence against women of colour is both gendered and racialized – as women of colour experience both the system of racism as a person of colour and patriarchy as a woman. Spillers approaches this intersection somewhat differently by considering how slavery and anti-blackness amounts to a form of 'ungendering'.

Ungendering to Spillers is the result of a 'theft of the body' and the reduction of the body to 'flesh'. She focuses on how enslavement, the conversion of African people into chattel (to be bought, sold, commodified), the conditions of the Middle Passage and the plantation economy subjected slaves to violence that worked directly on the body. In these extreme conditions at the birth of modernity, systems of gendered relations stopped making sense. If gender is the system of identification which white Europeans used to classify and mark people as persons and as political subjects, then through slavery black people were robbed of these systems of differentiation and subjectivity – including, profoundly, their own pronouns, names, their own languages. This follows a shared argument with black studies and decolonial theorists (such as Sexton 2008; Wilderson 2010; Wynter 2003) who argue that slavery severed people racialized as black (but also native and colonized peoples) from personhood and from theories and practices of political subjectivity and rights (see also Králová 2015). But what Spillers argues is that, in this instance, gender was also eviscerated as a marker of personhood. It is not that gender is 'enhanced' as another avenue of oppression in this act of violence (as in the figure of the 'woman of colour'). But gender disappears, resulting in what Spillers refers to as the severing of 'body' from 'flesh' (Spillers 1987: 67). Thus 'under these conditions, we lose at least gender difference in the outcome, and the female body and the male body become a territory of cultural and political manoeuvre, not at all gender-related, gender-specific' (Spillers 1987: 67; for a much earlier comparable argument, see Sojourner Truth's 'Ain't I a Woman' speech; Truth 2020).

It is in the extreme conditions of embodied violence that ungendering takes place. Spillers (1987: 66) reminds us of the multiple sites of violence against black bodies and normalized forms of everyday torture:

> A female body strung from a tree limb, or bleeding from the breast on any given day of field work because the 'overseer,' standing the length of a whip, has popped her flesh open, adds a lexical and living dimension to the narratives of women in culture and society. This materialized scene of unprotected female flesh – of female flesh 'ungendered' – offers a praxis and a theory, a text for living and for dying, and a method for reading both through their diverse mediations.

Ungendering is thus the process by which someone is subject to racialized violence that reduces them to flesh. Extending this focus on excessive violence, Saidiya Hartman (1997, 2008) argues that what underpins this anti-black racism is a 'libidinal economy' (see also Sexton 2012, 2016; Wilderson 2010) where the white master both desires and eroticizes the enslaved and in the same moment desires their excessive punishment as a form of hatred and self-empowerment (Hartman 2008). In this way, we can consider how ungendering structures both features of anti-black racism (the afterlife of the enslaved) and the privileges and investments of whiteness (the afterlife of the master).

To illustrate the power of ungendering as a historical condition but also a 'theory and praxis', it is useful to reflect on Spillers' discussion of family here. The social relations of family have long been a focus of feminist and queer scholarship – family encapsulates patriarchy, gender relations and heteronormativity; it reflects a space of disempowerment to radical feminists or a site of social reproduction and wageless labour to Marxists. Instead, Spillers shows how black people have been historically written out of the social relations of family or, more precisely, the dominant Euro-centred relations of kinship that we call 'family'. In unpacking this point, Spillers reminds us that central to slavery was the dispossession of patrilineal and matriarchal lineages of names, property, titles and, with these, motherhood and fatherhood. We should remember here that western modernity has been defined by the way that patriarchal lineages are passed on through systems of legal inheritance, from property to citizenship (Neti 2014; Peterson 2014). However, enslaved people could never be parents under law. Slaves could reproduce, but their children became property of their master. They had no rights of parentage or inheritance other than inheritance into slavery – although children also inherited freedom from freed parents (see also Burnham 1987 for more on this and Sharpe 2010 on intimacy and 'freedom'). This is significant because, whilst the family is usually viewed as heteronormative and patriarchal, it is more rarely theorized as a site of racism.

What is important for Spillers is how these historical processes organized the ongoing shape of anti-black racism and how this worked to structure the modern world. This leads Spillers to reflect on how the history of slavery and ungendering structures and normalizes contemporary discussion around the contemporary black family, for example, as a site of dysfunctionality and 'failure', connected with discussion of the 'welfare queen' (Cohen 2005; Nadasen 2007), the absent father, systems of 'gang culture' (Shabazz 2015) and violence, or as central to new technologies of fertility and reproductions (see Roberts 1997; Weinbaum 2019). To Spillers (1987: 69), such contemporary debate 'borrow[s] its narrative energies from the grid of associations, from the semantic and iconic folds buried deep in the collective past, that come to surround and signify the captive person'. This leads her to claim that the dominant understanding of the family is an active agent in dehumanizing and dispossessing black communities who are ejected from its claims of normal and moral existence.

From this brief synopsis, it may appear that the nature of Spillers' work focuses solely on dispossessive violence over agency and struggle. However, it would be a mistake to categorize her work in this way. As well as recognizing the political and psycho-analytical consequences of racialized violence, Spillers' conception of ungendering is also meant as an intervention into how we conceptualize the 'human'. In an interview in 2007, Spillers (Spillers et al. 2007) reflects on the power of the concept of ungendering by suggesting that it was designed as a means of showing how racism created the conditions through which black men and women were bound to a history of resistance and survival. She went on to argue that this meant they were in a unique position to resist the recreation of western and European patriarchy in their own communities. Such an emphasis on the potential for alternatives and other ways of thinking gender could be seen as connecting to the project of decolonial feminism discussed above.

The implications of Spillers' work are profound and far-reaching. On its publication, 'Mama's Baby, Papa's Maybe' had a powerful impact on black (feminist) studies (Spillers et al. 2007) but it had much less of an impact on wider feminist scholarship or on those scholars addressing issues of gender, migration, mobility or borders. But an engagement is necessary and, we argue, productive. In order to better understand how race and gender intersect in contemporary migration, we might use Spillers' work to ask how systems of migration governance work to *ungender*. Or, how notions of family are central to the structuring and normalization of ongoing forms of global racism. Consider, for instance, strategies of containment, abandonment and carceral regimes in the Global North and South. How are refugees from sub-Saharan Africa subject to anti-black violence whilst making the journey to Europe? How are bodies reduced to captive flesh by European visa regimes and Frontex operations that allow so many to drown at sea? How are people ungendered by practices of incarceration and detention in the United Kingdom or the United States, or in the 'cruddy' (Povinelli 2011) and everyday forms of abandonment in policies on destitution, asylum and welfare? And equally, how is this violence normalized and rendered accepted and necessary?

In her work, Christina Sharpe (2016), drawing on the legacy of Spillers, asks how the spatial metaphor of the 'hold' (the space where slaves were confined in the Middle Passage) continues to haunt people racialized as black today. Examining the practices of human traffickers in the Mediterranean, Sharpe shows how traffickers are keenly aware of the racist scales of ungendered inferior/superior human life. So much so that in order to be picked up by European authorities and to avoid being turned around and 'sent back' to North Africa, traffickers often force darker-skinned people into the bowels of boats – out of sight of authorities – thus making room for lighter-skinned refugees, and particularly lighter-skinned women and children, who are more visible as symbols of 'empathy'. Sharpe (2016) argues that we must be attuned to how victimhood and the figure of the 'good refugee' is thus organized around the afterlife of anti-blackness, thus gendered and racialized in particular ways. We can also consider how those forced into the 'hold' are ungendered and made more susceptible to death in case of the ship sinking, whilst other gendered bodies (lighter-skinned women and children recognized by systems of gender) are made more visible. The remnants of slavery and ungendering are still very much alive in such events.

Spillers' reflection on the family provides another rich stream of research questions, theory and praxis that challenges and helps us rethink work on family in migration studies. Rather than exploring how families are affected by borders, visa regimes, detention and deportation strategies (for example), Spillers' work asks us to consider how dominant heteronormative appeals to 'family' rely upon the evacuation of people racialized as black from the category of the human. Take the crisis at the US–Mexico border in 2019 caused by the Trump administration's restriction of asylum claims and border crossing. Widespread news coverage has focused on the cruel practice of splitting up families, separating children and parents, in different carceral institutions from detention centres and private-run prisons to secure housing. There are a number of ways in which this practice is gendered, sexualized and racialized and relies upon invocations of normative intimacy. What campaign groups and migrant solidarity organizations have fixated on is the cruelty and trauma experienced by families in these conditions. Such heteronormative appeals have social power because of idealization of the 'family', the place of children as the ultimate representation of the 'future' (Edelman 2004) and the gendered construction of victimhood where 'mothers' should not be subject to such conditions. All worthy and necessary work. However, we might ask what silences are present in these gendered and sexualized appeals and contestations, how single men, for example, or non-normative couples and dependencies and non-binary people are excluded from these campaigns and from wider regimes of empathy.

Drawing on Spillers' work forces us to explore other lines of analysis which foreground the place of race in this calculus. The legacies of slavery and anti-blackness are becoming more salient at the Mexico–US border in 2019, firstly because of the contingency of anti-black violence, secondly because the migration route through Central America has increasingly become a route for both Afro-descendants and people moving from sub-Saharan Africa to the United States. In this context, we might ask how the history of family has relied upon the exclusion of people racialized as black and brown from this dominant construction of intimacy. How might we understand the separations of kinships, dependencies, intimacies 'at the border' as part of a longer line of practices by colonizers, slave owners and settlers to dehumanize captive peoples? How might these carceral spaces 'at the border' share a common logic with other carceral institutions which create other captive populations? For example, supermax prisons, deportation centres, torture cells, inner-city projects and holding rooms. Ultimately, what does the practice of splitting up families, dependencies and kinships 'at the border' tell us about the way that gender works through racialization to offer some people limited forms of protection (i.e. those who can be recognized as families) whilst others are denied rights and recognition? This all points to the work that dominant claims to 'family' do to naturalize and make (un)recognizable systems of inequality and violence.

Equally, following Spillers' emphasis on survival and alternatives, we might ask how diasporic communities are forged through these global networks of movement and control. And how do people navigate new strategies of togetherness even in conditions of trauma and despair? Spillers' work provides a useful starting point for a re-evaluation of the kind of question we ask, as well as theoretical tools for unpacking these connections.

Queer-of-colour critique

We have so far focused largely on work taking place within feminism and with it some implications for queer theory. But we argue that debates regarding race within queer theory are productive in themselves and form a vital part of wider decolonial and postcolonial research agendas. Queer theory was largely influenced by postmodernist and post-structuralist theoretical debates during the 1980s (for an overview, see Warner 1991). Because of this, scholars tended to sideline analysis of race and coloniality. This was despite prominent Third World and Afro-feminist critiques of gender and sexuality which challenged preconceived notions that heterosexuality and the biological indicators of sex were fixed, ahistorical and timeless. For example, in her seminal work *Gender Trouble* (1990), Judith Butler makes no reference to black feminism, Afro-feminism or Third World feminist work (for example, Kapur 2005; Roy 2012) that disturbs the western binaries of gender and sex that she aims to unravel in her own work. However, queer activists and scholars have increasingly revealed the necessity to consider how sexuality and the construction of sexual 'normality' or hetero/homonormativity (key aspects of queer theory) intersect with race (see Macharia 2016a on queer theory in African scholarship; see McLelland and Mackie 2015 for sexualities and South East Asia). Roderick Ferguson's work provides a productive account of what is often called the 'queer-of-colour critique' (see also Gopinath 2005; Munoz 1999; Petzen 2012; Reedy 2011; on indigeneity and queer theory, see Driskill et al. 2011 and Rifkin 2015), an analysis that tackles the absence of questions of race in queer theory. (For queer theory work on colonialism, see Holden and Ruppel 2003.) Engaging with Ferguson's work is productive for engaging queer critiques of migration studies.

According to Ferguson, the queer-of-colour critique locates itself as an extension of women-of-colour feminism 'by investigating how intersecting racial, gender, and sexual practices antagonise and/or conspire with the normative investments of nation-states and capital' (2003: 4). What sets queer-of-colour critiques apart is the way this approach centres the materiality of race, gender and sexuality in the study of social relations. Ferguson's work relies on a rereading of historical materialism to reveal the silences and reproduction of colonial and bourgeois western categories and experiences in critical theory and Karl Marx's texts. If Marx reproduced racist, gendered and sexualized imaginaries of civilization and Eurocentric notions of progress, then queer critique can engage in deconstructing and reformulating historical materialism to appreciate how sexuality, race and gender structure contemporary capitalism (see also Blaney and Inayatullah 2009). Central to this re-evaluation of the history of capitalism is revealing how liberal colonial ideology in the nineteenth century used sexuality as a schema of civilizational progress. Ferguson (2003) argues that we need to understand how sexuality was used to produce 'taxonomies of perversion', perversions which are structured around hierarchies of race and claims to civilization. To understand this involves considering how/why heterosexual sex became 'normalized'.

Materialist accounts of the rise of heterosexuality as a dominant social relation tend to demonstrate how this is tied to the expansion of capitalism and the role capital had in promoting certain forms of reproductive sexuality (Hennessey 2006; Laslett and Brenner 1989). The argument goes that because heterosexual sex led to reproduction, the regeneration of labour and the inheritance of property and wealth, this form of intimacy was privileged above others. In this way, non-normative intimacies (such as the figure of the 'homosexual') were 'discovered', made deviant and regulated by various moral authorities because they were not conducive to or 'threatened' capitalist social relations. However, what Ferguson (2003) argues is that the emergence of deviancies and non-normative sexualities that were policed and disciplined was already fundamentally racialized. In European metropoles, prostitutes and 'homosexuals' were cast as threats not only to sexual reproduction but to racial purity and to civilization itself (for more on heteronormativity and colonialism, see Hoad 2007). Ferguson's 'taxonomy of perversions' helps demonstrate how claims about the 'sexual savagery' of black women, for example, worked to racialize colonized peoples as already perverse (Ferguson 2003: 10). Equally, when prostitution and homosexuality were conceived of as a 'sexual threat', this was already racialized as the perversity of these practices was cast as being in proximity to uncivilized peoples who were represented as sexually backward and regressive through colonization.

A key aspect of Ferguson's critique is showing how heteronormativity is fundamentally racialized. He demonstrates how this functions in the US context and in the construction of citizenship.

But the analysis has wider global resonance which picks up how Third World and decolonial feminists understand gender to function in settler-colonial and postcolonial states. 'As a technology of race,' Ferguson argues, 'US citizenship historically ascribed hetero-normativity to certain groups and non-heteronormativity and/or "perversity" to others. The state worked to regulate the gender and sexual non-normativity in these racialized groups in a variety of ways' (2003: 14). By linking sexuality to progress and perversity to race, Ferguson thus argues that black, Asian and Latino working-class subjects (and, as Morgensen 2011 reminds us, indigenous communities) have been historically viewed as non-heteronormative while white bourgeois subjects were viewed as heteronormative. This helps us understand how non-normative intimacies and sexual relations were viewed as backward (Reedy 2011). Further to this, heteronormativity, and the privileging of heterosexual intimacy as morally, economically and socially superior, was bound up with the maintenance of white supremacy.

Significantly for us, Ferguson shows how the development of heteronormativity in northern metropoles and settler states was expressed in the regulation of minority racialized peoples through immigration control, citizenship law and strategies of 'integration'. Ferguson argues that during the early twentieth century, being truly American and 'belonging' were judged on the emulation of white heteronormative ideals, for example, of family, domesticity, normative gender, child rearing and sexualized relations, which, it was proposed, supported a capacity for wage labour (see also Shah 2011). For example, in the case of Mexican immigrants in the early twentieth century, 'Americanization programs' (what we would call integration strategies today) 'attempted to reconstitute the presumably preindustrial Mexican home'. Doing so meant the Mexican mother 'had to be transformed into a proper custodian who would be fit for domestic labor in white homes, as well as her own' (Ferguson 2003: 14). Just as Lugones's work explores the imposition of gender in historical colonial contexts, here we can see how immigration law works in settler and postcolonial states to produce sexualized–racialized subjects who could reproduce the heteronor-mativity that structured American capitalism and produce migrants as 'good mothers' and/or 'domestic workers'.

Thinking with the queer-of-colour critique outlined by Ferguson is highly productive for work in migration studies. But this focus on heteronormativity needs to be qualified with recent work within queer-of-colour debates which extends this analysis by examining how 'homonormativity' also functions through race, gender and class. Homonormativity relates to heteronormativity; it is the idea that people identified as homosexual can claim normative sexuality by emulating particular forms of desire, behaviour and labour (Puar 2007). LGBTQ+ rights and queer social movements have forced liberal states not only to decriminalize homosexuality but to recognize social rights of sexual minorities (symbolized in the recognition of gay marriage, for example). Yet Puar and others (Duggan 2004; Reedy 2011) argue that this inclusion has been achieved through the co-option and instrumentalization of LGBTQ+ rights by liberal states (Ahmed 2011). To be included into this regime of rights and recognition, queer subjects are expected to emulate and perform traditional forms of normative sexuality – such as monogamous relationships, marriage, domesticity, social reproduction and commodified households, for example presented in the figuration of the good, wealthy, gay couple. Puar thus shows how homonormativity structures racialized forms of control and violence. For example, the United States, Britain and Israel draw upon discourses of protecting LGBTQ+ rights to legitimate imperial wars (Puar 2007), and respecting 'gay rights' has become a key criterion in justifying immigration restrictions, and in some European contexts reshaping citizenship naturalization processes (see Hertoghs and Schinkel 2018; Rao 2015, 2020).

Queer-of-colour critiques develop our understanding of how sexuality continues to be central to gender and race. To paraphrase Jin Haritaworn (2008), we argue that it is productive to consider how heterosexuality is racialized because it helps recognize how the regulation of sexuality leads to the control of different social groups who are considered 'non-normative': 'The queering of racialized straights by racialized queers reflects an awareness that all racialized people transgress dominant gender norms' (Haritaworn 2008: 5.1). We thus stress how heteronormativity, and with it homonormativity, have been powerful forces in producing categories of civilization, progress and belonging. At the same time, through the idea that dominant ideals of desire, intimacy and family are normal and universal, the creation of these categories and the violence and exclusion they create are often obscured and hidden.

Scholars working on migration and borders have begun to take up the insights of queer-of-colour critiques (see Luibhéid 2013; Luibhéid and Cantu 2005). Equally, work on homonormativity is being used to explore how, for example, visa regimes and asylum policy rely upon western and Eurocentric ideas of LGBTQ+ rights (Lewis 2014; Sabsay 2012; also Farris 2017 on gender rights). Expanding these research agendas is important, as is situating the queer-of-colour critique in dialogue with decolonial and black feminism, which, as we have highlighted, explores the global character of colonial heteronormativity and gender (see also Mendoza 2015). Kengura Macharia's recent work, for instance, has extended aspects of the queer-of-colour critique by arguing that struggles over sex, gender, desire and eroticism are central to black freedom struggles across Africa and Afro diasporas (Macharia 2019). Macharia (2016b) reminds us that studies of sexuality (even when they refer to a queer-of-colour critique) still often rely on knowledge produced by and for populations in the Global North, where regions and countries in Africa are reduced to 'cases' or sites for the extraction of data, rather than places of holding rich bodies of knowledge and scholarship.

This is important when we consider the link between heteronormativity, race and migration. Ferguson's work on 'taxonomies of perversion' is useful for exploring how sexuality is central to the regulation of global movement. Border regimes, integration strategies, citizenship practices, asylum policies, refugee resettlement schemes and camp structures continue to regulate the movement and treatment of people based on heteronormative and western ideals of value and worth. Considering questions of sexuality, we might ask, for example, how do family migration regimes or refugee resettlement schemes continue to privilege heteronormative ideals of kinship and intimacy – such as marriage, monogamy, child rearing – in the distribution of visas, citizenship and nationhood (Oswin 2010)? Ferguson's work reminds us that normative sexuality (family, domesticity, intimacy) works to exclude queer subjects but also queer racialized subjects. Exploring how migration and refugee resettlement regimes categorize and judge whether someone is in a 'genuine' couple or partnership, or is a true parent or 'good worker', means being attuned to the sexualized–racialized and colonial history of who can be a 'genuine couple', a 'real family' or a productive labourer and equally how this structures the exclusion of other modes of kinship, desire and intimacies (see Turner 2020 for more on this).

In the context of liberal states that may extend family rights to same-sex partnerships, we can also consider how work on homonormativity in the context of the 'taxonomy of perversions' may sustain and privilege particular groups and further exclude others. How might wealthy white gay partnerships be included in a way that harnesses the expulsion of other non-homonormative/ heteronormative relations? How are regimes of LGBTQ+ rights used to shore up and justify restriction on the movement of Muslim populations? How do migration regimes that foster domestic labour rely upon and produce heteronormative ideas of worth and value? How are these sexualized categories of value/worth reproduced by racialized capitalism and the ongoing unequal extraction of resources and accumulation of wealth (for example, see Lee 2018)?

If anyone was in doubt about the seriousness of issues of sexuality, which are too often reduced to questions of preference or desire, exploring sexuality as always already gendered and racialized helps remind us of the centrality of intimacies to world politics, the organization of modern states and material inequality (Peterson 2014, 2020). Under liberal imperial capitalism, global wealth remains distributed by birthright and access to citizenship, often of northern rich states (whose wealth is gained through colonialism). However, access to citizenship remains restricted (primarily) to reproduction and inheritance through parentage. So as V. Spike Peterson argues, who can gain access to rights of citizenship, through reproduction and through family law, remains a central method through which global racialized inequality is reproduced and sustained in the modern world (Peterson 2020). How sexualities and intimacies are regulated, permitted by law and given social and legal acceptance is not a small 'private question' but a question of the distribution of mobility and resources globally and of people's rights, access to resources, shelter, wealth, work and survival. Thinking through Ferguson's work on heteronormativity and citizenship thus helps us realize what is at stake in the regulation of sexualities globally and the colonial structuring of that regulation.

Conclusion

In this chapter, we have explored how decolonial, postcolonial and black feminisms and queer-of-colour scholarship can be drawn upon to consider questions of mobility and migration, or more precisely to rethink and produce alternatives to how migration studies produce knowledge on people on the move. We illustrated how we might connect important work in these traditions with burgeoning work on gender and sexuality in migration, borders, citizenship and refugee studies.

We argued that engaging with the work of Maria Lugones, Hortense Spillers and Roderick Ferguson is productive for providing new concepts and analytical positions that place colonialism, race and history at the centre of feminist and queer scholarship. Lugones's coloniality of gender provides tools to question the universality of gender, which ruptures white feminist scholarship but also, and as importantly, shows alternative ways of considering how heteropatriarchal systems of gender and sexuality continue to be imposed and structure dispossession and violence globally. This can be useful for considering how mobility is organized in terms of South–South relations but also in the experiences of indigenous communities, Afro diasporas and those subject to deracination by imperial and postcolonial states. Spillers' work asks us to consider how the violence and history of slavery provides a different story surrounding gender and feminism. Examining Spillers' notion of ungendering, we discussed how this concept can help us understand and rethink analysis of race and gender as well as of work looking at 'family' in migration studies. Last, we examined Ferguson's approach to queer-of-colour critique, which emphasizes the role of sexuality, normativity and desire in processes of racialization and producing race around 'taxonomies of perversion'. Ferguson's focus on historical materialism reminds us of the centrality of capitalism to the production and regulation of categories of bodies, intimacies, reproduction and labour. Following debates within queer-of-colour critique, we showed how a focus on racialized heteronormativity and homonormativity is productive for analysing policies on integration, asylum, visa regimes and so on.

These insights can not only help us better understand systems of mobility today and how they are gendered and sexualized, but they also challenge us to confront how we think of gender and sexuality as universal and naturalized lived experiences. In the spirit of these critiques, it is important to not divorce analysis present in these scholars' work from their commitments to social justice, including decolonial justice for 'migrant' groups and communities. In challenging the violence of colonial systems of gender and sexuality, which have defined people and groups as 'deviant' and perverse, this scholarship is also a call for the emergence of radical alternatives, not just of different performances of gender and sexuality but to remake the material structures of world politics that would also sustain and foster (rather than tolerate or 'recognize') different forms of gender relations, intimacy and desire.

8
Conclusion

We started this book with a series of provocations – that migration studies has historically failed to engage with past and ongoing forms of (neo)-colonialism and imperialism which shape mobility today, and has equally failed to substantially engage with scholarship that centres colonialism within theory and analysis. We called this failure a product of 'sanctioned ignorance' so as to recognize that this failure is systematic, institutional and thus a collective (rather than individual) phenomenon and responsibility. This book has thus attempted to provide migration studies scholars with resources to begin, to support and/or to enhance this necessary engagement. The guiding logic here has been to showcase debates and literatures which are relevant to questions around migration and mobility but rarely form part of the 'canon' of texts and theories which migration scholars are exposed to or that are taught to students. This has meant drawing upon diverse fields of scholarship from postcolonial, decolonial theory, TWAIL, black feminism and queer-of-colour critiques. In some instances, we have been able to highlight emergent debates from scholars working on issues of migration from these perspectives; in other cases, we have illustrated the need for and relevance of applying these perspectives to the various related interests of migration studies. The central argument we have put forward here is that it should not be possible to study migration without at least engaging with these approaches, and that our understanding of contemporary migration is made more historically accurate and analytically rigorous for doing so.

In order to develop an account of migration studies after colonialism, we proposed two interconnected ways to understand the role of colonialism today: (1) as a form of knowledge which shapes a Eurocentric understanding of modernity; (2) as an ongoing system of global power, inequality and racism. In the early chapters of the book, we set out theories and the key debates necessary for understanding this account of colonialism and we sought to show how it shapes both migration and mobility (who moves, where, why, how) and how we study migration and mobility.

We showed how migration studies, like most of the social sciences, remains firmly embedded in a Eurocentric account of linear (or developmental) progress and time. We then demonstrated how this shapes the meta-theoretical assumptions that underpin studies of migration, for example, that there are distinct nation-state units of analysis, and that migration is movement from one sovereign state to another, that migration is bound up with 'development', and so on. Whilst geographical movement is important to migration studies, so too is temporality, and we showed how this often replicates a mapping of the world where 'backward' peoples are viewed as travelling into or towards 'modernity'. Challenging this Eurocentric account of modernity which was produced through colonial accounts of the 'uncivilized', we propose that it might be more appropriate to think about multiple modernities (pluriverses) or 'connected' histories which powerfully subvert a singular and developmental account of world history as *European*. Rather than only critiquing the field as Eurocentric – as if it can't change – we highlighted ways of thinking which both reveal the problems with dominant narratives and seek to produce new forms of interconnected histories and recover subordinated forms of knowledge.

If we are to take Eurocentrism within migration studies seriously, this also means reckoning with histories of colonialism and with this the legacies and reformulations of colonial racism which relate to migration. Drawing upon theories of race and racialization, we showed how ideas around race were central to colonialism but also how 'migration' and mobility were central to the organization of colonial and imperial rule. We showed how ideas of race shaped who could move, where and under what conditions, whether through projects of settler colonialism, enslavement, genocide or indentured labour. Just as forms of colonial rule, violence, dispossession and accumulation forced peopled from their land, colonialism and imperialism have created economic dependencies and wealth inequalities within the global capitalist system which conditions contemporary patterns of movement today. Whilst migration studies have broadly sidestepped an analytics of race and racialization, we showed how race plays a central role in contemporary migration regimes, not just in immigration debates but in the forms of control and security used to govern people on the move, through processes of citizenship, rights and settlement, to the lived experiences of migrants and 'host' societies. On one hand, we propose that we need to understand how race shapes global mobility today because of both the legacies of colonialism and ongoing forms of neo-colonialism and imperialism. On the other, we proposed that we need to understand how race shapes how we understand 'migration' in the first place, including who can be recognized, identified or viewed as a 'migrant'. This is because the control of mobility from its inception was concerned with the control and management of people racialized as non-white. Migration and the control of migration we inherited today began as a system of control under European empire and has always been about racialized mobility. We need to start our analysis of contemporary migration by reckoning with this and its ongoing effects.

Understanding and critiquing Eurocentric knowledge formation and understanding the work that racialization does in contemporary migration formed two central themes that ran through this book. These two interconnected ideas were reflected upon as we explored different events, debates and processes that occupy contemporary migration studies (such as sovereignty, citizenship, forced migration, security, gender and sexuality). The emphasis here was on positively demonstrating and illustrating what engagement with work from postcolonial, decolonial, TWAIL and black studies (amongst other) scholars could do, the different perspective it offers, the different research agendas that could be enhanced and developed. One of the key themes we addressed was how the fundamental units of analysis at the heart of migration studies start to look very different once we take colonial histories, race and Eurocentrism seriously.

In chapter 4, we examined how it is important to historicize some of the fundamental concepts so central to research on migration studies (and cognitive fields such as border, citizenship, integration studies): sovereignty and citizenship. Drawing on critical work on racialized sovereignty and 'connected' sociologies, we showed how the nation-statist concept of sovereignty covers up a far more complex series of international dependencies that challenge how we think about the foundations of rights and 'inclusion/exclusion'. If we start with colonial histories which shape and continue into the present, the whole conception of 'migration' (i.e. a subject moving across international state borders) looks very different. We considered some of the implications for questions of mobility and rights once we recognize that sovereignty and citizenship have worked transnationally across different colonized spaces and peoples, creating global networks of dependencies new and old. This raises some important questions for how migration should be analysed by scholars today. For example, we could consider that the vast majority of mobility from the Global South to the Global North is not of 'migrants' but of 'postcolonial citizens' with a historical claim to the political rights of many northern metropoles. This then has important implications for how 'migration' is analysed globally, how 'migrant' and 'host' experiences are accounted for, and how 'integration' is theorized and practised (just some areas of research central to contemporary migration studies). Rethinking the categories of both 'citizen' and 'migrant' is of fundamental importance. However, we also stressed that this account is further complicated once we examine indigenous scholarship on sovereignty, which challenges both the rights of settlers and 'arrivants' (such as racialized migrants and enslaved populations) to settler-colonized lands. In this case, we showed how denaturalizing and challenging statist concepts of sovereignty and citizenship open up new possibilities for rethinking migration studies but also create new challenges and tensions.

In the same way that we challenged the core assumptions of migration studies in chapter 4, we sought to show how postcolonial and decolonial thought can help us rethink burgeoning literature on forced migration (chapter 5), security (chapter 6) and gender and sexuality (chapter 7). These literatures and debates were chosen because refugee and forced migration studies represent important sub-fields connected to migration studies. Equally, questions of border security have expanded in the context of the 'war on terror', and gender and sexuality are not only being 'mainstreamed' in migration studies but are also on the agenda of international organizations. Across all of these separate chapters, we set out to show how postcolonial and decolonial scholarship offered a new starting point from which to view forced migration, security and gender and sexuality. This allowed us to showcase debates 'outside' of migration studies and their relevance but also to highlight the emergent work within the field from scholars drawing upon postcolonial and decolonial perspectives.

We have focused on work that sought to historicize events, analyse the role of race and racialization, and decentre western and Eurocentric knowledge. In the context of refugee and forced migration studies, we examined how the concept of deracination and necropolitics could help us rethink the fundamentals of forced migration by challenging the presentism of current research. We showed how deracination places incidents of 'forced migration' inside a longer history of dispossession, violence and forced movement. Whilst deracination helps us understand the conditions of forced migrations differently, we proposed that necropolitics helps us recognize the global networks of containment and (often mundane) violence that structure 'refugee reception' in Europe, Australia and North America. In this way, we refute the idea that postcolonial theorizing somehow only concerns ex-colonies, or even just ex-colonies and metropoles. Colonialism was a global/local system. In a related fashion, we explored the role of anti-Muslim racism in organizing border security and showed how this is a continuity of colonial forms of control and dehumanization. As with 'forced migration', we demonstrated how border security needs to be placed in a longer history of colonial racism, imperial warfare and racialized capitalism and engage scholarship from the Global South which is so often ignored in existing (even critical) debates in migration, citizenship and security studies. The global 'war on terror' starts to look very different once we engage with the perspectives of those whose insecurity is produced by the North's 'security'. In the last chapter on gender and sexuality, we likewise sought to explore the often overlooked experiences of colonized populations and women racialized as non-white by engaging with decolonial, black feminist and queer-of-colour theorists. We aimed to challenge work in migration studies that presents gender and sexuality as either a 'variable' or a universal form of subjectivity. Instead, we examined how concepts of gender as coloniality, ungendering and taxonomies of perversion provide starting points for both theorizing gender, sexuality and movement differently (often through theories of colonial racism) and rethinking white western feminism.

Throughout these chapters, we have stressed how postcolonial, decolonial and TWAIL scholarship provides a different set of concepts, theories and research agendas ignored not only in mainstream migration studies but also in more self-declared 'critical' approaches, for example, post-structuralist-influenced approaches to border security, 'securitization' or forced migration, which have elided a deeper engagement with questions of race, coloniality and white supremacy. Feminist approaches, too, have engaged with questions of gender and sexuality as systems of power but failed to engage with feminists who have argued that gender is a particular European form of subjectivity, imposed upon colonized people through empire. This is important because the wider structures of academic research mean critical theories can also be subject to colonial amnesia. One of the key areas in which we attempted to confront 'critical scholarship' was in debates on 'open borders'. This has been a mainstay position of progressive political movements and critical scholars. Whilst sharing some sympathy with the intention of this type of strategy, we also showed how this often ignores some of the broader colonial inequalities that would make a truly 'open-border' world potentially problematic and regressive. And we highlighted aspects of indigenous scholarship on sovereignty which upholds the need for indigenous peoples to claim fundamental political and spiritual rights to their lands. These positions problematize the call to 'open borders', though they of course have not gone unchallenged.

One of the key intentions of the book was to help think migration through questions of the colonial. But as we have substantiated throughout, this is not solely about the critique of existing studies and theories. Instead, we have hopefully been steadfast in our commitment to introduce overviews of the positive impact that often neglected forms of knowledge can bring to this area of research. For example, how work on deracination provides a different starting point for an analysis of forced migration and refugee studies (chapter 5); or how Southern African scholarship provides a different set of meta-theoretical assumptions through which we gain a different insight into border security (chapter 6); or how 'connected histories' provide a set of tools to analyse mobility and 'migrant' experiences differently, challenging linear Eurocentric notions of time and progress (chapter 4). In some cases, this has meant exploring scholarship still often sidelined within western academic studies of migration (for example, postcolonial and decolonial theory), in other cases it has meant exploring knowledge which seeks to challenge the primacy of western academic research altogether (for example, debates in indigenous scholarship; see chapter 4). We do not read any of this work as critique for the sake of critique; we have sought to show how this represents a commitment to fundamentally disturb dominant views of the global power and knowledge bound to it. For example, in the case of engaging scholarship on 'Islamic resistance' (chapter 6), we aimed to show how a subordinated form of knowledge completely changes how we think of a vital concept such as 'terrorism'. The force of this kind of work is to focus on developing new strategies of research which work within and beyond Eurocentric accounts.

This equally relates to our own positionality, parochialisms and blind spots within this project. As we highlighted in the introduction, we are white, western, 'cis'-gender researchers working in elite institutions. We do not profess to be able to transcend these positionalities and colonial systems of power in the writing of this book. In this way, when we have engaged with forms of marginalized, postcolonial, southern and indigenous knowledge, we have done so to challenge the dominant, colonial, northern, western perspective and to also treat this knowledge as open to engagement and critique. We have tried to be reflexive and fair to those texts and present them in a way that does justice to the content of the argument. However, as we stated in the introduction, the point of this book is as a guide and a reference point to those texts for students and scholars who have not previously encountered such work, so we urge you – don't just trust our interpretations – please go read them yourself! Do not cite this book; please cite the original sources. Equally, far from being a fixed testament to this scholarship, we write this book to welcome further critique and to open up further productive lines of research and engagement, not to close them down.

Rather than substantiating and developing one overarching theoretical position throughout this book, we have instead been seeking to summarize and contextualize important debates and also to be clear about areas of tension and disagreement across different bodies of scholarship. Postcolonial, decolonial, TWAIL, black studies and Third World, black, decolonial feminist scholars follow different intellectual traditions. Not all of the positions we have articulated in this book naturally work together. As we highlighted in chapter 3 on race, there are debates between decolonial and black studies scholars which are not obviously or easily reconcilable. Equally, as we discussed in chapter 4, there are tensions and potential disagreements between TWAIL positions on postcolonial citizenship and reparations and indigenous scholarship on sovereignty. We do not seek to sidestep these tensions but instead reveal them as open areas of contestation which deserve further engagement. There is no one theory or pathway to a 'postcolonial' or 'decolonial' analysis. Instead, we have hoped to illustrate open threads to support reflexive insights, forms of learning and unlearning and, tentatively, the potential for new and exciting research agendas.

These tensions and potential contradictions are equally reflected in debates on decolonizing research and universities. Fraught discussions continue over levels of violence, complicity and radical versus conservative positions on questions of decolonizing. To many, decolonial projects are in danger of being co-opted by elite institutions and by elite (white) scholars who risk mainstreaming ideas in the search to appear 'diverse' or to catch 'hot topics' and increase their own social capital. Equally, the radical potential of decolonizing is potentially lost, as Tuck and Yang (2012) propose, when it is made into an intellectual exercise or becomes a question of knowledge production and, in the university context, is settled in practices of audits, reading lists and decolonizing seminars. Such perspectives have of course been contested, with Bhambra, Gebrial and Nişancıoğlu (2018) arguing that university is a key site of knowledge production and validation which has significant influence on broader discourse. Rather than silence those critical challenges, we have instead found their provocations a useful political and ethical strategy and have allowed them to remain largely unreconciled throughout the time of writing. It is important to recognize that activist challenges to scholarly efforts at centring colonialism in knowledge production cannot and should not be easily glossed over or forgotten, and to remind ourselves of the politicality of this research and writing process. Nevertheless, for us the bigger risk is that there is less reading of, dialogue with and influence from these important and necessary bodies of work, which seem surprisingly easy for some to ignore. Equally, and as noted in the introduction, writing books should never be the only work that we do.

Despite the fraught tensions that surround decolonizing debates, what we hope that readers will take away from this book is the need to take colonial histories and coloniality (ongoing forms of colonial power and knowledge) seriously. Migration scholarship not only exists in a deeply colonially inflected world but plays a part in how the world and those global systems of power are reproduced. As we have hopefully demonstrated, the subject matter of migration studies should be colonialism (or at least a central part of any research agenda!). Colonialism has shaped and birthed migration studies. Colonialism continues to condition why, how and where people move, just as it shapes the forms of knowledge we have about what migration *is* in migration studies (who is a migrant vs a citizen, what is sovereignty, the nation, etc.), as well as the fact that colonialism produced the forms of racialized management that control 'migration'. Whilst the majority of migration studies is firmly located in the 'here and now' and attuned to vital questions of our contemporary moment, what we need to suspend (and, perhaps more than this, unlearn) is the idea that being attuned to what seem like questions of 'history' and the 'past' are not important for understanding the 'here and now'. Instead, we need to recognize how colonialism is far from over. In terms of structural inequalities of migration, racialized capitalism and the structures of violence in our world, colonialism is very much alive and well. Issues of the 'past' continue to play out today, whether in forms of normalized dehumanization or ideas about who is 'deserving' of rights. In this context, doing historical analysis or uncovering structures of contemporary colonialism is far from an indulgence but is instead a vital and invaluable analytical practice.

References

Abbas, T. (2012) 'The Symbiotic Relationship between Islamophobia and Radicalisation', *Critical Studies on Terrorism* 5(3): 345–58.

Abrahamsen, R. (2018) 'Return of the Generals: Global Militarism in Africa from the Cold War to the Present', *Security Dialogue* 49(1–2): 19–31.

Achiume, E. T. (2019) 'Migration as Decolonization', *Stanford Law Review* 71(6): 1509–74.

Adeyanju, C. T. and Oriola, T. B. (2011) 'Colonialism and Contemporary African Migration: A Phenomenological Approach', *Journal of Black Studies* 42(6): 943–67.

Agathangelou, A. (2010) 'Bodies of Desire, Terror and the War in Eurasia: Impolite Disruptions of (Neo)Liberal Internationalism, Neoconservatism and the "New" Imperium', *Millennium* 38(3): 1–30.

Agathangelou, A. (2016) 'Throwing Away the "Heavenly Rule Book": The World Revolution in the Bandung Spirit and Poetic Solidarities', in Q. N. Pham and R. Shilliam (eds), *Meanings of Bandung: Postcolonial Orders and Decolonial Visions*. London: Rowman and Littlefield.

Agathangelou, A. M. and Killian, K. D. (2016) *Time, Temporality and Violence in International Relations: (De)fatalizing the Present, Forging Radical Alternatives*. Abingdon: Routledge.

Ahmed, S. (2000) *Strange Encounters: Embodied Others in Post-Coloniality*. London: Routledge.

Ahmed, S. (2011) 'Problematic Proximities: Or Why Critiques of Gay Imperialism Matter', *Feminist Legal Studies* 19(2): 119–32.

Ahmed, S. (2012) *On Being Included: Racism and Diversity in Institutional Life*. Durham, NC: Duke University Press.

Ahram, A. (2019) 'Sexual Violence, Competitive State Building, and Islamic State in Iraq and Syria', *Journal of Intervention and Statebuilding* 13(2): 180–96.

Ake, C. (2000 [1979]) *Social Science as Imperialism: The Theory of Political Development*. Ibadan, Nigeria: Ibadan University Press.

Alatas, S. F. (2006) *Alternative Discourses in Asian Social Science: Responses to Eurocentrism*. Thousand Oaks, CA: Sage.

Ali, N. and Whitham, B. (2018) 'The Unbearable Anxiety of Being: Ideological Fantasies of British Muslims beyond the Politics of Security', *Security Dialogue* 49(5): 400–17.

Alldred, P. (2003) 'No Borders, No Nations, No Deportations', *Feminist Review* 73(1): 152–7.

Allen, P. G. (1992 [1986]) *The Sacred Hoop: Recovering the Feminine in American Indian Traditions*. Boston, MA: Beacon Press.

Amadiume, I. (1989) *Male Daughters, Female Husbands: Gender and Sex in an African Society*. London: Zed Books.

Amar, P. (2013) *The Security Archipelago: Human-Security States, Sexuality Politics, and the End of Neoliberalism*. Durham, NC: Duke University Press.

Amighetti, S. and Nuti, A. (2016) 'A Nation's Right to Exclude and the Colonies', *Political Theory* 44(4): 541–66.

Amin, S. (1988) *Eurocentrism*. London: Zed Books.

Amoore, L. (2006) 'Biometric Borders: Governing Mobilities in the War on Terror', *Political Geography* 25(3): 336–51.

Anderson, B. (2013) *Us and Them? The Dangerous Politics of Immigration Controls*. Oxford: Oxford University Press.

Anderson, B. (2019) 'New Directions in Migration Studies: Towards Methodological De-nationalism', *Comparative Migration Studies* 7(36).

Anderson, B., Sharma, N. and Wright, C. (2009) 'Editorial: Why No Borders?', *Refuge* 26(2): 5–18.

Andrews, K. (2018) *Back to Black*. London: Zed Books.

Anghie, A. (2008) *Imperialism, Sovereignty, and the Making of International Law. Cambridge Studies in International and Comparative Law*. Cambridge: Cambridge University Press.

Anievas, A. and Nişancioğlu, K. (2013) 'What's at Stake in the Transition Debate? Rethinking the Origins of Capitalism and the "Rise of the West"', *Millennium Journal of International Studies* 42(1): 78–102.

Anievas, A. and Nişancioğlu, K. (2015) *How the West Came to Rule: The Geopolitical Origins of Capitalism*. London: Pluto Press.

Ansems de Vries, L., Coleman, L. M., Rosenow, D., Tazzioli, M. and Vázquez, R. (2017) 'Collective Discussion: Fracturing Politics (or, How to Avoid the Tacit Reproduction of Modern/Colonial Ontologies in Critical Thought)', *International Political Sociology* 11(1): 90–108.

Anzaldúa, G. (1987) *Borderlands/La Frontera: The New Mestiza*. San Francisco: Aunt Lute Books.

Appleyard, R. (2001) 'International Migration Policies: 1950–2000', *International Migration* 39(6): 7–20.

Arendt, H. (1951) *The Origins of Totalitarianism*. New York: Schocken Books.

Arunima, G. (1995) 'Matriliny and Its Discontents', *India International Centre Quarterly* 22(2/3): 157–67.

Arvin, M., Tuck, E. and Morrill, A. (2013) 'Decolonizing Feminism: Challenging Connections between Settler Colonialism and Heteropatriarchy', *Feminist Formations* 25(1): 8–34.

Asad, T. (1979) 'Anthropology and the Colonial Encounter', in G. Huizer and B. Mannheim (eds), *The Politics of Anthropology: From Colonialism and Sexism Toward a View from Below*. Paris: Mouton.

Austin, M. S. (1992) 'A Culture Divided by the United States–Mexico Border: The Tohono O'Odham Claim for Border Crossing Rights', *Arizona Journal of International and Comparative Law* 8: 97–116.

Baaz, M. E. and Verweijen, M. J. (2018) 'Confronting the Colonial: The (Re)Production of "African" Exceptionalism in Critical Security and Military Studies', *Security Dialogue* 49(1/2): 57–69.

Bacchetta, P., Maira, S. and Winant, H. (eds) (2018) *Global Raciality: Empire, PostColoniality, DeColoniality*. Abingdon: Routledge.

Baker, A. H., Diawara, M. and Lindeborg, R. H. (eds) (1996) *Black British Cultural Studies: A Reader*. Chicago: University of Chicago Press.

Baker, C. (2018) *Race and the Yugoslav Region: Postsocialist, Post-conflict, Postcolonial?* Manchester: Manchester University Press.

Balzacq, T. and Carerra, S. (2016) *Security versus Freedom? A Challenge for Europe's Future*. Abingdon: Routledge.

Banaji, J. (2007) 'Islam, the Mediterranean and the Rise of Capitalism', *Historical Materialism* 15: 47–74.

Barabantseva, E., Ní Mhurchú, A. and Peterson, V. S. (2019) 'Introduction: Engaging Geopolitics through the Lens of the Intimate', *Geopolitics*, DOI: 10.1080/14650045.2019.1636558\

Barber, M. and Ripley, S. (1988) 'Refugee Rights', in P. Sieghart (ed.), *Human Rights in the United Kingdom*. London: Human Rights Network.

Barkawi, T. (2016) 'Decolonising War', *European Journal of International Security* 1(2): 199–214.

Barker, M. (1981) *The New Racism*. London: Junction Books.

Bauder, H. (2014) 'The Possibilities of Open and No Borders', *Social Justice* 39(4): 76–96.

Bauman, Z. (2000) *Liquid Modernity*. Cambridge: Polity Press.

Bayat, A. (2010) *Life as Politics: How Ordinary People Change the Middle East*. Stanford: Stanford University Press.

Bell, D. (2016) *Reordering the World: Essays on Liberalism and Empire*. Princeton: Princeton University Press.

Bennett, C. and Thomas, F. (2013) 'Seeking Asylum in the UK: Lesbian Perspectives', *Forced Migration Review* 42. Available at https://www.fmreview.org/sogi/bennett-thomas

Berlant, L. (2007) 'Slow Death (Sovereignty, Obesity, Lateral Agency)', *Critical Inquiry* 33(4): 754–80.

Besteman, C. (2019) 'Militarised Global Apartheid', *Cultural Anthropology* 60(19): 526–38.

Bettini, G. and Gioli, G. (2016) 'Waltz with Development: Insights on the Developmentalization of Climate-induced Migration', *Migration and Development* 5(2): 171–89.

Bhabha, H. K. (2005 [1994]) *The Location of Culture*. London: Routledge.

Bhabha, J. (2004) 'Demography and Rights: Women, Children and Access to Asylum', *International Journal of Refugee Law* 16(2): 228–43.

Bhambra, G. K. (2007) *Rethinking Modernity: Postcolonialism and the Sociological Imagination*. Basingstoke: Palgrave Macmillan.

Bhambra, G. K. (2010) 'Historical Sociology, International Relations and Connected Histories', *Cambridge Review of International Affairs* 23(1): 127–43.

Bhambra, G. K. (2011) 'Historical Sociology, Modernity, and Postcolonial Critique', *American Historical Review* 116(3): 653–62.

Bhambra, G. K. (2014) *Connected Sociologies*. London: Bloomsbury.

Bhambra, G. K. (2017a) 'Brexit, Trump, and "Methodological Whiteness": On the Misrecognition of Race and Class', *British Journal of Sociology* 68(S1): 214–32.

Bhambra, G. K. (2017b) 'The Current Crisis of Europe: Refugees, Colonialism, and the Limits of Cosmopolitanism', *European Law Journal* 23(5): 395–405.

Bhambra, G. K. (2019) 'On European "Civilization": Colonialism, Land, Lebensraum', in Nick Aikens, Jyoti Mistry and Corina Oprea (eds), *Living with Ghosts: Legacies of Colonialism and Fascism*. L'Internationale, https://www.internationaleonline.org/bookshelves/living_with_ghosts_legacies_of_colonialism_and_fascism

Bhambra, G. K. (forthcoming) 'Colonial Global Economy: Towards a Theoretical Reorintation of Political Economy', *Review of International Political Economy*, special issue on 'Blind Spots in IPE'.

Bhambra, G. K., Gebrial, D. and Nişancıoğlu, K. (eds) (2018) *Decolonising the University*. London: Pluto Press.

Bhambra, G. K. and Holmwood, J. (2018) 'Colonialism, Postcolonialism and the Liberal Welfare State', *New Political Economy* 23(5): 574–87.

Bhambra, G. K. and Shilliam, R. (eds) (2008) *Silencing Human Rights: Critical Engagements with a Contested Project*. London: Palgrave.

Bhandar, B. (2018) *Colonial Lives of Property: Law, Land and Racial Regimes of Ownership*. Durham, NC: Duke University Press.

Bhatia, A. (2013) 'We Are All Here to Stay? Indigeneity, Migration and "Decolonizing" the Treaty Right to Be Here', *Windsor Year Book of Access to Justice* 3(1): 39–64.

Bhattacharyya, G. (2018) *Rethinking Racial Capitalism: Questions of Reproduction and Survival*. London: Rowman and Littlefield.

Bhui, H. S. (2016) 'The Place of "Race" in Understanding Immigration

Control and the Detention of Foreign Nationals', *Criminology and Criminal Justice* 16(3): 267–85.

Bialasiewicz, L. (2012) 'Off-Shoring and Out-Sourcing the Borders of EUrope: Libya and EU Border Work in the Mediterranean', *Geopolitics* 17(4): 843–66.

Bilge, S. (2013) 'Intersectionality Undone: Saving Intersectionality from Feminist Intersectionality Studies', *Du Bois Review* (10): 405–24.

Bilgen, P. (2016) *The International in Security, Security in the International*. Abingdon: Routledge.

Bilgin, P. and Herz, M. (2019) *Critical Security Studies in the Global South*. London: Palgrave Macmillan.

Bilgin, P. and Morton, A. D. (2002) 'Historicising Representations of "Failed States": Beyond the Cold-War Annexation of the Social Sciences?', *Third World Quarterly* 23(1): 55–80.

Biswas, S. and Nair, S. (2009) *International Relations and States of Exception: Margins, Peripheries, and Excluded Bodies*. London: Routledge.

Blackburn, R. (2013) *The American Crucible: Slavery, Emancipation and Human Rights*. London: Verso.

Blakeley, R. (2011) *State Terrorism and Neoliberalism: The North in the South*. Abingdon: Routledge.

Blanc-Szanton, C., Glick Schiller, N. and Basch, L. (1992) *Towards a Transnational Perspective on Migration: Nationalism Reconsidered*. Baltimore: Johns Hopkins University Press.

Blaney, D. and Inayatullah, N. (2009) *Savage Economics: Wealth, Poverty and the Temporal Walls of Capitalism*. London: Routledge.

Bledsoe, A. and Wright, W. J. (2019) 'The Anti-Blackness of Global Capital', *Environment and Planning D: Society and Space* 37(1): 8–26.

Bleich, E. (2005) 'The Legacies of History? Colonization and Immigrant Integration in Britain and France', *Theory and Society* 34(2): 171–95.

Bloch, A. and Dona, G. (eds) (2018) *Forced Migration: Current Issues and Debates*. London: Routledge.

Blomley, N. (2008) 'Enclosure, Common Right and the Property of the Poor', *Social & Legal Studies* 17(3): 311–31.

Bohmer, C. and Shuman, A. (2008) *Rejecting Refugees: Political Asylum in the 21st Century*. London: Routledge.

Bonilla-Silva, E. (2003) *Racism without Racists*. London: Rowman and Littlefield.

Bonilla-Silva, E. (2015) 'The Structure of Racism in Color-Blind, "Post-Racial" America', *American Behavioral Scientist* 59(11): 1358–76.

Bonjour, S. and Duyvendak, J. W. (2018) 'The "Migrant with Poor Prospects": Racialized Intersections of Class and Culture in Dutch Civic Integration Debates', *Ethnic and Racial Studies* 41(5): 882–900.

Boulila, S. (2019) *Race in Post-Racial Europe: An Intersectional Analysis*. London: Rowman & Littlefield International.

Brachet, J. (2016) 'Policing the Desert: The IOM in Libya Beyond War and Peace', *Antipode* 48(2): 272–92.

Branch, J. (2012) '"Colonial Reflection" and Territoriality: The Peripheral Origins of Sovereign Statehood', *European Journal of International Relations* 18(2): 277–97.

Brettell, C. and Hollifield, J. F. (2008) *Migration Theory: Talking across Disciplines*, 2nd edn. London: Routledge.

Broeck, S. and Saucier, P. K. (2016) 'A Dialogue: On European Borders, Black Movement, and the History of Social Death', *Black Studies Papers* 2(1): 23–45.

Brown, C. (1992) 'Marxism and the Transnational Migration of People: Ethical Issues', in B. Barry and R. E. Goodin (eds), *Free Movement: Ethical Issues in the Transnational Migration of People and of Money*. New York: Harvester Wheatsheaf, pp. 127–44.

Brown, W. (2008) 'Tolerance as Civilization/Discourse', *Nomos* 48: 406–41.

Brown, W. (2010) *Walled States, Waning Sovereignty*. New York: Zone.

Browne, S. (2010) 'Digital Epidermalization: Race, Identity and Biometrics', *Critical Sociology* 36(1): 131–50.

Browne, S. (2015) *Dark Matters: On the Surveillance of Blackness*. Durham, NC: Duke University Press.

Buckley-Zistel, S. and Krause, U. (2017) *Gender, Violence and Refugees*. Oxford: Berghahn Books.

Buffon, G. L. (1776) 'Des mulets', in *Suppléments à l'Histoire Naturelle*. Paris: Imprimerie Royale.

Burnham, M. A. (1987) 'An Impossible Marriage: Slave Law and Family Law', *Law & Inequality* 5(2): 187–225.

Busbridge, R. (2013) 'Performing Colonial Sovereignty and the Israeli "Separation" Wall', *Social Identities* 19(5): 653–69.

Butler, J. (1990) *Gender Trouble*. London: Routledge.

Butler, J. (2009) *Frames of War: When Is Life Grievable?* London: Verso.

Buur, L., Jensen, S. and Stepputat, F. (eds) (2007) *The Security–Development Nexus: Expressions of Sovereignty and Securitization in Southern Africa*. Cape Town: Nordiska Africa Institute/HSRC Press.

Byrd, J. A. (2011) *The Transit of Empire: Indigenous Critiques of Colonialism*. Minneapolis, MN: University of Minnesota Press.

Cabral, A., Njinya-Mujinya, L. and Habomugisha, P. (1998) 'Published or Rejected? African Intellectuals Scripts and Foreign Journals, Publishers and Editors', *Nordic Journal of African Studies* 7(2): 83–94.

Calhoun, C. (2002) 'The Class Consciousness of Frequent Travellers: Towards a Critique of Actually Existing Cosmopolitans', in Steven Vertovec and Robin Cohen (eds), *Conceiving Cosmopolitanism: Theory, Context and Practice*. Oxford: Oxford University Press.

Cameron, D. (2011) 'PM's Speech at Munich Security Conference', *Cabinet Office*, 5 February. Available at: https://www.gov.uk/government/speeches/pms-speech-at-munich-security-conference

Camiscioli, E. (2009) *Reproducing the French Race: Immigration, Intimacy, and Embodiment in the Early Twentieth Century*. Durham, NC: Duke University Press.

Cantu, L. (2009) *The Sexuality of Migration: Border Crossings and Mexican Immigrant Men*. New York: New York University Press.

Carby, H. (1982) 'White Woman Listen! Black Feminism and the Boundaries of Sisterhood', in B. Ashcroft, G. Griffiths and H. Tiffin (eds), *The Empire Writes Back: Theory and Practice in Postcolonial Literatures*. London: Hutchinson, pp. 212–35.

Carens, J. (2015) *The Ethics of Immigration*. Oxford: Oxford University Press.

Casey, J. P. (2010) 'Open Borders: Absurd Chimera or Inevitable Future Policy?', *International Migration* 48(5): 14–62.

Castles, S., de Haas, H. and Miller, M. J. (2014) *The Age of Migration: International Population Movements in the Modern World*, 5th edn. New York and London: Palgrave Macmillan.

Castles, S., de Haas, H. and Miller, M. (2020) *The Age of Migration*, 6th edn. London: Palgrave Macmillan.

Caygill, H. (2013) *On Resistance: A Philosophy of Defiance*. London: Bloomsbury.

Chakrabarty, D. (2008) *Provincializing Europe: Postcolonial Thought and Historical Difference*. Princeton: Princeton University Press.

Charett, C. (2019) *Performing Politics: Hamas, the EU and the 2006 Palestinian Elections*. London: Routledge.

Chari, S. and Verdery, K. (2009) 'Thinking between the Posts: Postcolonialism, Postsocialism, and Ethnography after the Cold War', *Comparative Studies in Society and History* 51(1): 6–34.

Chatterjee, P. (1993) *The Nation and Its Fragments: Colonial and Postcolonial Histories*. Princeton: Princeton University Press.

Chatterjee, S. (2019) 'Immigration, Anti-Racism, and Indigenous Self-Determination: Towards a Comprehensive Analysis of the Contemporary Settler Colonial', *Social Identities* 25(5): 644–61.

Chavez, K. (2011) *Queer Migration Politics: Activist Rhetoric and Coalitional Possibilities*. Chicago: University of Illinois Press.

Chi-Kwan, M. (2007) 'The "Problem of People": British Colonials, Cold War Powers, and the Chinese Refugees in Hong Kong, 1949–62', *Modern Asian Studies* 41(6): 1145–81.

Chilisa, B. (2012) *Indigenous Research Methodologies*. London: Sage.

Chimni, B. S. (1998) 'The Geopolitics of Refugee Studies: A View from the South', *Journal of Refugee Studies* 11(4): 350–74.

Chimni, B. S. (2006) 'Third World Approaches to International Law: A Manifesto', *International Community Law Review* 8: 3–27.

Chimni, B. S. (2009) 'The Birth of a "Discipline": From Refugee to Forced Migration Studies', *Journal of Refugee Studies* 22(1): 11–29.

Clemens, M. A. (2014) 'Does Development Reduce Migration?', in R. E. B. Lucas (ed.), *International Handbook on Migration and Economic Development*. Cheltenham: Edward Elgar.

Coburn, E. (2016) 'Alternatives: Theorizing Colonialism and Indigenous Liberation: Contemporary Indigenous Scholarship from Lands Claimed by Canada', *Studies in Political Economy* 97(3): 285–307.

Cohen, C. (2005) 'Punks, Bulldaggers, and Welfare Queens: The Radical Potential of Queer Politics?', in E. P Johnson and M. Henderson (eds), *Black Queer Studies: A Critical Reader*. Durham, NC: Duke University Press, pp. 22–51.

Cohen, R. and Deng, F. M. (eds) (1998) *The Forsaken People: Case Studies of the Internally Displaced*. Washington, DC: Brookings Institution Press.

Cohen, R. and Jonsson, G. (eds) (2011) *Migration and Culture*. Cheltenham: Edward Elgar.

Collyer, F., Connell, R., Maia, J. and Morrell, R. (2019) *Knowledge and Global Power: Making New Sciences in the South*. Clayton, Australia: Monash University Press.

Combahee River Collective (1983 [1977]) 'The Combahee River Collective Statement', in B. Smith (ed.), *Home Girls: A Black Feminist Anthology*. New York: Kitchen Table, Women of Color Press, pp. 272–82.

Connell, R. (2018) 'Meeting at the Edge of Fear: Theory on a World Scale', in B. Reiter (ed.), *Constructing the Pluriverse*. Durham, NC: Duke University Press.

Cooper, F. and Packard, R. (1997) *International Development and the Social Sciences: Essays on the History and Politics of Knowledge*. Berkeley, CA: University of California Press.

Cooper, F. and Stoler, A. L. (1997) *Tensions of Empire: Colonial Cultures in a Bourgeois World*. Berkeley, CA: University of California Press.

Coulthard, G. (2014) *Red Skin, White Masks: Rejecting the Colonial Politics of Recognition*. Minneapolis, MN: University of Minnesota Press.

Cowen, D. and Gilbert, E. (2008) 'Fear and the Familial', in R. Pain, S. Graham and S. Smith (eds), *Fear: Critical Geopolitics and Everyday Life*. London: Ashgate, pp. 49–58.

Cowen, D. and Lewis, N. (2016) 'Anti-Blackness and Urban Geopolitical Economy', *Society and Space*. Available at: https://www.societyandspace. org/articles/anti-blackness-and-urban-geopolitical-economy

Crawley, H. (2011) '"Asexual, Apolitical Beings": The Interpretation of Children's Identities and Experiences in the UK Asylum System', *Journal of Ethnic and Migration Studies* 37(8): 1171–84.

Crawley, H. and Skleparis, D. (2018) 'Refugees, Migrants, Neither, Both: Categorical Fetishism and the Politics of Bounding in Europe's "Migration Crisis"', *Journal of Ethnic and Migration Studies* 44(1): 48–64.

Crenshaw, K. (1989) 'Demarginalizing the Intersection of Race and Sex: A Black Feminist Critique of Antidiscrimination Doctrine, Feminist Theory and Antiracist Politics', *University of Chicago Legal Forum* 140: 139–67.

Crisp, J. (2003) 'The Refugee and the Global Politics of Asylum', *Political Quarterly* 74(1): 75–87.

Crooke, A. (2009) *Resistance: The Essence of the Islamist Revolution*. London: Pluto Press.

Cross, H. (2013) 'Labour and Underdevelopment? Migration, Dispossession and Accumulation in West Africa and Europe', *Review of African Political Economy* 40(136): 202–18.

Cusicanqui, S. R. (2012) '*Ch'ixinakax utxiwa*: A Reflection on the Practices and Discourses of Decolonization', *South Atlantic Quarterly* 111(1): 95–109.

Dahmoon, R. K. (2011) 'Considerations on Mainstreaming Intersectionality', *Political Research Quarterly* 64(1): 230–43.

Danewid, I. (2017) 'White Innocence in the Black Mediterranean: Hospitality and the Erasure of History', *Third World Quarterly* 38(7): 1674–89.

Danewid, I. (2020) 'The Fire This Time: Grenfell, Racial Capitalism and the Urbanisation of Empire', *European Journal of International Relations* 26(1): 289–313.

D'Aoust, A.-M. (2013) 'In the Name of Love: Marriage Migration, Governmentality and Technologies of Love', *International Political Sociology* 7(3): 258–74.

D'Aoust, A.-M. (2017) 'A Moral Economy of Suspicion: Love and Marriage Migration Management Practices in the United Kingdom', *Environment and Planning D: Society and Space* 36(1): 40–59.

da Silva, D. F. (2007) *Toward a Global Idea of Race*. Minneapolis, MN: University of Minnesota Press.

da Silva, D. F. and Chakravartty, P. (2012) 'Accumulation, Dispossession, and Debt: The Racial Logic of Global Capitalism – An Introduction', *American Quarterly* 64(3): 361–85.

Daulatzai, S. (2012) *Black Star, Crescent Moon: The Muslim International and Black Freedom beyond America*. Minneapolis, MN: University of Minnesota Press.

Davies, D. and Boehmer, E. (2019) 'Postcolonialism and South–South Relations', in E. Fiddian-Qasmiyeh and P. Daley (eds), *Routledge Handbook of South–South Relations*. London: Routledge.

Davies, T. and Isakjee, A. (2018) 'Ruins of Empire: Refugees, Race and the Postcolonial Geographies of European Migrant Camps', *Geoforum* 102: 214–17.

Davies, T., Isakjee, A. and Dhesi, S. (2017) 'Violent Inaction: The Necropolitical Experience of Refugees in Europe', *Antipode* 49(5): 1263–84.

Davis, A. (2003) *Are Prisons Obsolete?*, New York: Seven Stories Press.

Davis, A. (2016) *Freedom Is a Constant Struggle*. New York: Haymarket Books.

Davis, A. Y. (1981) *Women, Race and Class*. New York: Random House.

Davis, M. (2006) *The Planet of Slums*. London: Verso.

De Genova, N. (2013) '"We Are of the Connections": Migration, Methodological Nationalism, and "Militant Research"', *Postcolonial Studies* 16(3): 250–8.

De Genova, N. (ed.) (2017) *The Borders of 'Europe': Autonomy of Migration, Tactics of Bordering*. Durham, NC: Duke University Press.

De Genova, N. (2018) 'The "Migrant Crisis" as Racial Crisis: Do Black Lives Matter in Europe?', *Ethnic and Racial Studies* 41(10): 1765–82.

De Haas, H. (2010) 'Migration and Development: A Theoretical Perspective', *International Migration Review* 44(1): 227–64.

De Haas, H. (2012) 'The Migration and Development Pendulum: A Critical View on Research and Policy', *International Migration* 50(3): 8–25.

De Jong, S. (2013) 'Intersectional Global Citizenship: Gendered and Racialized Renderings', *Politics, Groups and Identities* 1(3): 402–16.

De Jong, S., Icaza, R. and Rutazibwa, O. (2019) *Decolonization and Feminisms in Global Teaching and Learning*. Abingdon, Routledge.

De Jong, S., Koevoets, S. and van Leeuwen, F. (2014) *Gendered Fortress Europe*. Amsterdam: Amsterdam University Press.

Deloria, V. (1988) *Custer Died for Your Sins: An Indian Manifesto*. New York: Macmillan.

De Noronha, L. (2018) 'The "Windrush Generation" and "Illegal Immigrants" Are Both Our Kin', 30 April. Available at: https://www.versobooks.com/blogs/3771-the-windrush-generation-and-illegal-immigrants-are-both-our-kin

De Noronha, L. (2019) 'Deportation, Racism and Multi-Status Britain: Immigration Control and the Production of Race in the Present', *Ethnic and Racial Studies* 42(14): 2413–30.

De Norohna, L. (2020) *Deporting Black Britons: Portraits of Deportation to Jamaica*. Manchester: Manchester University Press.

Devika, J. (2005) 'The Aesthetic Woman: Re-forming Female Bodies and Minds in Early Twentieth-Century Kerala', *Modern Asian Studies* 39(2): 461–87.

Dhamoon, R. K. (2011) 'Considerations on Mainstreaming Intersectionality', *Political Research Quarterly* 64(1): 230–43.

Dillon, M. and Reid, J. (2009) *The Liberal Way of War: Killing to Make Life Live*. London: Routledge.

Dillon, S. (2012) 'Possessed by Death: The Neoliberal–Carceral State, Black Feminism, and the Afterlife of Slavery', *Radical History Review* 1(112): 113–25.

Dirks, N. B. (2006) *The Scandal of Empire: India and the Creation of Imperial Britain*. Delhi: Permanent Black.

Distretti, E. (2018) 'The Colonial Mediterranean, Anonymity and Migration Control', in O. Rutazibwa and R. Shilliam (eds), *The Routledge Handbook of Postcolonial Politics*. Abingdon: Routledge.

Dixit, P. (2014) 'Decolonizing Visuality in Security Studies: Reflections on the Death of Osama bin Laden', *Critical Studies on Security* 2(3): 337–51.

Donato, K. and Gabaccia, D. (2015) *Gender and International Migration*. London: Sage.

Driskill, Q., Finley, C., Gilley, B., Morgensen (eds) (2011) *Queer Indigenous Studies: Critical Interventions in Theory, Politics, and Literature*. Tucson, AZ: University of Arizona Press.

Drnovšek Zorko, S. (2019) 'Articulations of Race and Genealogies of Encounter among Former Yugoslav Migrants in Britain', *Ethnic and Racial Studies* 42(9): 1574–91.

Du Bois, W. E .B. (1965) *The World and Africa: An Inquiry into the Part Which Africa Has Played in World History*. New York: International Publishing.

Dubow, S. (1989) *Racial Segregation and the Origins of Apartheid in Twentieth Century South Africa, 1919–36*. London: Macmillan.

Duggan, L. (2004) *The Twilight of Equality: Neoliberalism, Cultural Politics, and the Attack on Democracy*. Chapel Hill: Beacon Press.

Dunbar-Ortiz, R. (2014) *An Indigenous Peoples' History of the United States*. Boston, MA: Beacon Press.

Dussel, E. (1995) 'Eurocentrism and Modernity (Introduction to the Frankfurt Lectures)', in J. Beverley, J. Oviedo and M. Aronn (eds), *The Postmodernism Debate in Latin America*. Durham, NC: Duke University Press, pp. 65–77.

Eastwood, J. (2018) 'Rethinking Militarism as Ideology: The Critique of Violence after Security', *Security Dialogue* 49(1–2): 44–56.

Edelman, L. (2004) *No Future: Queer Theory and the Death Drive*. Durham, NC: Duke University Press.

Elden, S. (2009) *Terror and Territory: The Spatial Extent of Sovereignty*. Minneapolis, MN: University of Minnesota Press.

El-Enany, N. (2020) *(B)ordering Britain: Law, Race and Empire*. Manchester: Manchester University Press.

Elliott-Cooper, A. (2016) 'State Violence from Old to New: From Slavery to Serco', in K. Andrews and L. Palmer (eds), *Blackness in Britain*. London: Routledge.

El-Tayeb, Fatima (2011) *European Others: Queering Ethnicity in Postnational Europe*. Minneapolis, MN: University of Minnesota Press.

Enloe, C. (2017) *The Big Push*. Berkeley, CA: University of California Press.

Erel, U. and Acik, E. (2020) 'Enacting Intersectional Multilayered Citizenship: Kurdish Women's Politics', *Gender, Place & Culture* 27(4): 479–501.

Erel, U., Haritaworn, J. and Gutiérrez Rodríguez, E. (2011) 'On the Depoliticisation of Intersectionality Talk: Conceptualising Multiple Oppressions in Critical Sexuality Studies', in Y. Taylor, S. Hines and M. Casey (eds), *Theorizing Intersectionality and Sexuality*. Basingstoke: Palgrave Macmillan, pp. 56–77.

Escobar, A. (1995) *Encountering Development: The Making and Unmaking of the Third World*. Princeton, NJ: Princeton University Press.

Escobar, A. (2007) 'Worlds and Knowledges Otherwise', *Cultural Studies* 21(2/3): 179–210.

Esteva, G. and Babones, S. J. (2013) *The Future of Development: A Radical Manifesto*. Bristol: Policy Press.

Estévez, A. (2013) 'The Politics of Death in Mexico: Dislocating Human

Rights and Asylum Law through Hybrid Agents', *Glocalism: Journal of Culture, Politics and Innovation* 1.

Evans, B. (2010) 'Foucault's Legacy: Security, War and Violence in the 21st Century', *Security Dialogue* 41(4): 413–33.

Evans, B. and Duffield, M. (2011) 'Bio-spheric Security: How the Merger between Development, Security and the Environment [Desenex] is Retrenching Fortress Europe', in P. Burgess and S. Gutwirth (eds), *A Threat Against Europe? Security, Migration and Integration*. Brussels: VUB Press.

Faist, T. (2000) *The Volume and Dynamics of International Migration and Transnational Social Spaces*. Oxford: Oxford University Press.

Fanon, F. (1963) *The Wretched of the Earth*. London: Grove Press.

Fanon, F. (2008 [1952]) *Black Skin, White Masks*. London: Pluto.

Farris, S. (2017) *In the Name of Women's Rights: The Rise of Femonationalism*. Durham, NC: Duke University Press.

Fassin, D. (2011) 'Policing Borders, Producing Boundaries: The Governmentality of Immigration in Dark Times', *Annual Review of Anthropology* 40(1): 213–26.

Federici, S. (2004) *The Caliban and the Witch*. New York: Autonomedia.

Ferguson, R. (2003) *Aberrations in Black: Toward a Queer of Color Critique*. Minneapolis, MN: Minnesota University Press.

Ferreira, Nuno (2018) 'Reforming the Common European Asylum System: Enough Rainbow for Queer Asylum Seekers?', *GenIUS – Rivista di studi giuridici sull'orientamento sessuale e sull'identita' di genere* 2018(2): 25–42.

Fiddian-Qasmiyeh, E. (2015) *South–South Educational Migration, Humanitarianism and Development: Views from the Caribbean, North Africa and the Middle East*. London: Routledge.

Fiddian-Qasmiyeh, E. and Daley, P. (2019) *The Routledge Handbook of South–South Relations*. London: Routledge.

Fitzgerald, D. (2014) *Culling the Masses: The Democratic Origins of Racist Immigration Policy in the Americas*. Cambridge, MA: Harvard University Press.

Fitzgerald, D. (2019) *Refuge Beyond Reach: How Rich Democracies Repel Asylum Seekers*. Oxford: Oxford University Press.

Flahaux, M. and de Haas, H. (2016) 'African Migration: Trends, Patterns, Drivers', *Comparative Migration Studies* 4(1).

Fortier, A.-M. (2018) 'On (Not) Speaking English: Colonial Legacies in Language Requirements for British Citizenship', *Sociology* 52(6): 1254–69.

Fortier, C. (2013) 'No One Is Illegal: Movements in Canada and the Negotiation of Counter-National and Anti-Colonial Struggles from within the Nation State', in L. Goldring and P. Landolt (eds), *Producing and Negotiating Non-Citizenship: Precarious Legal Status in Canada*. Toronto: University of Toronto Press.

Foucault, M. (1991 [1975]) *Discipline and Punish: The Birth of the Prison*. London: Penguin.

Foucault, M. (1998 [1976]) *The Will to Knowledge: The History of Sexuality, Volume 1*, trans. R. Hurley. London: Penguin.

Foucault, M. (2003) *'Society Must Be Defended': Lecture Series at the Collège de France, 1975–76*, trans. D. Macey. New York: Picador.

Foucault, M., Davidson, A. I. and Burchell, G. (2008) *The Birth of Biopolitics: Lectures at the Collège de France, 1978–1979*. London: Springer.

Fournon, G. and Glick-Schiller, N. (2001) 'All in the Family: Gender, Transnational Migration, and the Nation-State', *Identities* 7(4): 539–82.

Fraser, N. (2000) 'Rethinking Recognition', *New Left Review*, May/ June. Available at: https://newleftreview.org/issues/II3/articles/nancy-fraser-rethinking-recognition

Freedman, J. (2007) *Gendering the International Asylum and Refugee Debate*. Basingstoke: Palgrave Macmillan.

French, J. H. (2013) 'Rethinking Police Violence in Brazil: Unmasking the Public Secret of Race', *Latin American Politics and Society* 55(4): 162–78.

Friedman, E. and Kelin, R. (2008) *Reluctant Refuge: The Story of Asylum in Britain*. London: The British Library.

Frowd, P. (2018) *Security at the Borders: Transnational Practices and Technologies in West Africa*. Oxford: Oxford University Press.

Frowd, P. M. and Sandor, A. J. (2018) 'Militarism and Its Limits: Sociological Insights on Security Assemblages in the Sahel', *Security Dialogue* 49(1/2): 70–82.

Gabaccia, D. (2014) 'Time and Temporality in Migration Studies', in C. Brettell and J. Hollifield (eds), *Migration Theory: Talking across Disciplines*. Abingdon: Routledge.

Gahman, L. (2020) *Land, God, and Guns: Settler Colonialism and Masculinity in the American Heartland*. London: Zed Books.

Gahman, L. and Hjalmarson, E. (2019) 'Border Imperialism, Racial Capitalism, and Geographies of Deracination', *ACME: An International Journal for Critical Geographies* 18(1): 107–29.

Gaibazzi, P., Dünnwald, S. and Bellagamba, A. (eds) (2017) *EurAfrican Borders and Migration Management: Political Cultures, Contested Spaces, and Ordinary Lives*. London: Springer.

Gamage, S. (2016) 'Academic Dependency on Western Disciplinary Knowledge and Captive Mind among South Asian Sociologists: A Critique', *Social Affairs* 1(5): 1–12.

Gandhi, L. (1998) *Postcolonial Theory: A Critical Introduction*. Edinburgh: Edinburgh University Press.

Gaztambide-Fernández, R. (2012) 'Decolonization and the Pedagogy of Solidarity', *Decolonization: Indigeneity, Education & Society* 1(1): 41–67.

Gebrial, D. (2018) 'Rhodes Must Fall: Oxford and Movements for Change', in G. K. Bhambra, D. Gebrial and K. Nisancioglu (eds), *Decolonising the University*. London: Pluto Press.

Geddes, A. and Scholten, P. (2016) *The Politics of Migration and Immigration in Europe*. London: Sage.

Gerver, M. and Millar, K. (2013) 'The Gendered Refugee Experience: Exploring Themes of Violence, Power Relations, Communities, and Empowerment', *St Antony's International Review* 9(1): 2–10.

Gibney, M. (2003) 'The State of Asylum: Democratisation, Judicialisation and Evolution of Refugee Policy', in S. Kneebone (ed.), *The Refugees Convention 50 Years On*. Aldershot: Ashgate.

Giddens, A. (1990) *The Consequences of Modernity*. Cambridge: Polity Press.

Gilman, S. (1985) *Difference and Pathology: Stereotypes of Sexuality, Race, and Madness*. Ithaca: Cornell University Press.

Gilmore, R. W. (2007) *Golden Gulag: Prisons, Surplus, Crisis, and Opposition in Globalizing*. Berkeley, CA: University of California Press.

Gilroy, P. (1993) *The Black Atlantic: Modernity and Double Consciousness*. Cambridge, MA: Harvard University Press.

Gilroy, P. (2002a) *Against Race: Imagining Political Culture Beyond the Color Line*. Cambridge, MA: Harvard University Press.

Gilroy, P. (2002b) *There Ain't No Black in the Union Jack: The Cultural Politics of Race and Nation*. London: Routledge.

Gilroy, P. (2003) '"Where Ignorant Armies Clash by Night": Homogeneous Community and the Planetary Aspect', *International Journal of Cultural Studies* 6(3): 261–76.

Gilroy, P. (2004) *After Empire: Melancholia or Convivial Culture?*, Abingdon: Routledge.

Giroux, H. A. (2008) 'Beyond the Biopolitics of Disposability: Rethinking Neoliberalism in the New Gilded Age', *Social Identities* 14(5): 587–620.

Global Justice (2017) 'Honest Accounts: How the World Profits from Africa's Wealth', *Global Justice*. Available at: https://www.globaljustice.org.uk/sites/default/files/files/resources/honest_accounts_2017_web_final_updated.pdf

Go, J. (2013) 'For a Postcolonial Sociology', *Theory and Society* 42(1): 25–55.

Goldberg, D. T. (1993) *Racist Culture: Philosophy and the Politics of Meaning*. Oxford: Wiley.

Goldberg, D. T. (2009) *The Threat of Race: Reflections on Racial Neoliberalism*. Oxford: Wiley-Blackwell.

Goldstein, J. (2013) '*Terra Economica*: Waste and the Production of Enclosed Nature', *Antipode* 45(2): 357–75.

Gomez, M. (2005) *Black Crescent: The Experience and Legacy of African Muslims in the Americas*. Cambridge: Cambridge University Press.

Gonzales, S. (2012) 'Colonial Borders, Native Fences: Building Bridges between Indigenous Communities through the Decolonization of the

American Landscape', in A. J. Aldama, M. B. Castellano and L. G. Najera (eds), *Comparative Indigeneities of the Américas: Toward a Hemispheric Approach*. Tucson, AZ: University of Arizona Press, pp. 307–20.

Goodfellow, M. (2019) *Hostile Environment: How Immigrants Became Scapegoats*. London: Verso.

Goodwin-Gill, G. S. (2001) 'After the Cold War: Asylum and the Refugee Concept Move On', *Forced Migration Review* 10: 14–16.

Gopal, P. (2019) *Insurgent Empire*. London: Verso.

Gopinath, G. (2005) *Impossible Desires: Queer Diasporas and South Asian Public Cultures*. Durham, NC: Duke University Press.

Gopinath, G. (2007) 'Queer Regions: Locating Lesbians in Sancharram', in G. E. Haggerty and M. McGarry (eds), *A Companion to Lesbian, Gay, Bisexual, Transgender and Queer Studies*. Oxford: Blackwell Publishing.

Gordon, A. (2011) '"I'm Already in a Sort of Tomb": A Reply to Philip Scheffner's *The Halfmoon Files*', *South Atlantic Quarterly* 110(1): 121–54.

Gordon, L. (1999) *Bad Faith and Antiblack Racism*. New York: Humanity Books.

Gray, H. and Franck, A. K. (2019) 'Refugees as/at Risk: The Gendered and Racialized Underpinnings of Securitization in British Media Narratives', *Security Dialogue* 50(3): 275–91.

Greenberg, J. A. (2002) 'Definitional Dilemmas: Male or Female? Black or White? The Law's Failure to Recognize Intersexuals and Multiracials', in T. Lester (ed.), *Gender Nonconformity, Race, and Sexuality: Charting the Connections*. Madison, WI: University of Wisconsin Press.

Gregory, D. (2004) *The Colonial Present: Afghanistan, Palestine, Iraq*. Oxford: Wiley-Blackwell.

Griffiths, M. and Repo, J. (2018) 'Biopolitics and Checkpoint 300 in Occupied Palestine: Bodies, Affect, Discipline', *Political Geography* 65: 17–25.

Grosfoguel, R. (2011) 'Decolonizing Post-Colonial Studies and Paradigms of Political Economy: Transmodernity, Decolonial Thinking, and Global Coloniality', *TRANSMODERNITY: Journal of Peripheral Cultural Production of the Luso-Hispanic World* 1(1). Available at: https://escholarship.org/uc/item/21k6t3fq

Grosfoguel, R. (2013) 'The Structure of Knowledge in Westernized Universities: Epistemic Racism/Sexism and the Four Genocides/Epistemicides of the Long 16th Century', *Human Architecture: Journal of the Sociology of Self-Knowledge* 11(1): 9–22.

Grosfoguel, R. (2016) 'What Is Racism?', *Journal of World Systems Research* 22(1): 9–15.

Grosfoguel, R., Oso, L. and Christou, A. (2015) '"Racism", Intersectionality and Migration Studies: Framing Some Theoretical Reflections', *Identities* 22(6): 635–52.

Gutiérrez Rodríguez, E. (2018) 'The Coloniality of Migration and the "Refugee Crisis": On the Asylum–Migration Nexus, the Transatlantic

White European Settler Colonialism-Migration and Racial Capitalism', *Refuge: Canada's Journal on Refugees* 34(1): 16–28.

Haddad, E. (2008) *The Refugee in International Society: Between Sovereigns.* Cambridge: Cambridge University Press.

Hage, G. (2017) *Is Racism an Environmental Threat?* Cambridge: Polity Press.

Haig-Brown, C. (2009) 'Decolonizing Diaspora: Whose Traditional Land Are We On?', *Cultural and Pedagogical Inquiry* 1(1): 4–21.

Hall, A. (2017) 'Decisions at the Data Border: Discretion, Discernment and Security', *Security Dialogue* 48(6): 488–504.

Hall, C. (2002) *Civilising Subjects: Metropole and Colony in the English Imagination, 1830–1867.* Cambridge: Cambridge University Press.

Hall, C., McClelland, K., Draper, N., Donington, K. and Lang, R. (2014) *Legacies of British Slave-Ownership: Colonial Slavery and the Formation of Victorian Britain.* Cambridge: Cambridge University Press.

Hall, S. (1978) 'Racism and Reaction', in Commission for Racial Equality, *Five Views of Multi-racial Britain.* London: Commission for Racial Equality.

Hall, S. (1991) 'Old and New Identities, Old and New Ethnicities', in A. D. King (ed.), *Globalisation and the World System.* London: Macmillan Educational, pp. 42–68.

Hall, S. (1992) 'New Ethnicities', in J. Donald and A. Rattansi (eds), *'Race', Culture and Difference.* London: Sage.

Hall, S. (1993) 'Culture, Community, Nation', *Cultural Studies* 7(3): 349–63.

Hall, S. (1996a) 'Race, Articulation and Societies Structured in Dominance', in Houston A. Baker Jr, Manthia Diawara and Ruth H. Lindeborg (eds), *Black British Cultural Studies: A Reader.* Chicago: Chicago University Press.

Hall, S. (1996b) 'The West and the Rest: Discourse and Power', in S. Hall, D. Held, D. Hubert and K. Thompson (eds), *Modernity: Introduction to the Modern Societies.* Oxford: Blackwell.

Hall, S. (1996c) 'When Was the Postcolonial? Thinking at the Limit', in I. Chambers and I. Curti (eds), *The Postcolonial Question.* London: Routledge.

Hall, S. (1996d) 'Gramsci's Relevance for the Study of Race and Ethnicity', in D. Morley and K. Chen (eds), *Stuart Hall: Critical Dialogues in Cultural Studies.* London: Routledge.

Hall, S. (2000) 'Conclusion: The Multicultural Question', in B. Hesse (ed.), *Un/settled Multiculturalisms: Diasporas, Entanglements, 'Transruptions'.* London: Zed Books, pp. 209–40.

Hall, S. (2017) *The Fateful Triangle: Race, Ethnicity, Nation.* Cambridge, MA: Harvard University Press.

Hall, S. (2019) *Essential Essays, Volume 2: Identity and Diaspora.* Durham, NC: Duke University Press.

Hall, S., Critcher, C., Jefferson, T., Clarke, J. and Roberts, B. (1978) *Policing the Crisis: Mugging, the State, and Law and Order.* London: Macmillan.

Hall, S. and Morley, D. (2019) *Stuart Hall: Selected Writings: Essential Essays, Volume 2: Identity and Diaspora.* Durham, NC: Duke University Press.

Hammerstad, A. (2014) *The Rise and Decline of a Global Security Actor: UNHCR, Refugee Protection and Security.* Oxford: Oxford University Press.

Hansen, P. and Jonsson, S. (2014) *Eurafrica: The Untold History of European Integration and Colonialism.* London: Bloomsbury.

Hansen, R. (2000) *Citizenship and Immigration in Post-war Britain.* Oxford: Oxford University Press.

Hansen, R. (2003) 'Migration to Europe since 1945: Its History and Its Lessons', *Political Quarterly* 74(1): 25–38.

Hansen, T. B. and Stepputat, F. (eds) (2005) *Sovereign Bodies.* Princeton, NJ: Princeton University Press.

Haritaworn, Jin (2008) 'Shifting Positionalities: Empirical Reflections on a Queer/Trans of Colour Methodology', *Sociological Research Online.* Available at: http://www.socresonline.org.uk/13/1/13.html

Harris, C. (2002) *Making Native Space: Colonialism, Resistance, and Reserves in British Columbia.* Vancouver: University of British Columbia Press.

Hartman, S. (1997) *Scenes of Subjection: Terror, Slavery, and Self-Making in Nineteenth Century America.* Oxford: Oxford University Press.

Hartman, S. (2007) *Lose Your Mother.* New York: Farrar, Straus and Giroux.

Hartman, S. (2008) 'Venus in Two Acts', *Small Axe* 12(2): 1–14.

Harvey, D. (2003) *The New Imperialism.* Oxford: Oxford University Press.

Harvey, D. (2010) 'The Right to the City: From Capital Surplus to Accumulation by Dispossession', in S. Banerjee-Guha (ed.), *Accumulation by Dispossession: Transformative Cities in the New Global Order.* London: Sage, pp. 17–33.

Hass, H., Castles, S. and Miller, M. (2019) *The Age of Migration: International Population Movements in the Modern World.* London: Red Globe Press.

Hathaway, J. C. (2007) 'Forced Migration Studies: Could We Agree Just to "Date"?', *Journal of Refugee Studies* 20(3): 349–69.

Hatton, J. (2018) 'Mars Attacks! A Cautionary Tale from the UK on the Relation between Migration and Refugee Studies (MARS) and Migration Control', *Movements: A Journal for Critical Migration and Border Regime Studies* 4(1).

Hay, C. (2002) *Political Analysis: Political Analysis.* Basingstoke: Palgrave Macmillan.

Hayter, T. (2001) 'Open Borders: The Case against Immigration Controls', *Capital and Class* 25: 149–56.

Headley, C. (2005) 'Otherness and the Impossible in the Wake of Sylvia Wynter's Notion of the "After Man"', in A. Bogues (ed.), *After Man, Towards the Human: Critical Essays on Sylvia Wynter*. Kingston, Jamaica: Ian Randle Publishers, pp. 57–75.

Heath-Kelly, C. (2013) 'Counter-Terrorism and the Counterfactual: Producing the Radicalisation Discourse and the UK PREVENT Strategy', *British Journal of Politics and International Relations* 15(3): 394–415.

Helliwell, C. and Hindess, B. (2011) 'The Past in the Present', *Australian Journal of Politics and History* 57(3): 377–88.

Hembrom, R. (2017) 'Reclaiming the Reproduction of Adivasi Knowledge: The Lens of an Adivasi Publisher', *LSE Blogs*. Available at: https://blogs.lse.ac.uk/inequalityandpoverty/files/2017/12/Reclaiming-the-Reproduction-of-Adivasi-Knowledge.pdf

Heng, G. (2018) *The Invention of Race in the European Middle Ages*. Cambridge: Cambridge University Press.

Hennessy, R. (2006) 'Returning to Reproduction Queerly: Sex, Labor, Need', *Rethinking Marxism* 18(3): 387–95.

Hertoghs, M. and Schinkel, W. (2018) 'The State's Sexual Desires: The Performance of Sexuality in the Dutch Asylum Procedure', *Theory and Society* 47: 691–716.

Hesketh, C. (2017) *Spaces of Capital/Spaces of Resistance: Mexico and the Global Political Economy*. Athens: University of Georgia Press.

Hesse, B. (2007) 'Racialized Modernity: An Analytics of White Mythologies', *Ethnic and Racial Studies* 30(4): 643–63.

Hickel, J. (2018) *The Great Divide: A Brief Guide to Global Inequality and Its Solutions*. London: Penguin.

Hiebert, D. (2003) 'A Borderless World: Dream or Nightmare?', *ACME: An International Journal for Critical Geographies* 2(2): 188–93.

Hill Collins, P. and Bilge, S. (2016) *Intersectionality*. Cambridge: Polity Press.

Hindess, B. (2005) 'Citizenship and Empire', in Thomas Blom Hansen and Finn Stepputat (eds), *Sovereign Bodies: Citizens, Migrants, and States in the Postcolonial World*. Princeton, NJ: Princeton University Press, pp. 241–56.

Hoad, N. (2007) *African Intimacies: Race, Homosexuality, and Globalization*. Minneapolis, MN: University of Minnesota Press.

Hobson, J. (2004) *The Eastern Origins of Western Civilisation*. Cambridge: Cambridge University Press:

Holborn, L. (1975) *Refugees: A Problem of Our Time*. Metuchen, NJ: The Scarecrow Press.

Holden, Philip and Ruppel, Richard J. (eds) (2003) *Imperial Desire: Dissident Sexualities and Colonial Literature*. Minneapolis, MN: University of Minnesota Press.

Holmwood, J. (2019) 'Claiming Whiteness', *Ethnicities* 20(1): 234–9.

Hönke, J. and Müller, M. (2012). 'Governing (In)Security in a Postcolonial

World: Transnational Entanglements and the Worldliness of "Local" Practice', *Security Dialogue* 43(5): 383–401.

hooks, b. (1992) *Black Looks: Race and Representation*. Boston, MA: South End Press.

hooks, b. (2004) *The Will to Change: Men, Masculinity, and Love*. New York: Washington Square Press.

Howell, A. and Richter-Montpetit, M. (2018) 'Racism in Foucauldian Security Studies: Biopolitics, Liberal War, and the Whitewashing of Colonial and Racial Violence', *International Political Sociology* 13(1): 2–19.

Howell, A. and Richter-Montpetit, M. (2020) 'Is Securitization Theory Racist? Civilizationism, Methodological Whiteness, and Antiblack Thought in the Copenhagen School', *Security Dialogue* 51(1): 3–22.

Huysmans, J. (2006) *The Politics of Insecurity: Fear, Migration and Asylum in the EU*. London: Routledge.

Hyndman, J. (2010) 'Introduction: The Feminist Politics of Refugee Migration', *Gender, Place & Culture* 17(4): 453–9.

Hyndman, J. and Giles, W. (2016) *Refugees in Extended Exile: Living on the Edge*. Abingdon: Routledge.

Icaza, R. and Vázquez, R. (2016) 'The Coloniality of Gender as a Radical Critique of Developmentalism', in W. Harcourt (ed.), *The Palgrave Handbook of Gender and Development*. London: Palgrave Macmillan.

Ignatiev, N. (1995) *How the Irish Became White*. New York and London: Routledge.

IMISCOE (2019) 'Standing Committee on Gender and Sexuality', *IMISCOE*. Available at: https://www.imiscoe.org/research/standing-committees/gender-and-sexuality-in-migration-research

Inayatullah, N. and Riley, R. (eds) (2006) *Interrogating Imperialism: Conversations on Gender, Race and War*. New York: Palgrave.

Ingiriis, M. H. (2008) 'The Invention of Al-Shabaab in Somalia: Emulating the Anti-Colonial Dervishes Movement', *African Affairs* 117(467): 217–37.

James, J. (1996) *Resisting State Violence: Radicalism, Gender, and Race in US Culture*. Minneapolis, MN: University of Minnesota Press.

Janmyr, M. (2017) 'No Country of Asylum: "Legitimizing" Lebanon's Rejection of the 1951 Refugee Convention', *International Journal of Refugee Law* 29(3): 438–65.

Jetten, J. and Esses, V. M. (2018) 'The Reception of Immigrants and Refugees in Western Countries: The Challenges of Our Time', *Journal of Social Issues* 74(4): 662–73.

Johnson, H. (2007) *Two Families: Treaties and Government*. Saskatoon: Putich Publishing.

Johnson, H. (2011) 'Click to Donate: Visual Images, Constructing Victims and Imagining the Female Refugee', *Third World Quarterly* 32(6): 1015–37.

Joly, D. (1996) *Haven or Hell? Asylum Policies and Refugees in Europe.* Basingstoke: Palgrave Macmillan.

Joly, D. (2002) 'Introduction', in D. Joly (ed.), *Global Changes in Asylum Regimes.* Basingstoke: Palgrave Macmillan.

Jones, R. C. (2009) 'Migration Permanence and Village Decline in Zacatecas: When You Can't Go Home Again', *Professional Geographer* 61(3): 382–99.

Joppke, C. (1999) *Immigration and the Nation-State: The United States, Germany, and Great Britain.* Oxford: Oxford University Press.

Jordan, W. (1974) *The White Man's Burden: Historical Origins of Racism in the United States.* Oxford: Oxford University Press.

Kahn, S., Alessi, E. J., Kim, H., Woolner, L. and Olivieri, C. J. (2018) 'Facilitating Mental Health Support for LGBT Forced Migrants: A Qualitative Inquiry', *Journal of Counseling & Development* 96(3): 316–26.

Kangas, A. and Salmenniemi, S. (2016) 'Decolonizing Knowledge: Neoliberalism beyond the Three Worlds', *Distinktion: Journal of Social Theory* 17(2): 210–27.

Kanwar, V. (2015) 'Not a Place, but a Project: Bandung, TWAIL, and the Aesthetics of Thirdness', in L. Eslava, M. Fakhri and V. Nesiah (eds), *Bandung, Global History and International Law: Critical Pasts and Pending Futures.* Cambridge: Cambridge University Press.

Kaplan, M. (1995) 'Panopticon in Poona: An Essay on Foucault and Colonialism', *Cultural Anthropology* 10(1): 85–98.

Kapoor, D. (2010) 'Learning from *Adivasi* (Original Dweller) Political–Ecological Expositions of Development: Claims on Forests, Land, and Place in India', in D. Kapoor and E. Shizha (eds), *Indigenous Knowledge and Learning in Asia/Pacific and Africa.* New York: Palgrave Macmillan.

Kapoor, N. (2018) *Deport, Deprive, Extradite: Twenty-First-Century State Extremism.* London: Verso.

Kapur, R. (2005) *Erotic Justice: Postcolonial Feminism Law Sexuality.* Abingdon: Routledge.

Kauanui, J. K. (2016) '"A Structure, Not an Event": Settler Colonialism and Enduring Indigeneity', *Lateral* 5(1). Available at: https://csalateral.org/issue/5-1/forum-alt-humanities-settler-colonialism-enduring-indigeneity-kauanui/

Kearney, M. (2000) 'Transnational Oaxacan Indigenous Identity: The Case of Mixtecs and Zapotecs', *Identities: Global Studies in Culture and Power* 7(2): 173–95.

Keely, C. B. (2001) 'The International Refugee Regime(s): The End of the Cold War Matters', *International Migration Review* 35(1): 303–14.

Keim, W., Çelic, E., Ersche, C. and Wöhrer, V. (eds) (2014) *Global Knowledge Production in the Social Sciences: Made in Circulation.* London: Routledge.

Kelley, R. D. G. (2017) 'What Did Cedric Robinson Mean by Racial

Capitalism?', *Boston Review*, 12 January. Available at: http://bostonreview. net/race/robin-d-g-kelley-what-did-cedric-robinson-mean-racial-capitalism

Kerner, I. (2017) 'Relations of Difference: Power and Inequality in Intersectional and Postcolonial Feminist Theories', *Current Sociology* 65(6): 846–66.

Keskinen, S. (2019) 'Intra-Nordic Differences, Colonial/Racial Histories and National Narratives: Rewriting Finnish History', *Scandinavian Studies* 91(1/2): 163–81.

Keskinen, S. and Andreassen, R. (2017) 'Developing Theoretical Perspectives on Racialisation and Migration', *Nordic Journal of Migration Research* 7(2): 64–9.

Kevles, D. (1995) *In the Name of Eugenics: Genetics and the Uses of Human Heredity*. Cambridge, MA: Harvard University Press.

Khalili, L. (2007) *Heroes and Martyrs of Palestine: The Politics of National Commemoration*. Cambridge: Cambridge University Press.

Khalili, L. (2013) *Time in the Shadows: Confinement in Counterinsurgencies*. Palo Alto, CA: Stanford University Press.

Kilkey, M., Merla, L. and Baldassar, L. (2018) 'The Social Reproductive Worlds of Migrants', *Journal of Family Studies* 24(1): 1–4.

Kivisto, P. and Faist, F. (2010) *Beyond a Border: The Causes and Consequences of Contemporary Immigration*. London: Pine Forge Press.

Klooster, D. (2013) 'The Impact of Trans-national Migration on Commons Management among Mexican Indigenous Communities', *Journal of Latin American Geography* 12(1): 57–86.

Knox, R. (1850) *The Races of Men: A Philosophical Enquiry*. London: Henry Renshaw.

Kofman, E. and Raghuram, P. (2015) *Gendered Migrations and Global Social Reproduction*. London: Palgrave Macmillan.

Koh, S. Y. (2015) 'Approaches to Migration in Asia: Reflections and Projections', *Geography Compass* 9(8): 432–44.

Koopmans, R. and Schaeffer, M. (2016) 'Statistical and Perceived Diversity and Their Impacts on Neighbourhood Social Cohesion in Germany, France and the Netherlands', *Social Indicators Research* 125(3): 853–83.

Koser, K. (2001) 'New Approaches to Asylum?', *International Migration* 39(6): 85–101.

Kotef, H. (2015) *Movement and the Ordering of Freedom: On Liberal Governances of Mobility*. Durham, NC: Duke University Press.

Kraler, A., Kofman, E., Kohli, M. and Schmoll, C. (2011) *Gender, Generations and the Family in International Migration*. Amsterdam: Amsterdam University Press.

Králová, J. (2015) 'What Is Social Death?', *Contemporary Social Science* 10(3): 235–48.

Krivonos, D. (2019) *Migrations on the Edge of Whiteness: Young Russian-Speaking Migrants in Helsinki, Finland*. PhD thesis, University of Helsinki.

Krivonos, D. and Näre, L. (2019) 'Imagining the "West" in the Context of

Global Coloniality: The Case of Post-Soviet Youth Migration to Finland', *Sociology* 53(6): 1177–93.

Kundnani, A. (2008) 'Islamism and the Roots of Liberal Rage', *Race and Class* 50(2): 40–68.

Kundnani, A. (2014) *The Muslims Are Coming: Islamophobia, Extremism, and the Domestic War on Terror*. London: Verso.

Kuppan, V. (2018) 'Crippin' Blackness: Narratives of Disabled People of Colour from Slavery to Trump', in A. Johnson, R. Joseph-Salisbury and B. Kamunge (eds), *Fire Now: Anti-Racist Scholarship in Times of Explicit Racial Violence*. London: Zed Books.

Kushner, T. (2006) *Remembering Refugees: Then and Now*. Manchester: Manchester University Press.

Lake, M. and Reynolds, H. (2008) *Drawing the Global Colour Line: White Men's Countries and the International Challenge of Racial Equality*. Cambridge: Cambridge University Press,

Laskar, P., Johansson, A. and Mulinari, D. (2016) 'Decolonising the Rainbow Flag', *Culture Unbound: Journal of Current Cultural Research* 8(3): 192–217.

Laslett, B. and Brenner, J. (1989) 'Gender and Social Reproduction: Historical Perspectives', *Annual Review of Sociology* 15: 381–404.

Lawrence, B. (2004) *'Real' Indians and Others: Mixed Blood Urban Native Peoples and Indigenous Nationhood*. Lincoln, NE: University of Nebraska Press.

Lawrence, B. and Dua, E. (2005) 'Decolonizing Antiracism', *Social Justice* 32(4): 120–42.

Lee, E. O. J. (2018) 'Tracing the Coloniality of Queer and Trans Migrations: Resituating Heterocisnormative Violence in the Global South and Encounters with Migrant Visa Ineligibility to Canada', *Refuge* 34(1): 60–74.

Lemberg-Pedersen, M. (2019) 'Manufacturing Displacement: Externalization and Postcoloniality in European Migration Control', *Global Affairs* 5(3): 247–71.

Lemke, T. (2011) *Biopolitics: An Advanced Introduction*. New York: New York University Press.

Lentin, A. (2020) *Why Race Still Matters*. Cambridge: Polity.

Lewis, G. (2013) 'Unsafe Travel: Experiencing Intersectionality and Feminist Displacements', *Signs* 38: 869–92.

Lewis, R. (2014) '"Gay? Prove It": The Politics of Queer Anti-deportation Activism', *Sexualities* 17(8): 958–75.

Lewis, R. (2019) 'LGBTQ Migration Crises', in C. Menjivar, M. Ruiz and I. Ness (eds), *The Handbook of Migration Crises*. Oxford: Oxford University Press.

Lewis, S. L. and Maslin, M. A. (2015) 'Perspective: Defining the Anthropocene', *Nature* 519: 171–80.

Li, D. (2018) 'From Exception to Empire: Sovereignty, Carceral Circulation, and the "Global War on Terror"', in C. McGranahan and J. Collins (eds), *Ethnographies of Empire*. Durham, NC: Duke University Press, pp. 456–77.

Li, D. (2019) *The Universal Enemy: Jihad, Empire, and the Challenge of Solidarity*. Stanford: Stanford University Press.

Linnaeus, C. (1964 [1735]) *Systema Naturae*. London: Coronet Books.

Lloyd, D. and Wolfe, P. (2015) 'Settler Colonial Logics and the Neoliberal Regime', *Settler Colonial Studies* 6(2): 109–18.

Locke, J. (1988 [1689]) *Two Treatises on Government*. Cambridge: Cambridge University Press.

Loescher, G. (1993) *Beyond Charity: International Cooperation and the Global Refugee Crisis*. Oxford: Oxford University Press.

Lorde, A. (1984) *Sister Outsider: Essays and Speeches*. New York: Crossing Press.

Losurdo, D. (2011) *Liberalism: A Counter History*. London: Verso.

Lowe, L. (2015) *The Intimacies of Four Continents*. Durham, NC: Duke University Press.

Lugones, M. (1992) 'On Borderlands/La Frontera: An Interpretive Essay', *Hypatia* 7(4): 31–7.

Lugones, M. (2007) 'Heterosexualism and the Colonial/Modern Gender System', *Hypatia* 22(1): 186–209.

Lugones, M. (2008) 'The Coloniality of Gender', *Worlds & Knowledges Otherwise* 2: 1–17.

Lugones, M. (2011) 'Toward a Decolonial Feminism', *Hypatia* 25(4): 742–59.

Luibhéid, E. (2013) *Pregnant on Arrival*. Minneapolis, MN: University of Minnesota Press.

Luibhéid, E. (2018) 'Same-Sex Marriage and the Pinkwashing of State Migration Controls', *International Feminist Journal of Politics* 20(3): 405–24.

Luibhéid, E. and Cantu, L. (2005) *Queer Migrations: Sexuality, US Citizenship, and Border Crossings*. Minneapolis, MN: University of Minnesota Press.

Luibhéid, E. and Chavez, K. (eds) (forthcoming) *Queer Migrations II: Detention, Deportation, and Illegalization*. Chicago, IL: University of Illinois Press.

Luna-Firebaugh, E. M. (2002) 'The Border Crossed Us: Border-Crossing Issues of the Indigenous Peoples of the Americas', *Wicazo Sa Review* 17(1): 159–81.

Lutz, H. (2004) 'Life in the Twilight Zone: Migration, Transnationality and Gender in the Private Household', *Journal of Contemporary European Studies* 12(1): 47–56.

Lutz, H., Phoenix, A. and Yuval Davis, N. (1995) *Crossfires: Nationalism, Racism and Gender in Europe*. London: Pluto Press.

Macharia, K. (2016a) 'On Being Area-Studied: A Litany of Complaint', *GLQ: A Journal of Lesbian and Gay Studies* 22(2): 183–90.

Macharia, K. (2016b) '5 Reflections on Trans* & Taxonomy', *Critical Arts* 30(4): 495–506.

Macharia, K. (2019) *Fottage*. New York: New York University Press.

Mack, A. N. and Na'puti, T. R. (2019) '"Our Bodies Are Not Terra Nullius": Building a Decolonial Feminist Resistance to Gendered Violence', *Women's Studies in Communication* 42(3): 347–70.

Maddison, A. (1971) *Class Structure and Economic Growth: India and Pakistan since the Moghuls*. London: George Allen & Unwin.

Magubane, Z. (2001) 'Which Bodies Matter? Feminism, Poststructuralism, Race and the Curious Theoretical Odyssey of the "Hottentot Venus"', *Gender and Society* 15(6): 816–34.

Mahmud, T. (2010) 'Colonial Cartographies, Postcolonial Borders, and Enduring Failures of International Law: The Unending Wars along the Afghanistan–Pakistan Frontier', *Brooklyn Journal of International Law* 36(1).

Mains, S. P., Gilmartin, M., Cullen, D. et al. (2013) 'Postcolonial Migrations', *Social and Cultural Geography* 14(2): 131–44.

Maldonado-Torres, N. (2007) 'On the Coloniality of Being', *Cultural Studies* 21(2/3): 240–70.

Mamdani, M. (1996) *Citizen and Subject: Contemporary Africa and the Legacy of Late Colonialism*. Princeton, NJ: Princeton University Press.

Manchanda, N. (2015) 'Queering the Pashtun: Afghan Sexuality in the Homo-nationalist Imaginary', *Third World Quarterly* 36(1): 130–46.

Marfleet, P. (2007) 'Refugees and History: Why We Must Address the Past', *Refugee Survey Quarterly* 26(3): 136–48.

Martiniello, M. and Rath, J. (eds) (2012) *An Introduction to International Migration Studies*. Amsterdam: Amsterdam University Press.

Marusek, S. (2016) *Faith and Resistance: The Politics of Love and War in Lebanon*. London: Rowman and Littlefield.

Marx, K. (1990 [1887]) *Capital, Vol. 1*. London: Penguin.

Mathieu, X. (2018) 'Sovereign Myths in International Relations: Sovereignty as Equality and the Reproduction of Eurocentric Blindness', *Journal of International Political Theory*. Available at: https://journals.sagepub.com/doi/10.1177/1755088218814072

Mau, S., Gülzau, F., Laube, L. and Zaun, N. (2015) 'The Global Mobility Divide: How Visa Policies Have Evolved over Time', *Journal of Ethnic and Migration Studies* 41(8): 1192–1213.

Mayblin, L. (2014) 'Colonialism, Decolonisation, and the Right to Be Human: Britain and the 1951 Geneva Convention on the Status of Refugees', *Journal of Historical Sociology* 27(3): 423–41.

Mayblin, L. (2017) *Asylum after Empire: Colonial Legacies in the Politics of Asylum Seeking*. London: Rowman and Littlefield.

Mayblin, L. (2019) *Impoverishment and Asylum: Social Policy as Slow Violence*. London: Routledge.

Maynard, R. (2017) *Policing Black Lives: State Violence in Canada from Slavery to the Present*. Winnipeg: Fernwood Publishing.

Mbembe, A. (2001) *On the Postcolony*. Berkeley, CA: University of California Press.

Mbembe, A. (2003) 'Necropolitics', *Public Culture* 15(1): 11–40.

Mbembe, A. (2017) *Critique of Black Reason*. Durham, NC: Duke University Press.

Mbembe, A. (2018) 'The Idea of a Borderless World', *Chimurenga*, transcript of a lecture given at Yale University. Available at: https://chimurengachronic.co.za/the-idea-of-a-borderless-world

McClintock, A. (1995) *Imperial Leather: Race, Gender, and Sexuality in the Colonial Conquest*. London: Routledge

McIlwaine, C. (2008) 'The Postcolonial Practices of International Migration: Latin American migration to London', working paper, http://www.geog.qmul.ac.uk/docs/staff/6312.pdf

McLelland, M. and Mackie, V. (eds) (2015) *Routledge Handbook of Sexuality Studies in East Asia*. Abingdon: Routledge.

McNevin, A. (2014) 'Beyond Territoriality: Rethinking Human Mobility, Border Security and Geopolitical Space from the Indonesian Island of Bintan', *Security Dialogue* 45(3): 295–310.

Meer, N. (2019) 'The Wreckage of White Supremacy', *Identities* 26(5): 501–9.

Mendez, X. (2015) 'Notes Toward a Decolonial Feminist Methodology: Revisiting the Race/Gender Matrix', *Transcripts* 5: 41–59.

Mendoza, B. (2016) 'Coloniality of Gender and Power: From Postcoloniality to Decoloniality', in L. Disch and M. Hawkesworth (eds), *The Oxford Handbook of Feminist Theory*, pp. 100–22.

Mendoza, R. (2015) *Metroimperial Intimacies: Fantasy, Racial–Sexual Governance, and the Philippines in US Imperialism, 1899–1913*. Durham, NC: Duke University Press.

Mezzadra, S. (2011) 'Bringing Capital Back In: A Materialist Turn in Postcolonial Studies?', *Inter-Asia Cultural Studies* 12(1): 154–64.

Michel, N. (2015) 'Sheepology: The Postcolonial Politics of Raceless Racism in Switzerland', *Postcolonial Studies* 18(4): 410–26.

Miège, J. L. (1993) 'Migration and Decolonization', *European Review* 1(1): 81–6.

Mies, M. (1999) *Patriarchy and Accumulation on a World Scale: Women in the International Division of Labour*. London: Zed Books.

Mignolo, W. (2000) *Local Histories/Global Designs*. Princeton, NJ: Princeton University Press.

Mignolo, W. D. (2005) 'Prophets Facing Sidewise: The Geopolitics of Knowledge and the Colonial Difference', *Social Epistemology* 19(1): 111–27.

Mignolo, W. (2007) 'Delinking: The Rhetoric of Modernity, the Logic of Coloniality and the Grammar of De-coloniality', *Cultural Studies* 21(2): 449–514.

Mignolo, W. (2009) 'Who Speaks for the "Human" in Human Rights?', *Hispanic Issues On Line* 5(1): 7–24.

Mignolo, W. (2011a) *The Darker Side of Western Modernity: Global Futures, Decolonial Options*. Durham, NC: Duke University Press.

Mignolo, W. (2011b) 'Geopolitics of Sensing and Knowing: On (De)coloniality, Border Thinking and Epistemic Disobedience', *Postcolonial Studies* 14(3): 273–83.

Mignolo, W. D. and Tlostanova, M. V. (2006) 'Theorizing from the Borders: Shifting to Geo- and Body-Politics of Knowledge', *European Journal of Social Theory* 9(2): 205–21.

Mills, C. (1997) *The Racial Contract*. Ithaca: Cornell University Press.

Mills, C. (2015) 'Unwriting and Unwhitening the World', in A. Anievas, N. Manchanda and R. Shilliam (eds), *Race and Racism in International Relations: Confronting the Global Colour Line*. Abingdon: Routledge.

Modood, T. and Werbner, P. (eds) (1997) *Debating Cultural Hybridity*. London: Zed Books.

Mohanty, C. (1988) 'Under Western Eyes: Feminist Scholarship and Colonial Discourses', *Feminist Review* 30(1): 61–88.

Moncada, E. (2010) 'Counting Bodies: Crime Mapping, Policing and Race in Colombia', *Ethnic and Racial Studies* 33(4): 696–716.

Mongia, R. (2018) *Indian Migration and Empire: A Colonial Genealogy of the Modern State*. Durham, NC: Duke University Press.

Moore, D. S. (1998) 'Subaltern Struggles and the Politics of Place: Remapping Resistance in Zimbabwe's Eastern Highlands', *Cultural Anthropology* 13(3): 1–38.

Moraga, C. and Anzaldúa, G. (eds) (1984) *This Bridge Called My Back: Writings by Radical Women of Color*. New York: Kitchen Table, Women of Color Press.

Moreton-Robinson, A. (2007) *Sovereign Subjects: Indigenous Sovereignty Matters*. Crows Nest, New South Wales: Allen & Unwin.

Moreton-Robinson, A. (2015) *White Possessive: Property, Power, and Indigenous Sovereignty*. Minneapolis, MN: University of Minnesota Press.

Morgan, G. and Poynting, S. (2012) *Global Islamophobia: Muslims and Moral Panic in the West*. London: Ashgate.

Morgensen, S. (2011) *Spaces between Us: Queer Settler Colonialism and Indigenous Decolonization*. Minneapolis, MN: University of Minnesota Press.

Morokvasic, M. (1991) 'Fortress Europe and Migrant Women', *Feminist Review* 39(1): 69–84.

Morsi, Y. (2017) *Radical Skin/Moderate Masks*. London: Rowland and Littlefield.

Mountz, A. (2011a) 'Where Asylum-Seekers Wait: Feminist Counter-Topographies of Sites between States', *Gender, Place & Culture* 18(3): 381–99.

Mountz, A. (2011b) 'The Enforcement Archipelago: Detention, Haunting, and Asylum on Islands', *Political Geography* 30(3): 118–28.

Mügge, L. and de Jong, S. (2013) 'Intersectionalizing European Politics: Bridging Gender and Ethnicity', *Politics, Groups, and Identities* 1(3): 380–9.

Munoz, J. E. (1999) *Disidentification: Queers of Color and the Performance of Politics*. Minneapolis, MN: University of Minnesota Press.

Mutua, M. A. (1994) 'What Is TWAIL?', *Proceedings of the Annual Meeting (American Society of International Law)* 94: 31–40.

NAACP (2020) 'Criminal Justice Fact Sheet', NAACP. Available at: https://www.naacp.org/criminal-justice-fact-sheet/

Nadasen, P. (2007) 'From Widow to "Welfare Queen": Welfare and the Politics of Race', *Black Women, Gender Families* 1(2): 52–77.

Narain, D. (2004) 'What Happened to Global Sisterhood? Writing and Reading "the" Postcolonial Woman', in S. Gillis, G. Howie and R. Munford (eds), *Third Wave Feminism: A Critical Exploration*. London: Palgrave Macmillan.

Nardin, T. (2003) 'Humanitarian Imperialism', *Ethics and International Affairs* 19(2): 21–6.

Nayak, M. (2015) *Who Is Worthy of Protection? Gender-Based Asylum and US Immigration Politics*. Oxford: Oxford University Press.

Nayaran, J. (2019a) 'British Black Power: The Anti-Imperialism of Political Blackness and the Problem of Nativist Socialism', *Sociological Review* 65(5): 945–7.

Nayaran, J. (2019b) 'Huey P. Newton's Intercommunalism: An Unacknowledged Theory of Empire', *Theory, Culture and Society* 36(3): 57–85.

Nayaran, J. (2020) 'Survival Pending Revolution: Self-Determination in the Age of Proto-neoliberal Globalization', *Current Sociology* 68(2): 187–203.

Ndlovu-Gatsheni, S. (2013) 'The Entrapment of Africa within the Global Colonial Matrices of Power: Eurocentrism, Coloniality, and Deimperialization in the Twenty-First Century', *Journal of Developing Societies* 29(4): 331–53.

Ndlovu-Gatsheni, S. (2018a) 'Racism and "Blackism" on a World Scale', in O. Rutazibwa and R. Shilliam (eds), *The Routledge Handbook of Postcolonial Politics*. Abingdon: Routledge.

Ndlovu-Gatsheni, S. J. (2018b) 'Decolonising Borders, Decriminalising Migration and Rethinking Citizenship', in H. H. Magidimisha et al. (eds), *Crisis, Identity and Migration in Post-Colonial Southern Africa*. Cham: Springer, pp. 23–37.

Ndlovu-Gatsheni, S. J. and Ojakorotu, V. (2010) 'Surveillance over a Zone of Conflict: AFRICOM and the Politics of Securitisation of Africa', *Journal of Pan African Studies* 3(6): 94–110.

Ndlovu-Gatsheni, S. J. and Zondi, S. (2016) *Decolonizing the University:*

Knowledge Systems and Disciplines in Africa. Durham, NC: Carolina Academic Press.

Nessa (2018) 'In Surveillance's Digital Age, Black Muslims Are Hit the Hardest', *The Establishment*. Available at: https://theestablishment.co/in-surveillances-digital-age-black-muslims-are-hit-the-hardest/index.html

Neti, L. (2014) 'Imperial Inheritances: Lapses, Love and Laws in the Colonial Machine', *Interventions* 16(2): 197–214.

Neumayer, E. (2005) 'Bogus Refugees? The Determinants of Asylum Migration to Western Europe', *International Studies Quarterly* 49(3): 389–410.

Nilsen, A. G. (2016) 'Power, Resistance and Development in the Global South: Notes Towards a Critical Research Agenda', *International Journal of Politics, Culture and Society* 29(3): 269–87.

Nisancioglu, K. (2019) 'Racial Sovereignty', *European Journal of International Relations*, DOI 10.1177/1354066119882991.

Nyamnjoh, F. (2004) 'A Relevant Education for African Development: Some Epistemological Considerations', *African Development* 29: 161–84.

Nyamnjoh, F. (2016) *#Rhodesmustfall: Nibbling at Resilient Colonialism in South Africa*. Bamenda, Cameroon: Langaa RPCID.

Obi, C. I. (2010) 'African Migration as the Search for a Wonderful World: An Emerging Trans-Global Security Threat?', *African and Asian Studies* 9(1/2): 128–48.

Obradovic, M. (2015) 'Protecting Female Refugees against Sexual and Gender-Based Violence in Camps', *United Nations University*. Available at: https://unu.edu/publications/articles/protecting-female-refugees-against-sexual-and-gender-based-violence-in-camps.html

Obradović-Wochnik, J. and Bird, G. (2019) 'The Everyday at the Border: Examining Visual, Material and Spatial Intersections of International Politics along the "Balkan Route"', *Cooperation and Conflict* 55(1).

Olund, E. N. (2002) 'From Savage Space to Governable Space: The Extension of United States Judicial Sovereignty over Indian Country in the Nineteenth Century', *Cultural Geographies* 9(2): 129–57.

Oswin, N. (2010). 'Sexual Tensions in Modernizing Singapore: The Postcolonial and the Intimate', *Environment and Planning D: Society and Space* 28(1): 128–41.

Pahuja, S. (2011) *Decolonising International Law: Development, Economic Growth and the Politics of Universality*. Cambridge: Cambridge University Press.

Paoline, E., Gau, J. M. and Terrill, W. (2018) 'Race and the Police Use of Force Encounter in the United States', *British Journal of Criminology* 58(1): 54–74.

Papadopoulos, D., Stephenson, N. and Tsianos, V. (2008) *Escape Routes: Control and Subversion in the Twenty-First Century*. London: Pluto Press.

Parashar, S. (2018) 'Terrorism and the Postcolonial "State"', in O. Rutazibwa and R. Shilliam (eds), *Routledge Handbook of Postcolonial Politics*. London: Routledge.

Parashar, S. (2019) 'Colonial Legacies, Armed Revolts and State Violence: The Maoist Movement in India', *Third World Quarterly* 40(2): 337–54.

Patterson, O. (1982) *Slavery and Social Death: A Comparative Study*. Cambridge, MA: Harvard University Press.

Paul, K. (1997) *Whitewashing Britain: Race and Citizenship in the Postwar Era*. New York: Cornell University Press.

Perera, S. and Razack, S. (eds) (2014) *At the Limits of Justice: Women of Colour on Terror*. Toronto: University of Toronto Press.

Perkowski, N. (2018) 'Frontex and the Convergence of Humanitarianism, Human Rights and Security', *Security Dialogue* 49(6): 457–75.

Peterson, V. S. (2014) 'Sex Matters', *International Feminist Journal of Politics* 16(3): 389–409.

Peterson, V. S. (2020) 'Family Matters in Racial Logics: Tracing Intimacies, Inequalities, and Ideologies', *Review of International Studies* 46(2): 177–96.

Petzen, J. (2012) 'Queer Trouble: Centring Race in Queer and Feminist Politics', *Journal of Intercultural Studies* 33(3): 289–302.

Picq, M. L. and Thiel, M. (2015) *Sexualities in World Politics*. Abingdon: Routledge.

Piekut, A., Pryce, G. and Van Gent, W. (2019) 'Segregation in the Twenty-First Century: Processes, Complexities and Future Directions', *Tijdschrift voor Economische en Sociale Geografie* 110(3): 225–34.

Pletsch, C. (1981) 'The Three Worlds, or the Division of Social Scientific Labor, circa 1950–1975', *Comparative Studies in Society and History* 23(4): 565–90.

Plonski, S. (2018) 'Material Footprints: The Struggle for Borders by Bedouin-Palestinians in Israel', *Antipode* 50(5): 1349–75.

Poliakov L. (1982) 'Racism from the Enlightenment to the Age of Imperialism', in R. Ross (ed.), *Racism and Colonialism: Comparative Studies in Overseas History*. Dordrecht: Springer.

Povinelli, E. (2011) *Economies of Abandonment: Social Belonging and Endurance in Later Liberalism*. Durham, NC: Duke University Press.

Pradella, L. and Taghdisi Rad, S. (2017) 'Libya and Europe: Imperialism, Crisis and Migration', *Third World Quarterly* 38(11): 2411–27.

Pratt, N. and Rezk, D. (2019) 'Securitizing the Muslim Brotherhood: State Violence and Authoritarianism in Egypt after the Arab Spring', *Security Dialogue* 50(3): 239–56.

Puar, J. (2007) *Terrorist Assemblages: Homonationalism in Queer Times*. Durham, NC: Duke University Press.

Puar, J. (2017) *The Right to Maim: Debility, Capacity, Disability*. Durham, NC: Duke University Press.

Puar, J. K. and Rai, A. S. (2002) 'Monster, Terrorist, Fag: The War on Terrorism and the Production of Docile Patriots', *Social Text* 20(3): 117–48.

Pulido, L. (2018) 'Geographies of Race and Ethnicity III: Settler Colonialism and Nonnative People of Color', *Progress in Human Geography* 42(2): 309–18.

Quijano, A. (2000) 'Coloniality of Power, Eurocentrism and Latin America', *Nepantla: Views from South* 1(3): 533–80.

Quijano, A. (2007) 'Coloniality and Modernity/Rationality', *Cultural Studies* 21(2/3): 168–78.

Raghuram, P. (2009) 'Which Migration, What Development? Unsettling the Edifice of Migration and Development', *Population, Space and Place* 15(2): 103–17.

Rahnema, M. and Bawtree, V. (1997) *The Post-Development Reader*. London: Zed Books.

Rajaram, P. K. (2018) 'Refugees as Surplus Population: Race, Migration and Capitalist Value Regimes', *New Political Economy* 23(5): 627–39.

Rangan, H. (2000) *Of Myths and Movements: Rewriting Chipko into Himalayan History*. Delhi: Oxford University Press.

Rao, R. (2015) 'Echoes of Imperialism in LGBT Activism', in K. Nicolaïdis, S. Berny and G. Maas (eds), *Echoes of Empire: Memory, Identity and Colonial Legacies*. London: I. B. Tauris, pp. 355–72.

Rao, R. (2020) *Out of Time: The Queer Politics of Postcoloniality*. New York: Oxford University Press.

Rashid, S. (2013) *Black Muslims in the US: History, Politics and the Struggle of a Community*. London: Palgrave Macmillan.

Razack, S. (2002) *Race, Space, and the Law: Unmapping a White Settler Society*. Toronto: Between the Lines.

Razack, S. (2008) *Casting Out: Race and the Eviction of Muslims from Western Law and Politics*. Toronto: University of Toronto Press.

Reedy, C. (2011) *Freedom with Violence: Race, Sexuality, and the US State*. Durham, NC: Duke University Press.

Reiter, B. (2018) 'Introduction', in B. Reiter (ed.), *Constructing the Pluriverse*. Durham, NC: Duke University Press.

Rhodes Must Fall Movement (2018) *Rhodes Must Fall: The Struggle to Decolonise the Racist Heart of Empire*. London: Zed Books.

Richmond, A. H. (1994) *Global Apartheid: Refugees, Racism, and the New World Order*. Toronto and Oxford: Oxford University Press.

Richter-Montpetit, M. (2014) 'Beyond the Erotics of Orientalism: Lawfare, Torture and the Racial–Sexual Grammars of Legitimate Suffering', *Security Dialogue* 45(1): 43–62.

Richter-Montpetit, M. (2018) 'Everything You Always Wanted to Know about Sex (in IR) but Were Afraid to Ask: The 'Queer Turn' in International Relations', *Millennium* 46(2): 220–40.

Rifkin, M. (2015) *When Did the Indians Become Straight?* Oxford: Oxford University Press.

Riley, J. L. (2008) *Let Them In: The Case for Open Borders*. New York: Gotham Books.

References

Rivera-Salgado, G. (1999) 'Mixtec Activism in Oaxacalifornia: Transborder Grassroots Political Strategies', *American Behavioural Scientist* 42(9): 1439–58.

Roberts, D. (1997) *Killing the Black Body: Race, Reproduction, and the Meaning of Liberty*. Toronto: Random House/Pantheon.

Robinson, C. (1983) *Black Marxism: The Making of the Black Radical Tradition*. Chapel Hill, NC: University of North Carolina Press.

Rodgers, N. (2007) *Ireland, Slavery and Anti-Slavery: 1612–1865*. London: Palgrave Macmillan.

Rodney, W. (2018 [1972]) *How Europe Underdeveloped Africa*. London: Verso.

Rodríguez, R. C. (2014) *Our Sacred Maíze Is Our Mother: Indigeneity and Belonging in the Americas*. Tucson, AZ: University of Arizona Press.

Rodriguez-Salgado, M. J. (2008) '"How Oppression Thrives Where Truth Is Not Allowed a Voice": The Spanish Polemic about the American Indians', in G. K. Bhambra and R. Shilliam (eds), *Silencing Human Rights: Critical Engagements with a Contested Project*. London: Palgrave Macmillan, pp. 19–42.

Rojas, C. (2016) 'Contesting the Colonial Logics of the International: Toward a Relational Politics for the Pluriverse', *International Political Sociology* 10(4): 369–82.

Rosa, M. (2018) 'Du'as of the Enslaved: The Malê Slave Rebellion in Bahía, Brazil', Yaqeen Institute, 28 April. Available at: https://yaqeeninstitute.org/margarita-rosa/duas-of-the-enslaved-the-male-slave-rebellion-in-bahia-brazil/

Rowe, M. (2004) *Policing, Race and Racism*. London: Routledge.

Roy, S. (2012) *New South Asian Feminisms: Paradoxes and Possibilities*. London: Zed Books.

Ruhs, M., Tamas, T. and Palme, J. (eds) (2019) *Bridging the Gaps: Linking Research to Public Debates and Policy-Making on Migration and Integration*. Oxford: Oxford University Press.

Rutazibwa, O. (2018) 'On Babies and Bathwater: Decolonizing International Development Studies', in S. de Jong, R. Icaza and O. U. Rutazibwa (eds), *Decolonization and Feminisms in Global Teaching and Learning*. London: Routledge, pp. 158–80.

Rutazibwa, O. (2020) 'Hidden in Plain Sight: Coloniality, Capitalism and Race/ism as Far as the Eye Can See', *Millennium: Journal of International Studies* 48(2).

Rutazibwa, O. and Ndushabandi, E. (2019) 'Agaciro: Re-centering Dignity in Development', in A. Escobar, A. Kothari, A. Salleh, F. Demaria and A. Acosta (eds), *Pluriverse: A Post-Development Dictionary*. New Delhi: Columbia University Press.

Ryan, L. (2011) 'Transnational Relations: Family Migration among Recent Polish Migrants in London', *International Migration* 49: 80–103.

Sabaratnam, M. (2017) *Decolonising Intervention: International Statebuilding in Mozambique*. London: Rowman and Littlefield.

Sabsay, L. (2012) 'The Emergence of the Other Sexual Citizen: Orientalism and the Modernisation of Sexuality', *Citizenship Studies* 16(5/6): 605–23.

Sachs, W. (1992) *The Development Dictionary: A Guide to Knowledge as Power*. London: Zed Books.

Saeidi, S. (2018a) 'Iran's Hezbollah and Citizenship Politics: The Surprises of Religious Legislation in a Hybrid Regime', in R. Meijer and N. Butenschon (eds), *The Middle East in Transition: The Centrality of Citizenship*. Cheltenham: Edward Elgar, pp. 223–48.

Saeidi, S. (2018b) 'A Passionate Pursuit of Justice: Towards an Ethics of Islamic Feminist Research Practice', *American Journal of Islamic Social Sciences* 35(2): 1–27.

Saeidi, S. and Vafa, A. (2019) 'After Isolation: Mirrors between Parallel Worlds and New Conceptual Spaces of Activism in Post-Revolutionary Iran', *Millennium: Journal of International Studies* 47(3): 417–43.

Said, E. W. (1995 [1978]) *Orientalism: Western Conceptions of the Orient*. London: Penguin.

Saini, A. (2019) *Superior: The Return of Race Science*. Boston, MA: Beacon Press.

Sajed, A. (2012) 'Securitized Migrants and Postcolonial (In)difference: The Politics of Activisms among North African Migrants in France', in Peter Nyers and Kim Rygiel (eds), *Citizenship, Migrant Activism and the Politics of Movement*. Abingdon: Routledge.

Sajed, A. and Seidel, T. (2019) 'Introduction: Escaping the Nation? National Consciousness and the Horizons of Decolonization', *Interventions: International Journal of Postcolonial Studies* 21(5): 583–91.

Salaita, S. (2016) *Inter/Nationalism: Decolonizing Native America and Palestine*. Minneapolis, MN: University of Minnesota Press.

Salamanca, O., Qato, M., Samour, S. and Rabie, K. (2013) 'Past Is Present: Settler Colonialism in Palestine', *Settler Colonial Studies* 2(1): 1–8.

Salem, S. (2018) 'Reading Egypt's Postcolonial State through Frantz Fanon: Hegemony, Dependency and Development', *Interventions* 20(3): 428–45.

Salem, S. (2020) *Anticolonial Afterlives in Egypt: The Politics of Hegemony*. Cambridge: Cambridge University Press.

Salter, M. (ed.) (2008) *Politics at the Airport*. Minneapolis, MN: University of Minnesota Press.

Sandler, S. (1999) *The Korean War: No Victors, No Vanquished*. Lexington, KY: University Press of Kentucky.

Santos, B. de Sousa (2008) 'The World Social Forum and the Global Left', *Politics & Society* 36(2): 247–70.

Santos, B. de Sousa (2014) *Epistemologies of the South: Justice against Epistemicide*. New York: Routledge.

Sardar, Z. (1999) 'Development and the Locations of Eurocentrism', in R. Munck and D. O'Hearn (eds), *Critical Development Theory: Contributions to a New Paradigm*. London: Zed Books, pp. 44–62.

Sassen, S. (1999) *Guests and Aliens*. New York: The New Press.

Satzewich, V. (1991) *Racism and the Incorporation of Foreign Labour: Farm Labour Migration to Canada since 1945*. London: Routledge.

Saucier, P. and Woods, T. (2014) 'Ex Aqua: The Mediterranean Basin, Africans on the Move and the Politics of Policing', *Theoria: A Journal of Social and Political Theory* 61(141): 55–75.

Scholten, P. (2018) 'Research-Policy Relations and Migration Studies', in R. Zapata-Barrero and E. Yalaz (eds), *Qualitative Research in European Migration Studies*. IMISCOE Research Series. London: Springer.

Schwartz, E. (2018) 'Flesh and Steel: Antithetical Materialities in the War on Terror', *Critical Studies on Terrorism* 11(2): 394–413.

Scott, D. (1995) 'Colonial Governmentality', *Social Text* 43: 191–220.

Scott, J. (2018) *The Common Wind: Afro-American Currents in the Age of the Haitian Revolution*. London: Verso.

Segre, A., Yimer, D. and Biadene, R. (dir.) (2008) *Come un uomo sulla terra [Like a Man on Earth]*. Film. Asinitas-ZaLab.

Seidel, T (2017) '"We Refuse to Be Enemies": Political Geographies of Violence and Resistance in Palestine', *Journal of Peacebuilding and Development* 12(3): 25–38.

Selwyn, B. (2015) 'Twenty-First-Century International Political Economy: A Class-Relational Perspective', *European Journal of International Relations* 21(3): 513–37.

Seth, S. (2013) '"Once Was Blind but Now Can See": Modernity and the Social Sciences', *International Political Sociology* 7(2): 136–51.

Sexton, J. (2008) *Amalgamation Schemes: Antiblackness and the Critique of Multiracialism*. Minneapolis, MN: University of Minnesota Press.

Sexton, J. (2012) 'Ante-anti-blackness: Afterthoughts', *Lateral 1*. Available at: https://csalateral.org/section/theory/ante-anti-blackness-afterthoughts-sexton/

Sexton, J. (2016) 'Afro-Pessimism: The Unclear Word', *Rhizomes* 29. Available at: https://doi.org/10.20415/rhiz/029.e02

Shabazz, R. (2015) *Spatializing Blackness*. Chicago, IL: Chicago University Press.

Shah, N. (2011) *Stranger Intimacy: Contesting Race, Sexuality and the Law in the North American West*. Berkeley, CA: University of California Press.

Shamir, R. (1996) 'Suspended in Space: Bedouins under the Law of Israel', *Law & Society Review* 30(2): 231–58.

Shamir, R. (2005) 'Without Borders? Notes on Globalization as a Mobility Regime', *Sociological Theory* 23(2): 197–217.

Sharma, N. (2006) 'White Nationalism, Illegality and Imperialism: Border Controls as Ideology', in Krista Hunt and Kim Rygiel (eds), *(En) Gendering the War on Terror: War Stories and Camouflaged Politics*. Aldershot: Ashgate Publishers, pp. 121–44.

Sharma, N. (2017) '"The New Order of Things": Immobility as Protection in the Regime of Immigration Controls', *Anti-Trafficking Review* 9: 31–47.

Sharma, N. (2020) *Home Rule: National Sovereignty and the Separation of Natives and Migrants*. Durham, NC: Duke University Press.

Sharma, N. and Wright, C. (2008–9) 'Decolonising Resistance, Challenging Colonial States', *Social Justice* 35(3): 120–38.

Sharp, J. (2011) 'A Subaltern Critical Geopolitics of the War on Terror: Postcolonial Security in Tanzania', *Geoforum* 42(3): 297–305.

Sharpe, C. (2010) *Monstrous Intimacies: Making Post-Slavery Subjects*. Durham, NC: Duke University Press.

Sharpe, C. (2016) *In the Wake: On Blackness and Being*. Durham, NC: Duke University Press.

Sheikh, F. (2016) *Islam and International Relations: Exploring Community and the Limits of Universalism*. London: Rowman and Littlefield.

Shilliam, R. (2006) 'What about Marcus Garvey? Race and the Transformation of Sovereignty Debate', *Review of International Studies* 32(3): 379–400.

Shilliam, R. (2008) 'What the Haitian Revolution Might Tell Us about Development, Security, and the Politics of Race', *Comparative Studies in Society and History* 50(3): 778–808.

Shilliam, R. (2015) *The Black Pacific: Anticolonial Struggles and Oceanic Connections*. London: Bloomsbury Academic Press.

Shilliam, R. (2018) *Race and the Undeserving Poor: From Abolition to Brexit*. London: Agenda Publishing.

Shilliam, R. and Pham, Q. (2016) *Meanings of Bandung: Postcolonial Orders and Decolonial Visions*. London: Rowman & Littlefield.

Shimazu, N. (1998) *Japan, Race and Equality: The Racial Equality Proposal of 1919*. London: Routledge.

Sigad, L. I. and Eisikovits, R. A. (2014) 'The Transnational Lives of American–Israeli Mothers', *Journal of International Migration and Integration* 8(16): 455–67.

Sinatti, G. and Horst, C. (2015) 'Migrants as Agents of Development: Diaspora Engagement Discourse and Practice in Europe', *Ethnicities* 15(1): 134–52.

Singha, R. (2000) 'Settle, Mobilize, Verify: Identification Practices in Colonial India', *Studies in History* 16(2): 151–98.

Skinner, Q. (1979) *The Foundations of Modern Political Thought: Volume 1*. Cambridge: Cambridge University Press.

Smith, A. (2015) *Conquest: Sexual Violence and American Indian Genocide*. Durham, NC: Duke University Press.

Smith, L. T. (2012) *Decolonizing Methodologies: Research and Indigenous Peoples*. London: Zed Books.

Smith, S. and Sender, J. (1983) 'A Reply to Samir Amin', *Third World Quarterly* 5(3): 650–6.

Soysal, Y. N. (1994) *Limits of Citizenship: Migrants and Postnational Membership in Europe*. Chicago and London: University of Chicago Press.

Spencer, M. (1995) *States of Injustice: A Guide to Human Rights and Civil Liberties in the European Union.* London: Pluto Press.

Spillers, H. (1987) 'Mama's Baby, Papa's Maybe: An American Grammar Book', *Diacritics* 17(2): 64–81.

Spillers, H., Hartman, S., Griffin, F., Eversley, S., and Morgan, J. (2007) '"Whatcha Gonna Do?": Revisiting "Mama's Baby, Papa's Maybe: An American Grammar Book": A Conversation with Hortense Spillers, Saidiya Hartman, Farah Jasmine Griffin, Shelly Eversley, and Jennifer L. Morgan', *Women's Studies Quarterly* 35(1/2): 299–309.

Spivak, G. C. (1988) 'Can the Subaltern Speak?', in C. Nelson and L. Grossberg (eds), *Marxism and the Interpretation of Culture.* Basingstoke: Macmillan Education.

Spivak, G. C. (1999) *A Critique of Postcolonial Reason: Toward a History of the Vanishing Present.* Boston, MA: Harvard University Press.

Squire, V. (2009) *The Exclusory Politics of Asylum.* London: Palgrave Macmillan.

Squire, V. (2017) 'Governing Migration through Death in Europe and the US: Identification, Burial and the Crisis of Modern Humanism', *European Journal of International Relations* 23(3): 513–32.

Stanley, A., Arat-Koc, S., Bertram, L. K. and King, H. (2014) 'Intervention – Addressing the Indigenous-Immigration "Parallax Gap"', *Antipode.* Available at: https://antipodefoundation.org/2014/06/18/addressing-the-indigenous-immigration-parallax-gap/

Stierl, M. (2017) 'Excessive Migration, Excessive Governance: Border Entanglements in Greek EUrope', in N. de Genova (ed.), *The Borders of 'EUrope': Autonomy of Migration, Tactics of Bordering.* Durham, NC: Duke University Press.

Stoking, G. (1995) *After Tylor: British Social Anthropology 1888–1951.* Madison: University of Wisconsin Press.

Subrahmanyam, S. (1997) 'The Eurasian Context of the Early Modern History of Mainland South-East Asia, 1400–1800', *Modern Asian Studies* 31(3): 735–62.

Tabar, L. (2017) 'From Third World Internationalism to "the Internationals": The Transformation of Solidarity with Palestine', *Third World Quarterly* 38(2): 414–35.

Talbot, I. and Singh, G. (2009) *The Partition of India.* Cambridge: Cambridge University Press.

Tawil-Souri, H. (2012) 'Uneven Borders, Coloured (Im)mobilities: ID Cards in Palestine/Israel', *Geopolitics* 17(1): 153–76.

Tazzioli, M. and Walters, W. (2016) 'The Sight of Migration: Governmentality, Visibility and Europe's Contested Borders', *Global Society* 30(3): 445–64.

Thapar, R. (2002) 'Cyclical and Linear Time in Early India', in K. Ridderbos (ed.), *Time.* Cambridge: Cambridge University Press, pp. 27–45.

Thiong'o, N. W. (1986) *Decolonising the Mind: The Politics of Language in African Literature.* Nairobi: East African Educational Publishers.

Thobani, S. (2007) 'White Wars: Western Feminisms and the "War on Terror"', *Feminist Theory* 8(2): 169–85.

Ticktin, M. (2017) 'A World without Innocence', *American Ethnologist* 44(4): 577–90.

Tilley, L. (2017) 'Resisting Piratic Method by Doing Research Otherwise', *Sociology* 51(1): 27–42.

Tilley, L. (2020) '"A Strange Industrial Order": Indonesia's Racialized Plantation Ecologies and Anticolonial Estate Worker Rebellions', *History of the Present* 10(1): 67–83.

Tilley, L. and Shilliam, R. (2018) 'Raced Markets: An Introduction', *New Political Economy* 23(5): 534–43.

Torpey, J. (2009) *The Invention of the Passport: Surveillance, Citizenship and the State*. Cambridge: Cambridge University Press.

Trexler, R. (1995) *Sex and Conquest: Gendered Violence, Political Order, and the European Conquest of the Americas*. Ithaca: Cornell University Press.

Trouillot, M.-R. (1995) *Silencing the Past: Power and the Production of History*. Boston, MA: Beacon Press.

Trujano, A. (2008) *Indigenous Routes: A Framework for Understanding Indigenous Migration*. Geneva: International Organisation for Migration, https://publications.iom.int/system/files/pdf/indigenous_routes.pdf

Truth, Sojourner (2020) 'Ain't I a Woman?', *The Sojourner Truth Project*. Available at: https://www.thesojournertruthproject.com

Tuck, E. and Yang, K. W. (2012) 'Decolonization Is Not a Metaphor', *Decolonization: Indigeneity, Education & Society* 1(1): 1–40.

Tuck, E., Guess, A. and Sultan, H. (2014) 'Not Nowhere: Collaborating on Selfsame Land', *Decolonization: Indigeneity, Education & Society* 11. Available at: https://decolonization.files.wordpress.com/2014/06/notnowhere-pdf.pdf

Tudor, A. (2018) 'Cross-Fadings of Racialisation and Migratisation: The Postcolonial Turn in Western European Gender and Migration Studies', *Gender, Place & Culture* 25(7): 1057–72.

Turhan, E. and Armiero, M. (2017) 'Cutting the Fence, Sabotaging the Border: Migration as a Revolutionary Practice', *Capitalism Nature Socialism* 28(2): 1–9.

Turner, J. (2015) 'The Family Migration Visa in the History of Marriage Restrictions: Postcolonial Relations and the UK Border', *British Journal of Politics and International Relations* 17(4): 623–43.

Turner, J. (2018) 'Internal Colonisation: The Intimate Circulations of Empire, Race and Liberal Government', *European Journal of International Relations* 24(4): 765–90.

Turner, J. (2020) *Bordering Intimacy: Postcolonial Governance and the Policing of Family*. Manchester: Manchester University Press.

Turner, L. (2017) 'Who Will Resettle Single Syrian Men?', *Forced Migration Review* 54: 29–31.

Turton, D. (2003) *Refugees, Forced Settlers and 'Other Forced Migrants': Towards a Unitary Study of Forced Migration*, Working Paper 94, Geneva: UNHCR.

Tyler, I. (2013) *Revolting Subjects: Social Abjection and Resistance in Neoliberal Britain*. London: Zed Books.

Tyrer, D. (2013) *The Politics of Islamophobia: Race, Power and Fantasy*. London: Pluto Press.

UNHCR (2019) 'Sexual and Gender Based Violence', UNHCR. Available at: https://www.unhcr.org/uk/sexual-and-gender-based-violence.html

UNRWA (2019) 'UNRWA in Figures', UNRWA. Available at: https://www.unrwa.org/resources/about-unrwa/unrwa-figures-2018-2019

Urry, J. (2007) *Mobilities*. Bristol: Polity Press.

Van den Boogaart, E. (1982) 'Colour Prejudice and the Yardstick of Civility: The Initial Dutch Confrontation with Black Africans, 1590–1635', in R. Ross (ed.), *Race and Colonialism*. London: Springer.

Van Ginkel, B. and Entenmann, E. (eds) (2016) *The Foreign Fighters Phenomenon in the European Union: Profiles, Threats and Policies*, The Hague: ICCT.

Vargas, J. C. and Alves, J. A. (2010) 'Geographies of Death: An Intersectional Analysis of Police Lethality and the Racialized Regimes of Citizenship in São Paulo', *Ethnic and Racial Studies* 33(4): 611–36.

Vaughan Williams, N. (2009) *Border Politics: The Limits of Sovereign Power*. Edinburgh: Edinburgh University Press.

Vázquez, R. (2011) 'Translation as Erasure: Thoughts on Modernity's Epistemic Violence', *Journal of Historical Sociology* 24(1): 27–44.

Vergara-Camus, L. (2014) *Land and Freedom: The MST, the Zapatistas and Peasant Alternatives to Neoliberalism*. London: Zed Books.

Vergara-Figueroa, A. (2018) *Afrodescendant Resistance to Deracination in Colombia: Massacre at Bellavista-Bojayá-Chocó*. Cham: Palgrave Macmillan.

Vigneswaran, D. (2020) 'Europe Has Never Been Modern: Recasting Historical Narratives of Migration Control', *International Political Sociology* 14(1): 2–21.

Virdee, S. (2019) 'Racialised Capitalism: An Account of Its Contested Origins and Consolidation', *Sociological Review* 67(1): 3–27.

Voltaire (1901) 'Essay surs les moeurs', in T. Smollett and W. Fleming (eds), *The Works of Voltaire*. New York: E. R. du Mont.

Walia, H. (2014) *Undoing Border Imperialism*. Oakland, CA: AK Press.

Wallerstein, I. (1974) 'The Rise and Future Demise of the World Capitalist System: Concepts for Comparative Analysis', *Comparative Studies in Society and History* 16(4): 387–415.

Wallerstein, I. (2004) *World-Systems Analysis: An Introduction*. Durham, NC: Duke University Press.

Walsh, C. (2002) 'The (Re)articulation of Political Subjectivities and Colonial

Difference in Ecuador: Reflections on Capitalism and the Geopolitics of Knowledge', *Nepantla* 3(1): 61–98.

Walters, W. (2006) 'No Border: Games with(out) Frontiers', *Social Justice* 33(1): 21–39.

Walters, W. (2008) 'Putting the Migration–Security Complex in Its Place', in L. Amoore and M. de Goede (eds), *Risk and the War on Terror*. London: Routledge, pp. 158–77.

Walters, W. (2010) 'Foucault and Frontiers: Notes on the Birth of the Humanitarian Border', in U. Brockling, B. Krasmann and T. Lemke (eds), *Governmentality: Current Issues and Future Challenges*. New York: Routledge, pp. 138–64.

Waltz, K. (1959) *Man, the State and War: A Theoretical Analysis*. New York: Colombia University Press.

Warner, M. (1991) 'Fear of a Queer Planet', *Social Text* 29: 3–17.

Weber, C. (2015) *Queer International Relations: Sovereignty, Sexuality and the Will to Knowledge*. Oxford: Oxford University Press.

Weerawardhana, C. (2018) 'Profoundly Decolonizing? Reflections on a Transfeminist Perspective of International Relations', *Meridians* 16(1): 184–213.

Weheliye, A. (2014) *Habeas Viscus: Racializing Assemblages, Biopolitics, and Black Feminist Theories of the Human*. Durham, NC: Duke University Press.

Weinbaum, A. E. (2019) *The Afterlife of Reproductive Slavery: Biocapitalism and Black Feminism's Philosophy of History*. Durham, NC: Duke University Press.

Weizman, E. (2003) 'Military Options as Human Planning: Interview with Philipp Misselwitz', in Eduardo Cadava and Aaron Lev (eds), *Cities without Citizens*. Philadelphia, PA: Slought Books.

Weizman, E. (2007) *Hollow Land: Israel's Architecture of Occupation*. London: Verso Books.

Wekker, G. (2016) *White Innocence: Paradoxes of Colonialism and Race*. Durham, NC: Duke University Press.

Wemyss, G. (2009) *The Invisible Empire: White Discourse, Tolerance and Belonging. Studies in Migration and Diaspora*. Farnham: Ashgate.

White, M. A. (2014) 'Archives of Intimacy and Trauma: Queer Migration Documents as Technologies of Affect', *Radical History Review* 1(120): 75–93.

Wilder, G. (2015) *Freedom Time: Negritude, Decolonization, and the Future of the World*. Durham, NC: Duke University Press.

Wilderson, F. (2010) *Red, White and Black: Cinema and the Structure of US Antagonisms*. Durham, NC: Duke University Press.

Williams, J. (2015) 'From Humanitarian Exceptionalism to Contingent Care: Care and Enforcement at the Humanitarian Border', *Political Geography* 47 (July): 11–20.

Wolfe, P. (2006) 'Settler Colonialism and the Elimination of the Native', *Journal of Genocide Research* 8(4): 387–409.

Wolfe, P. (2016) *Traces of History: Elementary Structures of Race.* London: Verso.

Wynter, S. (1990) 'Afterword: Beyond Miranda's Meanings: Un/silencing the "Demonic Ground" of Caliban's Woman', in C. B. Davies and E. S. Fido (eds), *Out of the Kumbla: Caribbean Women and Literature.* Trenton: Africa World, pp. 355–72.

Wynter, S. (2000) 'Africa, the West, and the Analogy of Culture: The Cinematic Text after Man', in J. Gianni and I. Baker (eds), *Symbolic Narratives/African Cinema: Audiences, Theory and the Moving Image.* London: British Film Institute and Palgrave Macmillan, pp. 25–75.

Wynter, S. (2003) 'Unsettling the Coloniality of Being/Power/Truth/Freedom: Towards the Human, after Man, Its Overrepresentation – an Argument', *New Centennial Review* 3(3): 257–337.

Yancy, G. (2016) *Black Bodies, White Gazes: The Continuing Significance of Race,* 2nd edn. Lanham, MD: Rowman & Littlefield.

Young, R. (2001) *Postcolonialism: An Historical Introduction.* Oxford: Wiley-Blackwell.

Zanker, F. (2019) 'Managing or Restricting Movement? Diverging Approaches of African and European Migration Governance', *Comparative Migration Studies* 7(17).

Zaragocin, S. (2019) 'Gendered Geographies of Elimination: Decolonial Feminist Geographies in Latin American Settler Contexts', *Antipode* 51(1): 373–92.

Zolberg, A., Suhrke, A. and Aguayo, S. (1989) *Escape from Violence: Conflict and the Refugee Crisis in the Developing World.* Oxford: Oxford University Press.

Index

aboriginal *see* indigenous
Africa
    African migration 16, 62–3, 69, 73,
        85, 89, 141, 148–50, 184
    African theory/philosophy 4, 24,
        155–7, 191
    anti-colonialism in 159, 191
    colonialism in 51, 60, 74, 151
    development in 40, 60
    IOM in Africa 11
    Maasi 101
    pan-Africanism 93, 156, 161, 164
    pre-colonial 177
    South Africa 4, 6, 70, 71, 117, 191
America
    African American 33, 99
    North 4, 53, 101, 117, 136, 147
    South 13, 20, 44, 55, 134
    the Americas 51, 59, 68, 69, 82,
        176
anti-blackness 54, 61–4, 72, 143,
    181, 185, 186
anti-Semitism 64
Asia 34, 36, 51, 93, 134, 149
asylum, asylum seekers 65, 73, 75,
    110–35, 142, 144, 169, 177,
    178, 185, 191, 193
Australia 26, 64, 70, 71, 94, 95–6,
    117, 147, 148, 199
borders
    and colonialism 7071, 75
    control policies 58, 62, 76, 48
    crossing 149

    and indigenous land 101
    no borders 79, 92–3, 103–10
    and race 67, 75, 82, 88
    and security 136–65

camps 70, 133, 191
capitalism
    colonial 32, 54, 59, 67, 96
    heteropatriarchal 159, 173, 188
    imperial 23, 50, 55, 70
    modern 26, 38
    neo-liberal 12, 41
    racial 15, 25, 72, 74–5, 137–8,
        144–7, 150, 156–7, 163, 168,
        188, 199, 203
    and socialism 84
China 69, 74, 116, 154
class 54, 56, 63, 69, 170, 171–2, 179,
    189, 190
connected histories 35, 38, 79, 83,
    99, 107, 129, 200

decoloniality
    coloniality/modernity 28, 31–2, 47,
        124, 127, 134
    decolonizing the university 5–7
    delinking 44–5
    and gender 167–8, 172–4, 178–84,
        189, 191; *see also* feminism
    overview 19–22
    perspective on borders *see* borders
    politics 101, 138, 159, 162, 164
    and race 54, 56

relation to world systems theory 13
development 5, 6, 15, 36, 37, 39–48,
    56, 59, 72, 101, 110, 127,
    129, 150

East 27, 36–7, 83
economic migration 87, 89
empires 1, 7, 56, 63, 67, 69, 70, 71,
    74, 87, 89, 90–2, 125, 146,
    156, 197, 200
enslavement *see* slavery/enslavement
epistemology 7, 44–6, 94, 98, 128
Eurocentrism
    alternatives to 5, 14, 43–7, 86, 147,
        150, 151, 157, 159, 164–5
    as colonial 27, 57, 79
    and gender/sexuality 174–6, 179,
        188, 191
    in social science 5, 7, 34–6, 39–40,
        81–2, 137–8, 148, 158
Europe
    European colonialism 177, 182
    European migrants 1, 11, 184–5
    European refugees 11, 110, 112,
        113, 116–19, 199
    migration to 13, 36, 132–6, 149,
        109
    and modernity 15, 18–22, 27–32,
        121, 131–2
    and race 39, 52–87, 121–2, 175

feminism 25, 49, 125, 140, 143,
    166–84, 187, 189, 191–3
First World
    relations with Third World 1, 36–7,
        45, 129
    relations with Fourth World 103,
        107
    and social sciences 6, 31, 36–7
    geographical complexity of 31, 79,
        80, 84, 103, 129, 146
    migration to 31, 87–92, 107–8,
        113–14, 119, 129
    wealth and exploitation 87, 90,
        119, 129
forced migration 14, 67, 72, 101,
    110–35, 178, 199

gender 10, 13, 25, 56, 63, 39, 129,
    140, 163, 166–94, 197–201

Global North
    and border security 114, 137, 147,
        150, 153, 164, 184
    geographical complexity of 27, 31,
        36
    migration to 12, 40, 59–60, 74–5,
        114, 150, 198
    and modernity 15, 28, 31, 37
    relations with Global South 24, 28,
        42–3, 59–60, 137, 198
    and social science 4, 9, 31, 34–7,
        110, 160, 191
    wealth and exploitation 60, 74–5,
        110
Global South
    and gender 178
    geographical complexity of 27, 31,
        36
    migration from 12, 34–6, 50, 67,
        110, 158, 164, 198
    and modernity 28, 42
    perspectives from 137, 147, 151,
        153–6
    relations with Global North 28,
        34–6, 114, 113, 138, 148
    and social science 31, 42, 43, 150,
        199
    and war 154

human 52–65, 69, 76, 147, 161, 173,
    175–6, 179, 184
human rights 5, 11, 26, 47, 103–24
human trafficking 110, 136, 143,
    168, 185
humanitarianism 111, 115, 125,
    128–9, 134, 149

India 6, 30, 32, 53, 55, 57, 69, 74,
    81, 86–7, 116–17, 177
indigenous
    gender and sexuality 170, 174–7,
        179, 189, 193
    immigrants 11, 35, 36, 45, 94,
        97–103, 119, 189
    and no borders 92–108, 105–7
    and racism 2, 53, 55, 59–61, 157
    and settler colonialism 7, 16, 17,
        45, 67, 69, 80, 92, 106, 158
    and social science 3, 16, 49, 56, 60,
        81, 201

sovereignty, 22–3, 56, 59, 79,
  92–108, 147, 198, 200
intersectionality 25, 167, 171–2, 177,
  179, 181
irregular migration 132
Islamophobia 135, 138–9, 163

Middle East 69, 134, 142, 145, 148,
  159, 160
modernity
  alternatives to 26–48, 154–7, 196
  colonial 121–4, 127, 147–8, 167,
    172, 177
  and development 40–3, 84, 86,
    121–4
  and Eurocentrism 19–20, 26–48,
    55–61, 74, 81, 127, 147, 162
  and racism 29–31, 50, 52, 53, 55,
    55–61, 65–8, 121–4, 182, 183
  and social science 5, 27–8

necropolitics 24, 60, 73, 111, 130–5,
  199
neo-colonial 6, 42, 79, 87, 89–93,
  107–8, 144, 197
no borders 79–80, 103–7, 155

Orientalism 18, 32, 138–9

pan-Africanism see Africa
passports 68, 88, 145

queer 22, 25, 49, 166–74, 183,
  187–93, 185, 199

race/racism
  absence of 2–3, 6–16, 25
  and capitalism 52, 53–7, 61–2,
    144, 153–5
  and colonialism 32, 48–77, 101,
    124
  intersectionality 167, 171–3,
    170–201
  as a structure 23, 27, 53–7, 61,
    131–4, 153
  and whiteness 62, 84–6, 96
  and security 137–9, 141–5
refugees see asylum
religion 44, 52, 58, 64, 76, 140–1,
  148, 160, 163–4

Second World 36–7, 40, 84, 115
Second World War 11, 12, 40, 115
security 66, 135–200
sexuality 56, 163, 166–200
slavery/enslavement
  contemporary legacies of 67–9,
    129–33, 143–6, 161
  and gender 175, 179–86, 193
  and mobility 60, 67–9, 74–5,
    99–100, 106, 129–33
  and modernity 29, 32, 53, 81,
    86–7, 99–100, 121–3
  and racism 50, 52–63, 106, 130,
    196, 198
  slave trade 1, 8, 60, 85, 151
sovereignty 12, 23, 78–109, 112, 118,
  132, 151, 155–6, 161, 164,
  179–80, 197–203
South Africa see Africa
space/spatial 19, 29, 34, 36, 38, 47,
  48, 53, 60, 69, 80–5, 96, 97,
  98, 100, 104, 107

terrorism 24, 42, 129, 135–64, 201
Third World
  geographical complexity of 31, 79,
    80, 84, 103, 129, 146
  migration from 31, 84–92, 107–8,
    113–14, 119, 129, 201
  relations with First World 35, 37,
    103, 146, 201
  relations with Fourth World 103,
    107
  resistance 43–5, 119, 146, 156–7
  and social sciences 6, 21, 31, 35–8
  wealth extraction and exploitation
    60, 87, 90, 119, 129, 146,
    163
Third World Approaches to
  International Law 3, 17, 21–4,
    79, 87, 108, 111, 125, 195,
    197, 199, 201
Third World feminism 170–1, 174,
  176, 187, 189
time/temporal 19, 26–48, 56–9, 80,
  84, 86, 196

university 5–11, 17, 202
uprooting 44, 60, 101, 121, 124–32,
  134, 178

visas 34, 63, 71, 88, 93, 136, 141–4, 155, 184–5, 191, 193

West, the
  and border thinking 44–56
  and colonialism 21, 37, 51, 58–9, 65
  decentring the West, 43–5, 147, 154–7, 161
  and Eurocentricism 27, 28, 37, 53, 56, 98, 134–44, 147–50
  and gender and sexuality 170–87
  and liberalism 42, 57, 134, 155
  migration to 15–16, 113–25
  modernity 27–41, 83–6, 199–201
  and Orientalism 18–19, 56, 134–44, 161
  privilege 69
world systems theory 13–14